ETHICS IN ARCHAEOLOGICAL PRACTICE

THE ANNUAL OF
THE AMERICAN SOCIETY OF OVERSEAS RESEARCH

Volume 78

Series Editor
William Caraher

ETHICS IN
ARCHAEOLOGICAL PRACTICE

edited by

Sarah Kielt Costello and Sarah Lepinski

American Society of Overseas Research • Alexandria, VA

THE ANNUAL OF THE AMERICAN SOCIETY OF OVERSEAS RESEARCH
VOLUME 78

Series Editor
William Caraher

ISBN: 978-0-89757-122-7 (hardcover)
ISBN: 978-0-89757-123-4 (PDF eBook)

Library of Congress Cataloging-in-Publication Data
Names: Costello, Sarah Kielt, 1971- editor. | Lepinski, Sarah, editor.
Title: Ethics in archaeological practice / edited by Sarah Kielt Costello,
    Sarah Lepinski.
Description: Alexandria, VA : American Society of Overseas Research, 2024.
    | Series: The Annual of the American Schools of Overseas Research ;
    volume 78 | Includes bibliographical references. | Summary: "This book
    targets current ethical questions pertaining to archaeology,
    specifically that of the Eastern Mediterranean region"-- Provided by
    publisher.
Identifiers: LCCN 2024025148 | ISBN 9780897571227 (hardback)
Subjects: LCSH: Archaeology--Moral and ethical aspects. |
    Archaeology--Moral and ethical aspects--Middle East. |
    Archaeology--Moral and ethical aspects--Mediterranean Region. |
    Antiquities--Collection and preservation--Moral and ethical aspects. |
    Archaeologists--Professional ethics. | Middle
    East--Antiquities--Collection and preservation--Moral and ethical
    aspects. | Mediterranean Region--Antiquities--Collection and
    preservation--Moral and ethical aspects.
Classification: LCC CC175 .E835 2024 | DDC 930.1--dc23/eng/20240718
LC record available at https://lccn.loc.gov/2024025148

Printed in the United States of America on acid-free paper

CONTENTS

Illustrations

Tables

For James

Introduction

Archaeological Ethics in the Twenty-first Century

Sarah Kielt Costello and Sarah E. Lepinski

ASOR and Ethics

While ethical decisions may not always be in the forefront of our professional minds, they are a part of everything we do in archaeology. The considerable number of volumes addressing ethics in archaeology underscore its importance to the field, particularly in the last quarter century (e.g., Hamilakis and Duke 2007; Lynott and Wylie 1995; McGill, Hollowell and Colwell-Chanthaphonh 2011; Meskell and Pels 2005; Scarre and Scarre 2006; Zimmerman, Vitelli and Hollowell-Zimmer 2003). Even with the growing attention to ethics in the field of archaeology, there is not a single volume focused specifically on the archaeology of ancient western Asia[1] and the Mediterranean region. Attention to principles of behavior within the professional practices of archaeologists working in these regions is timely; as a society, we are at a moment of multiple reckonings, especially related to race, gender, and the environment. Like many professional organizations, the American Society of Overseas Research (ASOR, an international association that supports archaeology in western Asia, north Africa, and

the Mediterranean) is confronting various ethical challenges, which are outlined further below. This book is intended to foreground a variety of ethical issues that are embedded in archaeological practice, which have significant resonance in this moment of social upheavals and historical reflection, particularly as they pertain to ASOR-affiliated scholars.

The notion of what constitutes "archaeological ethics" has changed dramatically over the centuries. From the Renaissance, when there was no distinction between archaeology and plundering, to Napoleon, whose looting was at least accompanied by an effort at scientific description, the early days of archaeology were not characterized by reflections on moral principles underlying professional conduct. Archaeology from across the Mediterranean, north Africa, and western Asia was closely tied to the colonial exploitation of those regions by European powers and by what Yannis Hamilakis characterizes as the commodification of archaeological artifacts and their transformation into national symbolic capital (2007: 17–18). While we (here, "we" refers loosely to the community of scholars researching these regions in antiquity) have made numerous changes to the way we do our work since that time, the legacy of our colonial past remains present throughout our work, from the terminologies we use, to ques-

---

[1] The "Near East" is the traditional scholarly term for western Asia, and the term currently in use by ASOR. The editors prefer "western Asia" since it does not assume a western perspective on the region.

tions of cultural patrimony and the relationships among excavators and local communities.

The traditional nature of our field and the way that archaeological projects frequently model themselves on their forbears mean that we are often slow to change and adapt. We tend to be gradual adopters of new theoretical approaches, for instance, and slow to adopt digital recording methodologies in the field. In the face of the broad social movements that are shaping society today, it has taken time for scholars to see how those conversations pertain ethically—and otherwise—to the often arcane work that we do in archaeology: we have been late to the racial justice movement, late to the #metoo conversation (we still never really had the feminism conversation, in fact), slow to admit that our field is dominated by white persons of privilege, even reluctant to acknowledge obvious problems, such as how difficult it is to carry out archaeological fieldwork while disabled, pregnant, or parenting, and how those difficulties affect our ability to gain or maintain a sustainable position in our field.

Recently, however, ASOR has undertaken a number of bold steps to address various ethical imperatives. The recent move to change ASOR's name illustrates both progress as well as the conservatism of our field. The "American School of Oriental Study and Research in Palestine" was founded in 1900. The association's name was changed in 1921 to The American Schools of Oriental Research. The acronym "ASOR" has long been used interchangeably with the longer name, in recent years in part to avoid the increasingly problematic term "Oriental," with its associated history of derogatory racial connotations. "Oriental" also put a limit on the directionality of the organization's research: people from the west studying people from the east. In recent decades a number of ASOR members argued for a name change, but it was not until 2021 that, as an organization, ASOR took the corrective step in making the change to the American Society of Overseas Research. In conversations, some scholars continue to insist that "Oriental" is not offensive, that it simply means "east," without acknowledging the implicit directionality and the historical

structures from which its use derives. The desire of some to keep things as they are, while ignoring the colonial implications of the name itself, illustrates the need for a re-examination of ethics—of the principles underlying behavior and established practices and perspectives—in all aspects of our work.

Addressing our directionality problem, in which scholars from "the west" study cultures from "the east," must go beyond a name change. As of 2022, 30% of ASOR membership was based outside the US, so making the annual meeting accessible via both funding and the virtual meeting is imperative to equity of access. The virtual meeting format, which started out of necessity during the Covid pandemic, will continue in the future as part of a new hybrid format for annual meetings. ASOR has raised funds to support attendance at the Annual Meeting for scholars from across the organization's geographic areas of study who might otherwise find travel costs to a meeting in the US prohibitive. The 2022 virtual meeting included sessions with Arabic and Farsi interpretation to broaden access to a wider audience.

Recent plenary addresses at the annual meeting signal the scope of ASOR's aspirational values. The 2021 plenary by Dr. Morag Kersel, "Living with Legacies: ASOR Archaeo-activism and a Future for 21st Century Archaeology," set out an array of ethical challenges along with examples of current scholarship that seeks to address them. The 2022 plenary by Dr. Solange Ashby, "Women of the Sacred South: Nubian Women in the Temple and Upon the Throne," signals ASOR's commitment to ASOR scholarship across a broader geographic expanse of the ancient world. ASOR has also instituted committees to address ethical issues; a standing DEI committee is developing initiatives including diversity scholarships to fund fieldwork and annual meeting attendance for scholars from underrepresented groups. An Ad Hoc Climate Impact Committee, recognizing that climate change impacts the organization's commitment to stewardship of cultural heritage, produced an extensive report in 2022 detailing the climate impact of ASOR activities, as well as the potential mitigation of possible solutions.

The ASOR mission is "to initiate, encourage, and support research into, and public understanding of, the cultures and history of the Near East and the wider Mediterranean, from the earliest times." Fostering fieldwork, scholarship, and education around the ancient cultures of the region of the eastern Mediterranean and beyond has long been the means to support that mission. In recent years, especially inspired by the tragic destruction wrought by recent wars in western Asia, ASOR has taken up the charge of education and advocacy for cultural heritage protections. The Cultural Heritage Initiative (CHI), instituted in 2014, partners with various government and non-government organizations to "document, protect, and preserve the cultural heritage of war-torn Syria, northern Iraq, and Libya" (asor.org).

Public outreach is also a component of the stated mission. The 2019 plenary address by Eric Cline took up that topic, addressing the need for work that reaches a broader public through popular publications and educational opportunities. In 2022, a new ASOR award was added, the Community Engagement and Outreach Award, to recognize such efforts. Public outreach is achieved, in part, through the growing resources available on ASOR's YouTube channel. Cultural heritage resources available there include numerous recorded lectures on the work of CHI, along with a "Tutorials for Cultural Heritage" series introducing open-source data management tools. The "educational resources" series offers videos on ancient Nubia; such videos are helpful to educators seeking to expand the traditional canon of their courses. The plenary lectures mentioned above, along with a number of other lectures, are also available to the public via the YouTube channel.

The significant developments within ASOR's professional structure and the broader focus of its programming provide a solid foundation with which to cultivate further ethical approaches in the field of archaeology. The editors hope that the chapters in this volume will inspire even deeper reflection on ways to advance the mission of ASOR, to protect cultural heritage, and to consider our role in supporting our colleagues and our communities, local and global.

ETHICS IN ARCHAEOLOGICAL PRACTICE

What does it mean to undertake archaeological practice in an ethical manner? If we know anything in the first years of the 2020s, it is that people are not in agreement about what constitutes ethical or moral behavior. Hot-button issues abound, including abortion, climate, racial justice, public health, gun violence, police violence, right down to what constitutes "truth." While the ethical issues facing archaeologists may be perceived as less controversial, they are nonetheless connected to larger, complex social issues that embody the challenges associated with equality, inclusivity, and politics.

In 2003, Randall McGuire observed that at the start of the 21st century, archaeological ethics became concerned with relations among people, rather than relations between archaeologists and things (McGuire 2003: vii). It was no longer enough to gather data ethically and to ensure its speedy publication. Organized and published by the Society for American Archaeology (SAA), the volume McGuire introduced took up ethics as they pertain to the archaeological record, to diverse publics, and to colleagues in the field (Zimmerman, Vitelli, and Hollowell-Zimmer 2003). Each of these areas remains vital, twenty years hence. And yet, the reckonings of recent years, with the history of racial, colonial, and gender-based violence in particular, as well the evident climate crisis we are facing, add urgency to particular aspects of archaeological practice. While our primary work involves understanding ancient societies and cultural practices through material culture, the editors argue that this work requires active engagement with current issues, as well as with sometimes volatile political and religious controversies. We must continue to assess the ethical principles that guide us and do our work in a way that furthers these principles.

What the editors are asking, through this volume, is that archaeologists recognize the many places in which our work intersects with ethical issues and consider how we can integrate ethical choices into our practices. Vigilant attention, not lip service, is required if we are to uphold our responsibilities as stewards of the cultures and people of the past and present. The editors ascribe to the view of Chris Scarre and Geoffrey Scarre as stated in their 2006 book on archaeological ethics, that ethics is not checking off the required boxes in the most minimal way, but rather about "energetically pursuing the good" (2006: 3) in all facets our work, including the way we work with one another, the manner in which we engage across institutional structures encompassed within the broader ecosystem in which archaeologists and aligned professionals work, and how we embrace the legacies and futures of our discipline.

Exploring the range of what is encompassed by the ethical "good" for professionals engaged in work in the field of archaeology of western Asia and the Mediterranean regions is part of the project of this volume. The scholars herein consider a range of archaeological practice—teaching, field work, grant writing, research, cultural heritage, and professional advocacy—and identify some of the myriad ethical issues we face in each of these areas. In most of the chapters, what the authors identify as "the good"—the ethical goal worth pursuing—is not particularly controversial. For instance, we should ensure that ourselves and our colleagues are safe and treated respectfully, and that opportunities are made available on an equitable basis. We should actively engage to identify and correct biased underpinnings in the discipline in which we work. We should reckon with the realities of climate change and how it intersects with our profession. We should strive to protect cultural heritage and in coordination with the appropriate communities. The chapters in this volume explore these ethical objectives and how we can work to further them.

It is in the details that we find space for debate. For example, in 2022, the ASOR Ad Hoc Climate Impact Committee administered a survey regarding the ASOR Annual Meeting and its carbon impact. The fact that the climate is changing and posing risks to society is no longer a subject for debate. The matter of how ASOR should ethically address the problem remains more challenging. Travel to an annual meeting carries a carbon impact. Furthermore, members whose location, finances, or physical challenges make it difficult to attend an in-person annual meeting are at a disadvantage. Remote meetings address both climate impact and equity issues; however, they limit the professional contact we find so valuable. Hybrid meetings are an ideal solution in many ways, though they may limit professional networking for those not attending in person. In decisions like this, members must choose how to weigh ethical issues against both cost and the professional aims of the organization. Similar "devil in the details" spaces are identified by many of the authors in this volume—the ethical "good" may be readily identified, but putting it in practice can be more complicated.

As professionals working in the field, in universities, in museums, and in other institutions and organizations, we are guided by various codes of ethics. In their book exploring ethics in anthropology as embedded practice, Lynn Meskell and Peter Pels outline the benefits and limits of codified professional ethics (2005: 2). Professionally, we are united by the desire to reveal and understand the past, to educate, and to share in that work with as broad a community as possible. But what does that mean, in practice? How accessible are our publications? What languages should we publish in? Who has the resources to pursue a PhD in our field? Theoretically (or generally), we agree that treating each other "well" is important, but what does that mean, in practice? How do hierarchies within our organizational structures—in the field and in our institutions—impact behaviors? Whose names go on the publications? How do we protect vulnerable members of our team? How do we support those in less formalized roles? How do we work productively and respectfully with the community in which our work is based?

This volume is not a comprehensive examination of all ethical issues in archaeology. It need not be; there are many excellent volumes on ethics in archaeology. Chris Scarre and Geoffrey Scarre's volume *The Ethics of Archaeology* (2006) pairs archaeologists with philosophers to address moral questions. The 2003 SAA volume on ethics mentioned above includes Alison Wylie's excellent theoretical formulation of ethics in archaeology, a history of the topic by Mark Lynott, and numerous case studies (Wylie 2003 and Lynott 2003 in Zimmerman, Vitelli, and Hollowell-Zimmer 2003). *Embedded Ethics* has anthropology more broadly as its subject but includes critical examinations of how archaeological practice intersects with living communities and the ethical responsibilities of archaeologists and heritage professionals (Meskell 2005 in Meskell and Pels 2005). Rather, the point of departure for the current volume sits squarely on candid discussions and reflections of current practices with the aim to explore pressing topics and issues surrounding archaeological work and to address professional responsibilities surrounding conduct and authority in archaeology. Within these discussions/reflections, the authors underscore the necessity for presenting ideas for paths forward and solutions.

CONTENTS OF THE VOLUME

The call for contributors to the volume generated a wide-range of papers reflecting ethics in practice from across a broad sweep of archaeological work and drawing from specific case studies and experiences. These papers range from a "look back" into efforts to raise consciousness within the ASOR membership regarding gender equality in the field, to looking forward, determining the kinds of training necessary for future archaeologists to conduct our work ethically in light of accelerating climate change, globally, and to ensure inclusivity in the field.

The chapter topics within represent a selection of issues scholars find pressing and relevant. Certain issues have emerged as urgent in the past few years, even during the last few months of our writing period: climate change, sexual harassment and assault with the #metoo movement, and racial justice with the Black Lives Matter movement. The country was mobilized, at last, by the brutal and tragic death of George Floyd in 2021. We must not wait until such moments of crisis to talk about how issues of human rights, safety, and justice intersect with our work.

The overarching goals for the volume are to gain deeper perspectives on current ethical practices and issues, to raise awareness of how archaeologists are addressing these issues, and to offer guidance and solutions where possible. The chapters that follow explore ethical challenges facing archaeologists and serve to illuminate potential paths forward for the ASOR community (and beyond) that are proactive rather than reactive, and which offer models of high standards of ethical practice for the 21st century.

The chapters are presented in three sections. The first, **Ethical Practices Towards One Another**, addresses how we treat our colleagues and how we ensure our field offers equal and safe opportunities to all scholars, in the classroom, the field, and in our professional organizations. Beth Alpert Nakhai opens the discussion with a look back at her activism over her years as an ASOR member, and how she has worked with ASOR towards greater gender equity. Her personal account reveals both how immediately ethical issues (in this instance, the lack of gender equity in archaeology) are felt, and how they affect the trajectory of our careers, but also how impactful each person's engagement with ethics can be. Laura Heath-Stout explores how archaeologists build ethical, diverse, and inclusive research communities, identifying the barriers that hinder recruitment and retention of marginalized peoples in archaeology. Grace Erny and Dimitri Nakassis address sexism and gender-based harassment in archaeology and academia, proposing concrete steps toward creating a more ethical and equitable discipline. Debby Sneed and Mason Shrader argue for active recruitment and inclusion of people with disabilities in archaeological fieldwork, demonstrating how existing structures and accommodations for nondisabled colleagues might serve as models moving forward.

The second section, **Ethical Practices Across the Discipline**, includes chapters that address the very immediate ways that we do our work and engage with our institutions and colleagues. Nadhira Hall and Maggie Beeler discuss the importance of teaching race and ethnicity in the ancient world and provide resources and context for instructors engaged in teaching inclusive and anti-racist archaeologies. Undergraduate teaching, especially to non-majors, is one of the ways that we as professionals and experts reach a wider audience. It is here that we can have a profound impact on how the ancient world is viewed and understood. Beyond the classroom, another critical point of engagement is in the museum and heritage space. Public and private collections of archaeological objects comprise an important part of our data about the ancient world and often serve as the entry point for interest in the subject among the general public. Sarah Kielt Costello addresses how we handle works that lack good information about findspot and argues against the polarizing term "orphan objects" and in favor of a more active engagement by scholars around the problems of unprovenienced objects. Tuğba Tanyeri-Erdemir takes up the challenging overlap between religious spaces and public heritage, looking at both museumification and de-museumification of such sacred spaces. In recognition that all of our professional work relies on funding, Christopher Thornton and Sarah Lepinski provide information to support the ethical application for, and awarding of, grants for archaeological research.

The chapters in the third section, **Legacies and Futures**, ask us to critically examine the foundations of the discipline and to consider our responsibilities looking forward. Just as the United States is slowly starting to reckon with the racism of our history and the ways racism has been institutionalized, we must likewise reckon with the racism that has been woven into our discipline for centuries. Annelies Van de Ven argues that we can herald the accomplishments of the early "heroes" of our discipline while still finding fault with their biases and actions. Louise Hitchcock digs into an early, and problematic, effort to decolonize Classics by revisiting Martin Bernal's *Black Athena* within the context of her pedagogical experiences. And finally, Benjamin Porter closes the volume by looking to the future, and how we as practitioners must work with the changing climate in mind.

This volume, if it is a critique of our field, is a friendly one issued by professionals working across institutional types and contributing to

the vibrant membership of ASOR and wider professional communities. The authors here in some cases suggest best practices or ways forwards; there are undoubtedly other paths, other solutions, and other ways to frame these issues. You are invited to consider the perspectives presented here and reflect on your own practices.

The challenges of compiling this volume during the pandemic of 2020 and following meant that some of the chapters originally slated for inclusion could not be written, as authors faced numerous personal and professional challenges, from expanded and intensified workloads to a lack of childcare, increasing institutional responsibility, loss of financial security, and general anxiety. We are living in what is daily referred to as an "unprecedented time." A time of pandemic, climate change, racial reckoning, sexual misconduct reckoning, and political violence in the paragon of stable democracy. Indeed, many of those "unprecedented moments" played out as the volume was being written, and it changed as a result—papers were withdrawn and some topics shifted as issues emerged. There are countless ethical issues not addressed here, in part due to the failure of the editors to find contributors to address them as pressures facing prospective authors mounted. In some cases, there was simply a lack of appeal for engaging in a reflective essay on a sensitive and complex topic, particularly in the face of multiple professional responsibilities. For example, we would have liked to hear from an excavation PI about the various ethical challenges encountered when directing a project, from safety in the field to publication practices. We also would have liked to explore responsibilities in engaging with the local communities in an area of study. Ethics surrounding digital resources, publication, and data management form another fundamental topic in the field that we had hoped to include in the volume. Ethical approaches and perspectives in conservation and cultural heritage protection and preservation are also missing here.

As we reflect on what this volume achieves and where it falls short, we find that while we were able to bring in a range of voices at different stages in their careers and from a variety of perspectives, the book lacks equitable representation of scholars from western Asia and the Mediterranean. Overall, however, we are encouraged by the trend towards open-access publication and of providing translations of work in the languages of the area of study in journals and online resources in particular. Changing the directionality of our organization's name is not enough; we must work towards broader inclusivity in our work, both in terms of whose voices we hear and who has access to our research products.

We hope that readers will find this book helpful, thought-provoking, and ultimately inadequate. We hope, that is, that it encourages deeper introspection and inspires further writing on ethics in archaeological practice We ask you to join the conversation: contribute a paper to a future volume on ethics, organize a session at a future meeting. We hope this is the first of more volumes on the subject, and that the reexamination of our profession through an ethical lens becomes a standard part of the work of ASOR-affiliated archaeologists.

ACKNOWLEDGMENTS

The editors would like to thank the contributing authors for engaging in this project with us and for sharing your insights, reflections, and research on archaeological practices. We recognize that, in many instances, addressing pressing issues surrounding ethical behaviors and principles in our discipline required courage and commitment.

REFERENCES

ASOR
  https://www.asor.org/chi/. ASOR Cultural Heritage Initiative. Accessed December 12, 2022.

Hamilakis, Y.
2007   Archaeology and Capitalism: From Ethics to Politics. Pp. 15–40 in *Archaeology and Capitalism: From Ethics to Politics,* ed. Y. Hamilakis and P. Duke. Walnut Creek, CA: Taylor & Francis.

Hamilakis, Y., and Duke, P. (eds.)
2007   *Archaeology and Capitalism: From Ethics to Politics.* Walnut Creek, CA: Taylor & Francis.

Lynott, M. J., and Wylie, A. (eds.)
1995   *Ethics in American Archaeology: Challenges for the 1990s.* Washington, DC: Society for American Archaeology.

McGuire, R. H.
2003   Forward. Pp. vii–ix in *Ethical Issues in Archaeology,* ed. L. J. Zimmerman, K. D. Vitelli, and J. Hollowell-Zimmer. Walnut Creek, CA: Altamira.

Meskell, L., and Pels, P. (eds.)
2005   *Embedding Ethics.* New York: Berg.

McGill, D.; Hollowell, J.; and Colwell-Chanthaphonh, C. (eds.)
2011   *Ethics in Action: Case Studies in Archaeological Dilemmas.* Washington, DC: Society for American Archaeology.

Scarre, C., and Scarre, G. (eds.)
2006   T*he Ethics of Archaeology: Philosophical Perspectives on Archaeological Practice.* Cambridge: Cambridge University Press.

Zimmerman, L. J.; Vitelli, K. D.; and Hollowell-Zimmer, J. (eds.)
2003   *Ethical Issues in Archaeology.* Walnut Creek, CA: Altamira.

I. Ethical Practices Towards One Another

Chapter 1

From Consciousness Raising to Community Action

Addressing Gender Inequality in ASOR and in Our Field

Beth Alpert Nakhai

ABSTRACT

When I first began attending ASOR's annual meetings in the 1980s, gender equality, a goal for which many of us had long struggled, was neither a value nor an expectation within Near Eastern archaeology. Not many women attended the meetings and fewer still held leadership positions either within ASOR or on excavations; women with tenure lines at academic institutions were rare. Change, slow as it has been, has resulted in more women pursuing careers in archaeology, participating in ASOR meetings, assuming leadership positions within ASOR and in the field, and (perhaps) experiencing less danger and discrimination in field settings. When I look back on those changes in which I have played a part, I view them within a continuum that, for me, has roots in the Consciousness Raising groups of my post-college years.

A commitment to equality is not a matter of personal choice; it is a moral and ethical imperative, an obligation to which we all must commit. Equality is mandated by law in the United States and elsewhere throughout the world. Equality means more than equity, more than numerical parity. The lack of gender equality within our field reflects an ethical failing that has, by dint of the deep ways in which gender-based discrimination is embedded within scholarship, led to false narratives about the past. Only by embracing diversity and inclusivity in the present can we, scholars of the past, hope to reconstruct that past in all its richness and complexity.

This essay considers those changes that have helped to place gender equality at the forefront of our work, and that have facilitated advances toward gender equality within ASOR. My choice of first-person narrative reflects my conviction that activism for equality is a moral and ethical responsibility that each of us must personally assume—and that our personal convictions and actions cannot be separated from our professional accomplishments.

Introduction: Consciousness Raising and Other Paths to Action

I entered college in 1968, a year famous—or infamous—enough to have an enduring mystique and a bibliography of its own.[1] Once I graduated, I moved into a carriage house outside Boston with a bunch of friends—something like a hippie commune—with lots of homemade granola, sprouting beans and heady conversations, but not much money. I paid my bills by working in the headquarters of a chain of discount drug stores, first as a secretary, then promoted to assistant buyer. Female secretaries were, of course, *de rigueur* in the early seventies—but female buyers were not. The men's world of mass merchandising was *terra incognita* for me. I was shocked by the crassness of the workplace: men with *Playboy* pinups on their walls, married men taking their secretaries to strip clubs at lunch, my bosses' banter about who "really" needed free samples of extra-large rubbers (as condoms were called in those days) from the sales reps for Trojan and Ramses.

This was, of course, a good number of years into the Women's Lib movement. Many of my female friends worked in settings like mine—and one way we dealt with the overt sexism (no need to be covert in those days) was to get together in Consciousness Raising (C-R) groups.[2] Friends, and friends of friends, we sat together in each other's kitchens and living rooms and we talked. Sexism, patriarchy and discrimination, friendship and romance, sex and sexuality, good books and good music, work—everything was on the table. We struggled to extrapolate from the personal, to understand that what each of us experienced, whether diminishment, dismissal, or other forms of discrimination, derived from systemic social injustice. We believed, passionately, that we were living in a time of change, and that we could think, talk, march—and vote—our way to a better world. We weren't naïve. We had witnessed Buddhist monks burn themselves to death on the streets of Saigon, and American soldiers, our brothers and cousins and friends and lovers, volunteers and draftees alike, be killed and kill in Vietnam. We had experienced, in the course of five short years, the assassinations of John F. Kennedy, Malcolm X, Martin Luther King Jr., and Robert F. Kennedy. None of us thought that "Peace & Love"—or Woodstock—would change the world, but we did think that change for women would happen. Our conversations, our commitment, the way we lived our lives, the constancy of our struggle, would, we believed, create change. Our C-R groups were our secure base and, to some extent, our methodology—conversation not as process, but as the catalyst for change.

Lessons learned: commit to activism; work in community to eradicate gender-based inequality.

1   A cursory list includes:
    1988. Kaiser, Charles. *1968 in America: Music, Politics, Chaos, Counterculture, and the Shaping of a Generation.* New York: Weidenfeld & Nicolson.
    1969. White, Theodore H. *The Making of the President, 1968.* New York: Atheneum.
    1995. Haldeman, Joe W. *1968: A Novel.* New York: Morrow.
    2004. Kurlansky, Mark. *1968: The Year That Rocked the World.* New York: Ballentine.
    2004. Kusch, Frank. *Battleground Chicago: The Police and the 1968 Democratic National Convention.* Westport, CT: Praeger.
    2009. Kaufman, Michael T. *1968.* New York: Roaring Brook.
    2017. Bowden, Mark. *Hûé 1968: A Turning Point of the American War in Vietnam.* New York: Grove.
    2017. Jones, Howard. *My Lai: Vietnam, 1968, and the Descent into Darkness.* New York: Oxford University.
    2017. O'Donnell, Lawrence. *Playing with Fire: The 1968 Election and the Transformation of American Politics.* London: Penguin.
    2018. Colt, George Howe. *The Game: Harvard, Yale, and America in 1968.* New York: Scribner.
    2018. Longley, Kyle. *LBJ's 1968: Power, Politics, and the Presidency in America's Year of Upheaval.* New York: Cambridge University.
    2018. Vinen, Richard. *The Long '68: Radical Protest and its Enemies.* London: Allen Lane.

2   "In C-R, women answer a question using examples from their personal lives, then the group uses these personal testimonies to draw conclusions about the political root of women's so-called 'personal' problems."

"C-R is used to: Collect and analyze data (e.g., women's life experiences); Get to the root of sexism—figure out who benefits and who pays; Understand that the pain and struggles in our lives are not our individual problems and we cannot solve them on our own; Take action (using C-R conclusions as the basis for our theory and strategy)" (https://womensliberation.org/priorities/feminist-consciousness-raising/; see also Sarachild 1979).

Talking and listening, observing and reflecting, assessing and reassessing—these became not only reflexes, but tools that I (and others) would later use to advocate for gender equity and inclusivity within ASOR and in the field of Near Eastern archaeology. Identifying inequality would provide no challenge, and as I (and others) began to speak openly, to develop community within and beyond ASOR, our efforts to actuate change would become increasingly effective.

When I left retailing and entered Harvard Divinity School to pursue a career in Near Eastern archaeology, my life changed. Gone were the days of Consciousness Raising. Now, the conversations that mattered most were about ancient history, ancient languages and literatures, and great archaeological discoveries. I note with chagrin that I don't remember thinking about gender bias while I was pursuing my master's degree. There were a few women in my classes, but Harvard did not have a single female professor in its biblical and ancient Near Eastern Studies programs, neither at the Divinity School nor in its Department of Near Eastern Languages and Civilizations.[3] Amidst the framed photos of male founders and deans that bedecked the Divinity School halls, it was hard not to notice gender disparities. At the time, though, I failed to articulate the problem or to consider its consequences. In retrospect, I attribute this to the intensity of my studies and to the fact that I was intimidated by the "Harvardness" of Harvard; my only goal there was to do as well as humanly possible. How much richer—how much more honest and accurate—our education would have been had the study of women and of gender been part of it.

While completing my Master of Theological Studies degree and afterwards, I "commuted" between Boston and Israel, studying, working on digs, making a living. My next move was to Tucson, to the University of Arizona, where I completed another masters, and then a PhD. My doctoral advisor, William G. Dever, selected several female students, myself included, to codirect excavations in Israel and Jordan.[4] That he used his position to advance female and not only male students is noteworthy, since senior (male) faculty at other American universities were not supporting their female students in this way. He underwrote our digs with university funding that he could have used for his own excavation work, and our excavation licenses included his name, meaning that he put his reputation on the line for us. I never heard Dever discuss his decision to support female grad students as way of advancing gender equity but, as they say, actions speak louder than words.

During this same period of time, my personal life changed dramatically, as I married and had a daughter. Throughout my last years in grad school, while I was completing my dissertation, I held a half-time job as the assistant director of Tucson/Pima County Community Profile (Community Profile), a multi-year county-wide social services planning project. Based at the United Way of Southern Arizona, Community Profile brought together some 1300 volunteers from all walks of life, organized into 22 task forces that focused on community issues, interests, and needs. Task force members (professionals, service providers and those whom they served, politicians, and other concerned individuals) met regularly over the course of a year and more, working together to pinpoint obstacles to success in their areas of engagement, to identify modes of improvement, and to craft plans for making our incredibly diverse part of the American Southwest a better place for everyone. My work at Community Profile involved bringing together a range of leaders and stakeholders; facilitating discussions of obstacles and opportunities; listening to myriad, diverse, and often conflicting voices; supporting the development of consensus regarding best practices and next steps; and building community (Kha and Peckham 1994). In its own way, despite its businesslike, solution-oriented, accountability-driven approach, Community Profile was not

---

3   The prestigious Hancock Professor of Hebrew and Other Oriental Languages at Harvard Divinity School was founded in 1764. To date, the Chair has never been held by a woman.

4   Bonnie Magness Gardiner and Steven Falconer at Tell el-Hayyat in Jordan; Bonnie Wisthoff, J. P. Dessel, and Beth Alpert Nakhai at Tell el-Wawiyat in Israel.

dissimilar to the Consciousness Raising groups of yore.[5] As for me, in addition to meeting amazing people and learning so much about the region I had come to call home, I received exceptional training in working with diverse communities, in engaging with leaders and stakeholders, and, perhaps most important, in both listening and hearing. I relished the contrast to my academic work, which by then focused on my dissertation research. Later, I would be able to bring what I learned at Community Profile to ASOR, where I (and others) would engage in public discourse over issues of ethics, gender equality, inclusion, and best practices in institutional and field settings.

FINDING WOMEN IN ASOR[6]

In 1993, doctorate in hand, finding employment in academia was a challenge. Of course, in 1968, the U.S. Equal Opportunity Employment Commission had ruled gender discrimination in the workplace illegal, and since 1972, Title IX of the U.S. Education Amendments had prohibited discrimination based on sex. Gone were job ads like the one recently reprinted in the *New York Times*, a "Help Wanted" advertisement from 1968, the year I entered college. Under "Help Wanted – Female," the ad read:

> TWA Flight Hostess. Enjoy this rewarding career with TWA, and gain the full travel advantages of flying within the U.S.A. and also to Europe. Job Qualifications: Minimum Age 19½; Single; Excellent Health; Unblemished Complexion; Height 5'2"- 5'9" with Proportionate Weight by TWA Standard; Glasses Permitted. (Dry 2019)

It was no longer 1968 when I entered the job market but even so, while I may not have needed

to be single, in excellent health and with an unblemished complexion to find a job, academia remained a man's world. While some women had long held positions in Classics and Assyriology, few could be found in biblical studies or in Near Eastern archaeology. Female archaeologists of my generation, at least in the States, were just beginning to push past the barrier of gender discrimination to obtain academic positions and even, in a few fortunate cases, tenure lines. For most, however, stable positions in academia would remain elusive.

My own next steps were slow, incremental, frustrating, and difficult. I spent 1994–1995 as a half-time adjunct, then nine years as a full-time adjunct, teaching six courses in the academic year and two over the summer—and finally, hallelujah, in 2003, a tenure line—all this at the University of Arizona, where I had received my PhD. In order to obtain that first adjunct position, I had proposed a course on "Women in Ancient Israel." Not that I had ever studied this topic—or, heaven forfend, heard so much as a word about women in antiquity while in grad school—but I'm a woman and I was (and remain) really interested in the topic, so why not? In the mid-1990s, the relevant bibliography was only a few pages long, and virtually all the work was being done by women who focused their attention on the Hebrew Bible, New Testament, extrabiblical texts, and inscriptions. Carol Meyers' 1988 *Discovering Eve: Ancient Israelite Women in Context* was the single book that considered evidence for gender gleaned from the archaeological record of Iron Age Israel (Meyers 1988). As has become increasingly clear, the risks that these inspirational women took as they righted wrongs, publishing on subjects that men had long dismissed, have been rewarded by the growing attention to women as normative members of ancient society. They are rewarded, as well, by the growing realization that scholarship published before the "discovery" of women is failed scholarship; its failures are not only intellectual and academic, but also ethical.

Time, finances, and family responsibilities permitting, I continued attending ASOR's annual meetings. In those days, ASOR met jointly

---

5   The principles that guided the work of Tucson/Pima County Community Profile were "Community, Coalition, Consensus, and Commitment" (Kha and Peckham 1994: 7).

6   The various studies discussed in the article will be published in a book I am now completing, *Women in Levantine Archaeology: Why the Present Matters, and How It Affects Our Knowledge of the Past* (Routledge).

with the Society of Biblical Literature (SBL) and the culture was overwhelmingly male—perhaps even more so in ASOR than in SBL, which had, in 1989, convened its Committee on the Status of Women in the Profession (CSWP).[7] I was eager to learn more about women in antiquity, so I kept my eyes open at ASOR's annual meetings for relevant papers and—"surprise"—there weren't any. Curious, I looked through several decades of past program books and discovered that there had been plenty of papers on pigs, and even some on goddesses, but none on women. In 1999, I introduced a new session, "The World of Women: Gender and Archaeology."[8] Now called "Gender in the Ancient Near East," it has become a standing session, in its third decade with its third program chair. Just as this session has promoted research into women in antiquity, it has also, I believe, helped to facilitate purposeful thinking about contemporary women and, therefore, about changes in ASOR's gendered culture.

The more annual meetings I attended, the more aware I became of the paucity of women attending ASOR conferences and serving in leadership roles within ASOR. In early September 2001, I attended ASOR's "Strategic Initiatives Retreat," and I left the Retreat committed to making a difference in ASOR's gender dynamic. In 2002, I joined the Board of Trustees, where I was one of a few women—and where the concerns of women working in Near Eastern archaeology were not a priority.[9] Educated in the tenets of processual and post-processual archaeology, working with scholars who thought deeply about process in all its permutations, I found it ironic that as an institution, ASOR had little process for identifying its gender-based problems and for implementing long-overdue systemic changes. At the same time, though, the disconnect I experienced between

my present occupation and my past work and life experiences meant that it took me time to reconnect with the methodologies and tools of C-R groups and Community Profile task forces, and to apply them to ameliorating these problems of gender-based discrimination.

Parity is not simply a practical goal but also an ethical mandate. Parity is both a statement about equivalence and a statement about human values. Within our field, the metrics for parity must include equality of opportunity, of access to professional advancement, of position and title, of areas of responsibility, of salary and benefits, of respect, and of professional and public visibility and recognition. I wondered to what extent ASOR, a 120-year-old non-profit organization with U.S. Federal 501(3)(c) status and all the attendant legal responsibilities,[10] had achieved gender parity. Gender balance within ASOR's membership is difficult to determine since ASOR does not systematically collect personal information. Even so, those of us who have attended annual meetings for decades realize that many more women are present nowadays than in the past.

Over the years, I have looked at gender balance within ASOR leadership, including the officers, trustees, and committee chairs.[11] I began speaking about gender bias in ASOR leadership at the annual meeting in 2007 and I have discussed it many times since then. I used my position on ASOR's Board Nominations Committee to help redress this imbalance.[12] It was not until 1973 that a woman served as an ASOR trustee (Joy Ungerleider Mayerson; Director, The Jewish Museum, New York City). Now, almost half a century later, about half the Board trustees

---

7 https://www.sbl-site.org/SBLCommittees_CSWP_
   Activities.aspx

8 I served first as chair (1999–2012) and, with Stephanie Langin-Hooper, as co-chair (2013–2014). After Langin-Hooper's term as chair, Stephanie Budin assumed the role and was recently joined by Debra Foran.

9 In 2002, ASOR's Board included seven male officers and one female officer; 18 male trustees and six female trustees.

10 https://www.irs.gov/charities-non-profits/charitable-
    organizations/exemption-requirements-501c3-organi
    zations

11 Much of the data have I used in this research can be found in ASOR program books, in ASOR Archives, and in the *Bulletin of the American Schools of Oriental Research* (*BASOR*). For example, the names of trustees are published in *BASOR*, as were the names of committee members. Now, information on recent years is accessible on the ASOR website. The only data not publicly available is from my Survey on Field Safety (2014; 2015; 2019).

12 Member 2002–2010; Chair 2010–2013.

are women.[13] The movement of women into positions of Board leadership has been similarly slow. In 1985, architectural historian Elizabeth Brennan Moynihan became the first woman to serve as Chair of the Board.[14] In 2014, Susan Ackerman (Dartmouth College) became the first woman to serve as ASOR president and in 2020, Sharon Herbert became the second. By way of comparison, the Archaeological Institute of America elected its first female president in 1965 (Margaret Thompson; American Numismatic Society), and the Society of Biblical Literature elected its first female president in 1987 (Elisabeth Schuessler Fiorenza; Episcopal Divinity School).

FINDING WOMEN ON EXCAVATIONS

I have looked, as well, at women in leadership positions on excavations, focusing on those affiliated with ASOR through its Committee on Archaeological Research and Policy (CAP).[15] CAP records for countries throughout the Middle East and North Africa begin in 1967.[16] In 1971, the first woman co-directed a CAP-affiliated excavation (Anita Walker; Idalion, Cyprus); only in 1976 did a woman direct a CAP-affiliated excavation (Robin Brown; Araq el-Amir, Jordan). Change has been uneven; in some countries, men would continue to direct or co-direct all CAP-affiliated

excavations, but in other countries, the situation began to change. By the turn of the century, almost one-quarter of CAP-affiliated directors/co-directors were women, and that percentage has now increased to one-third.[17]

FINDING WOMEN IN ACADEMIC PUBLICATIONS

Publishing, as well we know, is a litmus test for professional success. Neither laudable professional and community service (both of which are disproportionately undertaken by women), nor excellence in teaching (evaluations of which are well known to be biased against women) promote an academic career in the same way as does a strong record of publications. The metrics for evaluating a publication dossier can vary; books, peer reviewed articles in journals and in edited volumes, the number of citations in other scholars' work (despite the well-known devaluation of women's research in citation counts),[18] and more, are ranked differently by different institutions. In thinking about equity, parity, and women's professional success, gender-based publication and citation disparities cannot be ignored.[19]

I am considering publications from a different vantage, as well, looking at commemorative volumes (*Festschrift*s and memorials), which have become increasingly important in biblical and Near Eastern studies. Organized by colleagues or by

---

13 By the mid-1980s, almost one-quarter of ASOR's trustees were women but not every subsequent Board maintained that modest standard. At the start of the twenty-first century, male trustees outnumbered female trustees by approximately 3:1. In 2013 and 2014, the proportion of men to women stood at approximately 2:1 (Nakhai 2014d; 2014e).

14 In 1986, Anne Cabot Ogilvy (Board trustee, American Center of Oriental Research, Amman) became ASOR's first female officer (assistant treasurer). In 1992, Lydie Shufro (Board trustee, W. F. Albright Institute of Archaeological Research, Jerusalem) became ASOR's first female vice president (for Development).

15 CAP affiliation is voluntary, not mandatory, for projects directed by ASOR members (https://www.asor.org/about-asor/committees/standing-committees/committee-on-archaeological-research-policy-2021/).

16 Records for most—but not all—years between 1967–2020 can be found in the ASOR Archives, and for recent years, on the ASOR website. My thanks to ASOR Archivist Cynthia Rufo, and to Abbe Alpert, for their help with the CAP records in the ASOR Archives.

17 My then-student, Valerie Schlegel (now, Prelee), worked with me on this project. She presented the interim results of our work at the ASOR annual meeting in 2014 (Schlegel 2014a; 2014b; see also Nakhai 2014c; 2014d; 2015c; Ebeling 2011).

18 In response to a discussion about gender parity in citations at a meeting of the ISW Steering Committee, Jennie Ebeling (University of Evansville) and Leanne Pace (Wake Forest University) undertook a study of citations in ASOR publications. They reported their findings at ASOR's 2014 annual meeting (Ebeling and Pace 2014). For other work on this problem, see, inter alia, West et al. 2013; Dion, Sumner, and Mitchell 2018. I confess that once I read "Self-Citation and Gender" (King et al. 2017), I began forcing myself to generously self-cite (as I have in this article), something that I never would have done before!

19 The bibliography is large. For archaeology, see, inter alia, Bolger 2003; Bardolph 2014; Fulkerson and Tushingham 2019.

former students, commemoratives honor scholars on special occasions or memorialize a lifetime of distinguished scholarship. *Festschrift*s originated in the last decades of the nineteenth century but did not become common until the 1990s and, since then, their popularity has grown exponentially. Women were honored in just under ten percent of the more than 150 commemorative volumes from Israel, Jordan, and Palestine, spanning the years 1908–2018. Further underscoring the extent of the gender-based bias in scholarship, the first volume honoring a woman was published in 1978, and the single volume memorializing a woman was published in 2012 (Bauer and Nakhai 2018).[20]

ADVANCING ETHICAL BEHAVIORS: WOMEN'S RIGHTS ARE HUMAN RIGHTS

At the 1995 United Nations Fourth World Conference on Women, in Beijing, Hillary Rodham Clinton famously asserted that "Women's Rights are Human Rights."[21] As an ASOR Trustee (2002–2015), I became concerned that, to accommodate acquiescence to cultural norms in some countries across the Middle East and North Africa, ASOR's Committee on Archaeological Research and Policy (CAP) might affiliate excavations that chose to exclude women from high visibility positions. I proposed to the Board that ASOR prohibit any actions within the United States or abroad that would violate Federal Equal Employment Opportunity Commission (EEOC) legislation.[22] By unanimous vote, the Board included the following in its 2005 *Case Statement*: "In its operations abroad, ASOR should not violate human rights legislation that binds all of us in this country (equal opportunity legislation)." Now, ASOR's website contains a "Non-Discrimination

Policy," which reproduces the EEOC language.[23]

In 2010, ASOR President Timothy Harrison (University of Toronto) charged an *ad hoc* Ethics Working Group to "help the Board develop a single, comprehensive ethics policy to replace ASOR's piecemeal and sometimes competing ethics policies."[24] In its 2013 workshop, "The Values of ASOR: Developing a Comprehensive Ethics Policy," Jennie Ebeling (University of Evansville) and I spoke about "ASOR's Role in Fostering Gender Equity in Near Eastern Archaeology" (Ebeling and Nakhai 2013). In 2015, ASOR adopted a "Policy on Professional Conduct," which states, in part, that:

"...ASOR members endeavor to:
C.4. refuse to practice discrimination based on categories such as gender, religion, age, race, disability, and sexual orientation in assembling a research team;
C.5. take all necessary steps to minimize personal risks and hazards to co-workers, the public, and the environment; including, but not limited to, avoiding harassment based on categories noted in paragraph C.4; and developing action plans in the event of civil or military disturbance, or injury."[25]

Significant as it is, the policy lacks mechanisms for monitoring and enforcement. In addition, it does not fully address what has become an increasingly conspicuous problem, that of gender-based harassment, intimidation, and violence in fieldwork settings, a topic to which I will return.

---

20 My then-student, Amanda Bauer, worked with me on this project, and we co-presented the interim results of our work at the ASOR annual meeting in 2018 (Bauer and Nakhai 2018).

21 Rodham Clinton was not, of course, the first to make this assertion, but her public declaration reverberated worldwide.

22 https://www.eeoc.gov.

23 "ASOR is an Equal Opportunity Employer. ASOR affirms its commitment to equality of opportunity and pledges that it will not practice or permit discrimination in employment on the basis of race, color, gender, national origin, age, religion, creed, disability, veteran's status, sexual orientation, or gender identity" (http://www.asor.org/about-asor/policies/non-discrimination-policy/).

24 http://www.asor.org/blog/2013/04/05/asor-and-archaeological-ethics/.

25 http://www.asor.org/about-asor/policies/policy-on-professional-conduct/.

LISTENING AND TAKING ACTION

The primary tenet of Consciousness Raising—and of Tucson/Pima County Community Profile—was sitting together, talking, and listening before crafting plans for action. In 2007, there were not enough papers to fill ASOR's "Gender" session and I decided to use that unfilled time to do what C-R and Community Profile had taught me to do: create a space for people to talk, share their thoughts, ideas, and feelings, identify problems, and arrive at ways of resolving them. Jennie Ebeling and I co-chaired a special session that we called "Open Mic on the Status of Women in Near Eastern Archaeology," and we made sure that it was included in the ASOR program book, so that people could incorporate it into their busy meeting schedules (Ebeling and Nakhai 2007). Some 75 individuals, mostly but not exclusively women, attended. Complaints were voiced, ideas offered, and solutions proffered.

In the years that followed, I maintained my focus on the status of women in ASOR and on gender equality in Near Eastern archaeology. In 2011, ASOR president Tim Harrison created an *ad hoc* committee, the Initiative on the Status of Women in ASOR (ISW), to address ethics and equity as they relate to women within ASOR, and he asked me to serve as its chair.[26] This great honor has provided me with a platform from which I could expand my efforts to promote ethical behaviors and to foster gender equality in our professional world. In March 2012, I emailed ASOR's membership to learn more about members' concerns as they relate to issues of gender in Near Eastern studies. Their responses were, as one might imagine, diverse, and they reflected what we had learned from the open-mic session of 2007 and from many subsequent discussions. Responses clustered around four topics: the field of archaeology; academia; ASOR; and the Middle East. Only two respondents raised concerns about physical safety in fieldwork settings. While some comments

were positive, women overall felt disadvantaged. They found limited opportunities to attain top-level positions in academia, fieldwork, and at ASOR; they were burdened by the complexities of balancing work and family; they noted the lack of access to funding sources, which follow people in premier academic and archaeological positions; and they commented on the paucity of senior women in Near Eastern studies. Among their suggestions for ASOR were to provide childcare at the annual meetings; advocate for family-friendly excavations; promote gender equity at colleges, universities, and seminaries that are ASOR's institutional members; facilitate mentoring between senior and junior women; create a database to track the professional status of women in ASOR and in Near Eastern archaeology; and engage in concerted efforts to effect change (Nakhai 2012a; 2012b). Even seemingly simple actions, like providing access to childcare at ASOR's annual meetings, have proven complicated—and all of it is work that must be accomplished in community (for more on this topic, see Heath-Stout's "Building an Ethical and Inclusive Research Community," this volume).

THE POWER OF PERSON-TO-PERSON CONNECTIONS

To develop and prioritize goals, create action plans, and actualize change, ASOR needed a working group. I launched a Steering Committee for the Initiative on the Status of Women; it convenes every year at ASOR's November meeting. In 2012, I worked with ASOR staff to develop an interactive "Women of ASOR" map, which shows women's academic and employment settings and their field projects.[27] In 2013, I launched the first of the ISW Mentoring Lunches, designed to bridge barriers by informally connecting junior and emerging scholars with senior women. They are held annually, during the November meeting. Donor underwriting ensures that the Mentoring Lunch is accessible to everyone, regardless of budgetary constraints. The ISW Facebook page,

---

26 http://www.asor.org/about-asor/committees/ad-hoc-asor-committees/asor-initiative-on-the-status-of-women/.

27 http://www.asor.org/initiatives-projects/women-of-asor-map/.

launched in 2015, is a way of sharing information, ideas, and observations; the group, not limited to ASOR members, now has almost 300 members.[28] I also introduced a series of workshops, which have served as a forum for discussions of women in the workplace. All are designed to provide (primarily but never exclusively) women with venues in which they can reflect upon their own experiences and learn about what other women have experienced, as well.[29]

KEEPING WOMEN—AND MEN—SAFE IN THE FIELD

Fieldwork has, of course, always had gender-based problematics. I remember a situation some decades ago when several women on an excavation approached the director to complain about male staff members who persisted in making unwanted physical advances. They were advised to put up with them because the men were venerable members of the project and, in at least one instance, of the local community. Stories like this circulated every summer, but in those days, no one in charge thought that they mattered, let alone that they highlighted a problem requiring immediate and systemic repair. It is easy to wonder, in retrospect, why we all were not more vocal, more persistent in our complaints, more adamant in our demands, but that was, let us say, a different time.

Despite the many oft told and well-known stories, I, like most of us, never thought comprehensively about field safety for women. That changed in 2013, though, in response to the work done by four bioanthropologists, Kate Clancy, Robin Nelson, Julienne Rutherford, and Katie Hinde. At the annual meeting of the American Association of Physical Anthropologists, Clancy stated that

"undergraduates, graduate students, postdocs, and faculty report sexual harassment and assault not only by their peers, but by their bosses and mentors in the field" (Clancy 2013a). They have published their work in (inter alia) *Scientific American* (Clancy 2013b), *PLoSONE* (Clancy et al. 2014) and *American Anthropologist* (Nelson et al. 2017), and in 2018 Clancy testified before the U.S. Congressional Subcommittee on Research and Technology, at its hearing on Sexual Harassment and Misconduct in the Sciences (Clancy 2018).

The moment that I read about their work, I committed myself to investigating the problem of safety in the field for female archaeologists working in the Middle East and North Africa—and to making it possible for everyone to engage in fieldwork across our broad region without fear of intimidation, harassment, and violence based on gender, sexual orientation, or gender identity. I realized that to get started, I would need to quantify the problem. I completed Institutional Review Board (IRB) training (required for work with human subjects), and in 2014, 2015, and 2019, I used Qualtrics to circulate the *Survey on Field Safety: Middle East, North Africa, and The Mediterranean Basin* (Nakhai 2014b; 2015b; 2019a).

The multi-year survey received more than 650 responses from people in two dozen countries. According to respondents, in 2019 more digs had codes of conduct than they had in 2014 and 2015, and the codes increasingly contained language defining and prohibiting sexual violations. Responsibility for reporting violations was increasingly mandated, as were repercussions. Nonetheless, acceptance of sexual violations remained a problem, as did drug abuse and alcohol abuse, violence, racial and/or religious harassment, theft, vandalism, and more. So, too, did expropriation of professional contributions, and harassment, intimidation, and discrimination in fieldwork and post-fieldwork assignments and opportunities based on gender, sexual orientation, and/or gender identity. Perpetrators of assaults and other violations included individuals in positions of authority (for more on this topic, see Erny and Nakassis' "Gender and Power in the Practice of Mediterranean Archaeology," this volume).

---

28 https://www.facebook.com/groups/1469401773364915/.

29 "Women in Near Eastern Archaeology: An Open Forum" brought four senior women together to discuss their experiences in the field (Nakhai 2012c). Stephanie Langin-Hooper and I co-chaired "Women at Work: Making One's Way in The Field of Near Eastern Studies" (Langin-Hooper and Nakhai 2014). Five years later, Jennie Ebeling and I organized another workshop, "Talking About: Jobs, Fieldwork, and Family" (Ebeling and Nakhai 2019).

In their survey responses, some people recounted violations of their physical and/or emotional integrity that they had never before discussed, and they noted their appreciation at finally being able to talk about them. I have spoken with respondents and others—excavation directors, staff, and volunteers—who have shared their own stories and, sometimes, sought advice for handling difficult situations.[30] My experience with Consciousness Raising groups, Tucson/Pima County Community Profile task forces, and life has taught me that sometimes people need to say a thing out loud—and have someone hear what they say—in order to process it themselves. In this way, the act of listening becomes a conduit to justice.

One point reiterated by Community Profile task force members from underrepresented and marginalized communities is that one cannot expect a community in pain to bear the sole responsibility for resolving the obstacles it faces. Lesson learned: it was incumbent upon me—and others, too—not only to identify problems but also to follow up within and beyond ASOR. When I first discussed sexual assault, harassment, and discrimination in archaeological field settings with the ASOR Board in 2013, I had faced skepticism, but survey data blunted much of the doubt. I spoke about the myriad problems at ASOR's annual meetings (Nakhai 2014a; 2014d).[31] I organized and moderated two ASOR workshops on the topic (Nakhai 2017d; 2018c). I spoke in non-ASOR venues in the United States and in Europe.[32] I published survey results in professional and public venues.[33] In 2017, I was interviewed by Rebecca Greenberg for *Game Plan*, a Bloomberg podcast; the episode was entitled *The Harvey Weinstein in Your Industry* (Greenberg and Nakhai 2017).

Final Reflections

I conclude this essay with some final thoughts. I highlight, first, a problem that requires urgent attention and decisive action—the widely-acknowledged lack of inclusivity in Near Eastern studies and within ASOR, with regard to (and here I employ U.S. EEOC language) "race/color," "national origin," "sexual orientation," and "gender identity."[34] Since the time of Napoleon, the field of Near Eastern studies has been dominated by men, virtually all white, Protestant, and heterosexual. Although this demographic has been somewhat transformed in the last half century, the transformation is inadequate. The imperative for activism with the goal of full inclusivity is incumbent upon us, and upon our professional societies and places of employment. Toward this goal, ASOR recently launched a Task Force on Diversity, Equity, and Inclusion, to recruit and support people within BIPOC (Black, Indigenous, and People of Color) communities.[35]

A second problem that must be addressed is the question of whether ASOR (or any professional society), given its Federal 501(3)(c) status, can continue to support academic institutions that themselves are not committed to gender equality. Here, I am thinking about seminaries and other Christian-affiliated institutions that bar women from certain faculty positions, such as those that entail teaching Bible, and that do not promote women to leadership positions on excavations

---

30 I have never, of course, violated the complete confidentiality of all those who have shared information and stories with me, whether by means of the surveys, emails, personal meetings, phone calls, or other modes of communication.

31 I have, as well, spoken with the Board, and with ASOR's Committee on Archaeological Research and Policy (CAP), which disseminated information to directors of ASOR-affiliated excavations.

32 Center for Middle Eastern Studies at University of Arizona (Tucson, AZ; Nakhai 2016); Second Workshop on Gender, Methodology and the Ancient Near East, Universitat de Barcelona (Spain; Nakhai 2017a); Society for American Archaeology (Washington, DC; Nakhai 2018a); Third Workshop on Gender, Methodology and the Ancient Near East, Ghent University (Belgium; Nakhai

2019b); European Association of Archaeologists (Nakhai 2020).

33 These include an ASOR Blogpost (Nakhai 2015a) and print and online journals (GenderStudies.Science [Nakhai 2017b]; *Mar Shiprim: Newsletter of the International Association for Assyriology* [Nakhai 2017c]; and *The Chronicle of Higher Education* [Nakhai 2018b]).

34 https://www.eeoc.gov/discrimination-type.

35 https://www.asor.org/about-asor/committees/dei-task-force.

(Ebeling 2019) and within ASOR. These entities, once they make the requisite donation to ASOR and become institutional members, fail to appoint women to ASOR's Board of Trustees. However, since they are institutional members, ASOR supports job discrimination by providing them with platforms on which to advertise job openings.[36] This needs to change.

This essay contains, I know, more personal narrative than is customary in professional publications but ethics are, of course, deeply personal. For me, as for many of us, the imperative to behave ethically is deeply rooted in familial and religious values. In my work relating to safety from sexual harassment and violence, I have been powerfully motivated by the fact that as children, my sisters and I— and perhaps many other girls—were molested by a (now long deceased) family member. Our ongoing efforts to seek justice were finally realized, within the last few years.[37] As we stepped forward, first advocating for justice, and later publicizing our story and connecting our names to it, I developed an even more profound respect for all those who have come forth to stand against gender-based violence, harassment, and discrimination in our field.

I close this essay by acknowledging, first of all, the climate of change that is afoot in Near Eastern archaeology—and in archaeology around the globe. Women, and concerned men, are addressing threats to field safety, the dismissal of women's contributions in the field and in post-excavation settings, impediments to women's advancement in academia and in professional societies, discrimination in publishing, and more. There is power in the growing number of people (including the editors of this volume and those contributing to it) who are willing to take

time from their own pressing professional and personal responsibilities to engage in the hard work of effecting change—by bringing people together, doing the research, speaking out about what they have learned, and publishing their results. They—we—advocate for differences that will alter not only the world in which we live and work but also our ability to understand the past. I do not see how we can honor the voices of the people who came before us if we do not honor the voices of each one of us today.

I want, too, to acknowledge the discomfort I have felt while writing this essay, even as I thank Sarah Lepinski and Sarah Costello for having invited me to contribute to *Ethics in Archaeological in Practice.* Their description of this book hooked me immediately: "The proposed volume will explore pressing topics and issues surrounding archaeological ethics as currently practiced, particularly as they relate to the ASOR membership, and address the principles of ethics in practice and professional responsibility surrounding conduct and authority in archaeology."[38] I am enthusiastic about this opportunity to highlight ethical concerns and to consider solutions to gender-based problems within ASOR and in our field. Even as I have thought about those personal circumstances that have empowered me, impeded me, and shaped my actions, I also recognize the great capacity for creating change that comes from engaging with a community of colleagues and friends.

REFERENCES

Bardolph, D. N.
2014   A Critical Evaluation of Recent Gendered Publishing Trends in American Archaeology. *American Antiquity* 79.3: 522-40.

Bauer, A. L., and Nakhai, B. A.
2018   "In Honor or Memory of" Whom? Exploring the Gendered Nature of Festschrifts and Memorial Volumes. Paper presented at the 2018 Annual Meeting of the American Schools of Oriental Research.

---

36 http://www.asor.org/memberships/institutional-memberships/.

37 For full discussion, see https://www.hadassahmagazine.org/2021/05/04/sisters-sexually-abused-renowned-cantor-speak-publicly-first-time/. My thanks to reporter Rahel Musleah and *Hadassah Magazine* editor Lisa Hostein for their commitment to exposing and ending abuse in Jewish institutions, and for their work on this article (Musleah 2021). See also https://www.jewishvirtuallibrary.org/putterman-david.

38 Email of June 13, 2019.

Bolger, D.
2003   Epilogue: Cypriot Archaeology—Who Tells the Story? Pp. 199–212 in *Gender in Ancient Cyprus: Narratives of Social Change on a Mediterranean Island*, by D. Bolger. Walnut Creek, CA: AltaMira.

Clancy, K. B. H.
2013a   Ethics of Field Site Management and Oversight. Paper given at the 82nd Annual Meeting of the American Association of Physical Anthropologists. *American Journal of Physical Anthropology* 150.S56: 39.
2013b   I Had No Power to Say That's Not Okay: Reports of Harassment and Abuse in the Field. *Scientific American: Context and Variation.* April 13, 2013. https://blogs.scientificamerican.com/context-and-variation/safe13-field-site-chilly-climate-and-abuse/
2018   A Review of Sexual Harassment and Misconduct in Science: Written Testimony. Address to U.S. House Subcommittee on Research and Technology Hearing on Sexual Harassment and Misconduct in Science. Feb. 27, 2018. https://www.congress.gov/event/115th-congress/house-event/106873

Clancy, K. B. H.; Nelson, R. G.; Rutherford, J. N.; and Hinde, K.
2014   Survey of Academic Field Experiences (SAFE): Trainees Report Harassment and Assault. *PLoS ONE* 9.7: e102172. https://doi.org/10.1371/journal.pone.0102172

Dion, M. L.; Sumner, J. L.; and Mitchell, S. M.
2018   Gendered Citation Patterns across Political Science and Social Science Methodology Fields. *Political Analysis* 26.3: 312–27.

Dry, R. (ed.)
2019   In Her Words (column). *New York Times.* Aug. 19, 2019.

Ebeling, J.
2011   Where Are the Female Dig Directors in Israel? The Bible and Interpretation. https://bibleinterp.arizona.edu/opeds/ebeling358011
2019   Archaeological Views: Missing from the Picture: American Women in Biblical Archaeology. *Biblical Archaeology Review* 45.4: 22–24.

Ebeling, J., and Nakhai, B. A.
2007   Open Mic on the Status of Women in Near Eastern Archaeology. Session organizers and co-moderators; 2007 Annual Meeting of the American Schools of Oriental Research.
2013   ASOR's Role in Fostering Gender Equity in Near Eastern Archaeology. Workshop organizers and co-moderators; 2013 Annual Meeting of the American Schools of Oriental Research.
2019   Talking About: Jobs, Fieldwork, and Family. Workshop organizers and co-moderators; 2019 Annual Meeting of the American Schools of Oriental Research.

Ebeling, J., and Pace, L.
2014   Writing It Right: The Inclusion of Women in ASOR Publications. Paper presented at the 2014 Annual Meeting of the American Schools of Oriental Research.

Fulkerson, T. J., and Tushingham, S.
2019   Who Dominates the Discourse of the Past? Gender, Occupational Affiliation, and Multivocality in North American Archaeology Publishing. *American Antiquity* 84.3: 379–99.

Greenberg, R., and Nakhai, B. A.
2017   The Harvey Weinstein in Your Industry. Interview for Bloomberg podcast, *Game Plan*; host Rebecca Greenfield. https://www.bloomberg.com/news/articles/2017-10-25/the-harvey-weinstein-in-your-industry-j9742fly

Kha, S., and Peckham, C. (eds.)
1994   *A Call to Action: Tucson/Pima County Community Profile.* Tucson, AZ.

King, M. M.; Bergstrom, C. T.; Correll, S.; Jacquet, J.; and West, J.
2017   Men Set Their Own Cites High: Gender and Self-citation across Fields and over Time. *Socius* 3: 1–22.

Langin-Hooper, S., and Nakhai, B. A.
2014   Women at Work: Making One's Way in The Field of Near Eastern Studies. Workshop organizers and co-moderators; 2014 Annual Meeting of the American Schools of Oriental Research.

Meyers, C. L.
1988   *Discovering Eve: Ancient Israelite Women in Context.* New York: Oxford University.

Musleah, R.
2021   Childhood Abuse, Adult Reckoning: Sisters Find Solace in Posthumous Fall of Renowned Cantor. *Hadassah Magazine* 102.6: 20–23.

Nakhai, B. A.
2012a On the Professional Advancement of Women in Near Eastern Archaeology. *The Bible and Interpretation.* https://bibleinterp.arizona.edu/articles/nak368016
2012b The Status of Women in ASOR. ASOR blogpost. http://asorblog.org/?p=2631
2012c Women in Near Eastern Archaeology: An Open Forum. Session chair; 2012 Annual Meeting of the American Schools of Oriental Research.
2014a Keeping Field Work Safe from Sexual Harassment and Physical Violence. Paper presented at the 2014 Annual Meeting of the American Schools of Oriental Research
2014b *Survey on Field Safety (2014): Middle East, North Africa, and The Mediterranean Basin.* http://bit.ly/FieldSafety
2014c Symposium on Women in Archaeology. Symposium participant. University of Pennsylvania.
2014d Women in ASOR: ASOR Leadership and CAP-Affiliated Excavations. Paper presented at the 2014 Annual Meeting of the American Schools of Oriental Research.
2014e Women on ASOR's Board of Trustees. ASOR blogpost. http://asorblog.org/?p=7080
2015a Keeping Fieldwork Safe from Sexual Harassment and Violence. ASOR blogpost. http://asorblog.org/2015/03/20/keeping-fieldwork-safe-from-sexual-harassment-and-physical-violence/
2015b *Survey on Field Safety (2015): Middle East, North Africa, and The Mediterranean Basin.* http://bit.ly/FieldSafety2015
2015c Women in Archaeology and the Archaeology of Women. Conference on Pioneering Women in Fields of Knowledge. Brigham Young University.
2016   Safety in the Field: Perspectives from Anthropology, Archaeology, and Journalism. Panelist; Center for Middle Eastern Studies, University of Arizona.
2017a Keeping Field Work Safe from Sexual Harassment and Physical Violence. Second Workshop on Gender, Methodology and the Ancient Near East, Universitat de Barcelona. Barcelona, Spain.
2017b Keeping Archaeological Field Work Safe from Sexual Harassment and Physical Violence. http://www.genderstudies.science/2017/05/21/keeping-archaeological-field-work-safe-from-sexual-harassment-and-physical-violence/
2017c Keeping Archaeological Field Work Safe from Sexual Harassment and Physical Violence. *Mar Shiprim: Newsletter of the International Association for Assyriology.* https://iaassyriology.com/field-work-safe/
2017d Talking About: How to Handle "Situations." Workshop organizer and moderator; 2017 Annual Meeting of the American Schools of Oriental Research.
2018a Gender-based Violence and Discrimination in Middle Eastern and North African Fieldwork. Paper presented at the 2018 Annual Meeting of the Society for American Archaeology.
2018b How to Avoid Gender-Based Hostility during Fieldwork. *The Chronicle of Higher Education.* Print 20 July 2018; online 15 July 2018. https://www.chronicle.com/article/How-to-Avoid-Gender-Based/243912?key=Bj9VwqXvQvYd6fLOxLcWg-78FoZKfqTPQnPI-dXlIMwmSm4xLfDQHEZXkglma5ifTXJSZGxVSzJ1SlBqRFF6Yjd3cmVaLWM1NEd1WE5URVB1NkNIQXN0Y0JxNA
2018c Talking About: How to Make Fieldwork Safe from Gender-based Violence, Ha-

rassment and Discrimination. Workshop organizer and moderator; 2018 Annual Meeting of the American Schools of Oriental Research.

2019a Survey on Field Safety (Update 2019): Middle East, North Africa, and The Mediterranean Basin. FieldSafety2019.

2019b Violence, Harassment, Intimidation, and Discrimination in Archaeological Field Settings. Third Workshop on Gender, Methodology and the Ancient Near East. Ghent University. Ghent, Belgium.

2020 Gender-based Intimidation, Harassment and Violence in Field Settings: Results from the 2014, 2015 and 2019 Surveys. European Association of Archaeologists, virtual conference.

Nelson, R. G.; Rutherford, J. N.; Hinde, K.; and Clancy, K. B. H.

2017 Signaling Safety: Characterizing Fieldwork Experiences and Their Implications for Career Trajectories. *American Anthropologist* 119/4: 710–22. https://doi.org/10.1111/aman.12929

Sarachild, K.

1979 Consciousness-Raising: A Radical Weapon. Pp. 144–50 in *Feminist Revolution: An Abridged Edition with Additional Writings*, ed. K. Sarachild, C. Hanisch, F. Levine, B. Leon, and C. Price. New York: Random House.

Schlegel, V.

2014a Breaking In: Women's Representation in Archaeology. Paper presented at the 2014 Annual Meeting of the American Schools of Oriental Research.

2014b Breaking In: Women's Representation in Archaeology. ASOR blogpost. http://asor-blog.org/?p=7096

West, J.; Jacquet, J.; King, M. M.; Correll, S.; and Bergstrom, C. T.

2013 The Role of Gender in Scholarly Authorship. *PLoS ONE* 8/7: e66212. https://doi.org/10.1371/journal.pone.0066212

Chapter 2

Building an Ethical and Inclusive Research Community

Insights from Interviews with Archaeologists

Laura E. Heath-Stout

ABSTRACT

Archaeological ethics have historically been framed with a focus on the preservation of sites and artifacts, and archaeologists' responsibilities to various stakeholder communities. Rarely, however, do publications on archaeological ethics explore how archaeologists treat one another. In this chapter, I explore the practices that archaeologists use to build research communities that are ethical, diverse, and inclusive, whether in the context of field projects, laboratories, museums, or academic departments. I draw from my qualitative interview study with a diverse sample of 72 archaeologists (many of whom conduct research in the Mediterranean or the Middle East); interviews focused on my interlocutors' career paths, research trajectories, and perceptions and experiences of privilege and oppression in the discipline. These interviews allowed me to identify the barriers that prevent marginalized people from being recruited into and retained in archaeological careers. I present concrete steps that leaders and participants in archaeological research communities can take in order to make those communities more open, diverse, ethical, and rigorous. If we all do our parts, we can build a discipline as diverse as the human past we study.

INTRODUCTION

In 2016, the Society for American Archaeology (SAA) added a ninth statement to its Principles of Archaeological Ethics:

Archaeologists in all work, educational, and other professional settings, including fieldwork and conferences, are responsible for training the next generation of archaeologists. Part of these responsibilities involves fostering a supportive and safe environment for students and trainees. This includes knowing the laws and policies of their home nation and institutional workplace that pertain to harassment and assault based upon sex, gender identity, sexual orientation, ethnicity, disability, national origin, religion, or marital status. SAA members will abide by these laws and ensure that the work and educational settings in which they have responsible roles as supervisors are conducted so as to avoid violations of these laws and act to maintain safe and respectful work and learning environments. (Society for American Archaeology n.d.)

When the proposal to add this principle was sent to the membership, some archaeologists argued that these concerns should not be considered part of archaeological ethics. For example, Michael Smith (2016) published a blog post titled "Why I voted NO on SAA ethics principle 9." His first objection was that "these are not archaeological principles. They do not concern sites or artifacts or fieldwork or the archaeological record."

Indeed, disciplinary ethics have usually been framed in the terms that Smith uses: "sites, artifacts, fieldwork, [and] the archaeological record," as well as relationships between archaeologists and the descendants of their research subjects. A brief perusal of the tables of contents of a variety of books on archaeological ethics shows that many are focused on how we treat archaeological sites, museum collections, descendant communities, and various publics, but lack discussion of how archaeologists treat one another (e.g., Gnecco and Lippert 2016; Green 1984; Ireland and Schofield 2015; Lynott and Wylie 2000; Scarre and Scarre 2006; Vitelli and Colwell 2006), although there are some exceptions (e.g., Zimmerman, Vitelli, and Hollowell-Zimmer 2003). Given this disciplinary context, it is not surprising that there would be disagreement among archaeologists about whether the creation of safe workplaces should be considered part of archaeological ethics. The majority of SAA members disagreed with Smith, however, and voted in favor of adding the statement (Gifford-Gonzalez 2016), and so it became part of the Society's official Principles.

Of course, adding a principle to an ethics statement does not immediately change the practices of the discipline; indeed, as Sara Ahmed (2012; 2017) has compellingly argued, institutional statements about diversity and inclusion may be red herrings in our attempts to build justice. As she puts it,

Institutions might name things or say yes to something in order not to bring some things into effect. We too as diversity workers might labor for something (a new policy, a new document), and these things can provide yet more techniques whereby institutions appear to do something without doing anything. This is difficult: our own efforts to transform institutions can be used by institutions as evidence that they have been transformed. (Ahmed 2017: 103)

The standard set by Principle 9 is modest: I have higher hopes for archaeology's disciplinary culture than an absence of violent crimes committed against one another! The work of creating an ethical and equitable archaeology goes beyond writing or living up to particular statements, as I discuss in this article.

Regardless of its effectiveness in changing archaeologists' individual behaviors or institutional policies, the vote on Principle 9 signaled a shift in the ways that archaeologists see our responsibilities: we now see building safe, respectful, and diverse professional communities as part of ethical practice. Our ethical responsibilities are not only to sites and artifacts, but to the people we interact with as we do our work: colleagues, students, employees, collaborators, stakeholders, and community members. Archaeological research is nearly always conducted in collaborative groups, making ethical treatment of each other especially salient to our practice. Furthermore, archaeologists in positions of power have the ethical responsibility to ensure that those they work with, teach, and supervise treat one another well, regardless of their different identities.

This is an important charge, but a difficult one. How can academic departments, research projects, professional organizations, and individuals work toward the goal of creating a discipline of archaeology that is diverse, inclusive, and safe? In this chapter, I draw on interviews with a diverse sample of archaeologists about their career paths and their experiences of privilege and discrimination in the discipline (Heath-Stout 2019). I demonstrate that marginalized people (e.g., women, people of color, queer people) face barriers to both entering and succeeding in archaeological career paths, and provide suggestions for how archaeologists can proactively lower these barriers in order to recruit and retain a diverse new generation of researchers.

Methods

In this chapter, I present data from the qualitative interview study completed as part of my dissertation research (Heath-Stout 2019). I conducted in-depth interviews with a diverse sample of archaeologists, exploring their career paths, research interests, and experiences and perceptions of race, gender, and sexuality issues in the field. The sample consisted of 72 archaeologists, all of whom are affiliated with universities in the United States. Informants were recruited through a mixture of social media announcements, invitations in relevant conference interest group meetings, and snowball sampling. Interviews focused on the informants' career trajectories, research interests, and experiences of gender, race, and sexuality in the discipline. They were recorded, transcribed, and analyzed using a grounded theory approach (Charmaz 2014). This study was approved by the Boston University Institutional Review Board (protocol number 4381X). See the dissertation (Heath-Stout 2019: ch. 8) for a more detailed description of the sample and methods.

Lowering Barriers to Entry and Recruiting Diverse Archaeology Students

Our efforts to diversify the discipline must begin with who we recruit to become archaeologists. My interviewees formed two groups: those who had discovered archaeology before entering college and those who discovered it as undergradu-

ates. The children who decide to become archaeologists must be exposed to the idea in order to set that goal for themselves. My interviewees encountered archaeology through school curricula, museum and site visits, and media ranging from *Indiana Jones* to PBS documentaries. Since pre-college experiences are fertile ground for recruiting the new generation of archaeology students, we should be thoughtful about who has access to them. Currently, wealthy children have more access to archaeology curricula in schools, and high-income families have more time and money to spend on trips to museums, public archaeology programs, archaeological sites, or similar activities. In order to lower these barriers, archaeologists must be more thoughtful and proactive in our public outreach. More of us should consider actively offering high-quality archaeology programs to under-resourced public schools, and these programs should be free, easily accessible, and widely advertised to diverse communities. We can also ensure that underfunded public libraries and public school libraries have high-quality books and other media about archaeology, to make those resources available to a broader range of students.

Although the archaeologists with cute stories of dreaming of archaeology as children like to tell those stories, most archaeologists—especially archaeologists of color and those with low socioeconomic statuses—find their career paths in college, and so the college classroom is an important place for the creation of a more diverse discipline. Unfortunately, the introductory and general education courses that bring students into archaeology careers are often seen as low priorities by administrators and faculty who value publications over teaching and the mentoring of graduate students over the teaching of undergraduates, especially at research universities (Childress 2019; Long, Allison, and McGinnis 1993; Marshall and Rothgeb 2011; Moosa 2018; Gentry and Stokes 2015). We must resist this metric- and research-focused value system and do our best work in our introductory courses, incorporating diverse cultures and perspectives in order to appeal to a diverse group of students.

Finally, fieldwork is an essential part of the recruitment of new generations of archaeologists. Those who first encountered archaeology in general education classrooms often had their interest cemented by field experiences. Others attended field schools as a way to have a fun and educational summer, and caught the bug. Unfortunately, the high costs of most field schools make them inaccessible to students without deep resources, or who must work for wages during the summer, and the small number of scholarships available are insufficient in both number and amount of financial support (Heath-Stout and Hannigan 2020). There are solutions, however: one informant, now a postdoctoral researcher, who has been working on the same project since he was an undergraduate, noted that this project had never charged fees for student volunteers. He told me,

> If I went to this info session and the professor had said, "And it's a $5000 program fee," I don't think I ever would have become an archaeologist. I honestly don't know where that path would have led, because I had saved enough money from working to get a flight over, I could do that, and I think I got some kind of grant or something from the university. So, that's always been in place, and that's important. And we've maintained that through, I just write a s*** ton of grant applications.

By covering the costs for field school students, this project recruited an archaeologist who now brings a critical eye to socioeconomic stratification in the ancient settlement he studies, and who is willing to write a "s*** ton" of grant applications to keep the project free as he has entered leadership. Other projects are even able to pay students for their research work, through programs like the National Science Foundation's Research Experience for Undergraduates grants (National Science Foundation n.d.). Expensive field schools reproduce the wealthy demographics of the discipline, and in order to change the field, we must make field research experiences available to students of all class backgrounds.

Overall, lack of access to sites, museums, and high-quality archaeology media creates a barrier to entry for many children and teenagers from low socioeconomic backgrounds. The cost of college and of field schools makes it difficult for many to find archaeology, although undergraduate coursework tends to recruit a more diverse group of aspiring archaeologists than pre-college exposure. We must lower these barriers to entry through public archaeology, collaborations with under-resourced public schools, the creation of high-quality media for public audiences, and making field schools affordable to a wider group of students.

Retaining Marginalized Archaeologists

Once students enter archaeological career paths, some of them remain on that path longer than others. While there are many reasons why an archaeologist might leave the discipline for a different career, many of my interviewees discussed leaving particular subfields and even considering leaving the discipline because of hostility, harassment, or bullying. These instances of mistreatment fell along a spectrum from small comments to outright violence.

Many of these incidents were microaggressions: "brief, everyday exchanges that send denigrating messages to certain individuals because of their group membership" (Sue 2010: xvi; see also Lilienfeld 2017). Women often experienced the microaggression of having their authority undermined. One woman discussed being the principal investigator for cultural resource management projects: "I know this is a stereotypic story, but I'd be out there with a field crew, and somebody would come by and say, 'Let me talk to the director. I want to talk to the director,' and I'm saying, 'I'm the director.' They would say, 'No, you're not the director. You can't be the director, because you're a girl.'"

Sometimes sexist microaggressions seem well-intentioned, especially when they take the form of chivalry. Many of my women interlocutors, especially those who work in the Mediterranean or the Middle East, mentioned the problem of carrying buckets or other objects on field sites. Male workers consistently take buckets out of women's hands, and although this may be intended to be helpful, the fact that they do not do so with male archaeologists suggests that they believe that women are unable to carry the buckets. A friend of mine tells this story: while working on a Middle Eastern site, she challenged herself to carry an object across the entire site without having a man take it out of her hands, at least once by the end of the field season. On the final day, she had not yet achieved this, so she ran across the site carrying a bucket, with various men trying to take it from her and being confused about why she was running: she finally made it. Many women archaeologists pride themselves on their physical strength and capability to do the hard labor of fieldwork, so this "helpful" act can be hurtful.

Microaggressions are not just about gender. Interviewees of color also told stories of being undermined as scholars, and their achievements questioned. A Black man I interviewed told me that, "I can definitely tell that there are people that will wonder if I get the certain opportunities I get because I'm a Black archaeologist and I'm sure that comes up a lot. I don't really care what they think about it [laughs]." Queer interviewees also shared stories of heterosexist microaggressions in work settings, often taking the form of homophobic jokes, assumptions of heterosexuality, or explanations that microaggressions were not in fact homophobic. These microaggressions might seem minor when considered individually, but they add up to create a hostile work environment for marginalized people, undermining our authority and suggesting that our colleagues may not respect us as people.

Many of the instances of sexism, racism, and heterosexism that my interviewees described went well beyond microaggressions. Sometimes the actions were explicitly related to a marginalized identity of the target, but other times it was not so clear. One interviewee became the scapegoat for a troubled project when he was a graduate student. Whenever something went wrong, the director would tell him to sit in the cab of the pickup truck with her, and then would

drive around screaming at him that it was all his fault. Years later, he wonders if he was the scapegoat because he was the only person of color on the project.

These instances of mistreatment may or may not be related to identity and structural oppression, but they contribute to the overall unwelcoming environment for marginalized people. One Mesoamericanist related a story of a classmate's experience as an undergraduate at a field school:

> We had two women on our trip to [field site]. One of them went home on the second day because people thought it would be fun to take a dead fer de lance [a poisonous snake] and wrap it around her while she was sleeping. That was the end of her as an anthropologist at [our university]. She abandoned the program altogether. Never saw her back in the school again. And that was sort of seen as a playful hazing ritual. Well, why was she singled out?

My interlocutor was not able to answer that question: it was unclear to him whether this was intended as a sexist action against the woman. Regardless of the intent, it was clearly a deeply upsetting incident that caused that woman to leave anthropology. We can also imagine how it might have felt to be the other woman on the project, and to have the only other woman driven out by bullying. Did she feel safe staying there, as the sole woman surrounded by men who thought putting dead snakes in people's beds was a funny but insignificant joke? We cannot know how the victim of this prank feels now, or how the other woman felt, but my interlocutor remembers the incident years later, and particularly when he sees bullying or sexual harassment in the field. When sexual harassment occurred on his current project, he reflected that,

> People's past experiences, too, were starting to become sort of more...What's the word I'm looking for? Just more visible. Like we'd all had really weird experiences in the past with things...So I think we

were all starting kind of have these weird flashbacks of terrible experiences we'd had when this was going on.

Each incident of bullying or sexual harassment builds on previous incidents, compounding previous traumas.

My interviews showed that sexual harassment and assault are endemic in archaeology, corroborating previous literature on the topic in both archaeology and related field sciences (Adler 2017; Clancy 2013; Clancy et al. 2014; 2017; Colannino et al. 2020; Kelsky 2017; Kloß 2017; Meyers et al. 2018; Nelson et al. 2017; L. Smith et al. 2018; Wright 2002; 2008). Of my 51 cisgender women interviewees, nearly all told stories of sexual harassment when asked about gender issues in the field, and the topic also commonly came up in interviews with men. In most cases, the harassment took place in the context of fieldwork, although there were also instances that took place in universities, laboratories, or offices. Many of these harassers were archaeologists themselves, often superiors to the women they targeted. In some projects, it is expected that young women will sleep with senior men, and the pressure to do so and the power imbalance make it hard to determine whether these relationships are consensual, as Erny and Nakassis (this volume) discuss in more detail. In other cases, the harassment comes from peers or equals within the structure of a field project.

Caitlin, a woman professor, told me this story about a friend and colleague harassing her:

> It was the end of the day and he had been drinking, probably not that much, to be honest. But he had recently been married, and he hit me on the butt, in front of my students. I'm like, "what?" At the time, I'm like, "Did that just happen? What is going on here?" And you know, he probably learned that it was appropriate on the other field seasons that he's been on his whole career... it definitely made me feel lesser than him and I think the students probably

thought something was going on between us. I'm like, "No, that's not..." I mean, we really get along, but it was like, that moment I was like, "You really think of me that way that you would do that in front of people?" And I wish that at the time I had confronted him... And I'm mad that I didn't say anything at the time, but you know what? He's someone that shouldn't have done it. So I've warned people, like: "Hey, if you're in the field with this person, this is what happened to me." And I'm sure it's gotten back to him. I probably should take it up with him. It just feels like it's another thing to do, right? It's more emotional labor to deal with this person. He doesn't deal with any of my students and he's not in a position where he would be anymore. So, that's good.

Caitlin's story is typical in many ways. First, her experience shows that harassers are not always obviously-creepy men: women are in danger of harassment from people they consider good friends. These harassers often use alcohol and the party culture of field schools to evade responsibility for their actions. Being harassed diminishes a women's sense of professional authority: in this case, being harassed in front of her students was an important part of why Caitlin was upset. Although many interviewees expressed a belief or hope that archaeology is "getting better" as each new generation comes of age, Caitlin points out that her colleague had learned this behavior from previous generations of men. Women also often related not knowing how to respond to harassment in the moment, and spent a lot of time in the interviews analyzing their responses to harassment and whether they had reacted correctly, in ways that preserved their own dignity and safety, held harassers accountable, and protected other women from them. Each of these elements came up over and over again in my interviews with women who had survived sexual harassment or assault.

Microaggressions, bullying, sexual harassment, and sexual assault are essential components of many marginalized archaeologists' careers. Many of my interlocutors had changed their research projects or specializations in order to avoid people who had mistreated them, and some had considered leaving archaeology altogether. One interviewee, a Black queer woman, was taking a leave of absence from graduate school and was not sure she would return to her program because of the hostility of the environment.

How to Retain Marginalized Archaeologists

In order to retain marginalized archaeologists, we must build a disciplinary culture in which bullying and harassment are not acceptable. Our professional communities should create and enforce anti-harassment policies if they have not already done so: this work is currently being done in the American Society of Overseas Research (n.d.), the Society for American Archaeology (Hays-Gilpin et al. 2019), and other professional organizations. It must also be done in every archaeology department, program, field project, laboratory, and professional organization.

Not all of this cultural change can be imposed from the top down, however: some of what we must do is to listen to, believe, and support survivors of harassment, bullying, and assault. For example, Jordan, a queer woman PhD student whose Latin American co-director assaulted her, relied on a circle of close friends who conducted fieldwork in the same country and would check up on her to offer support. One of her friends, Greg, would drive hours to spend weekends with her in the aftermath of her assault. When I interviewed Greg, he at first said that he thought he might not be a good interlocutor since, as a straight white cisgender man, he had had a relatively easy time as an archaeologist. After I reassured him that I wanted a variety of perspectives on diversity issues in the field, not just from the most marginalized people, we proceeded with the interview. He told me stories about experiences he had watched his wife and his women friends, including Jordan, experience in the

field. Many men I interviewed mentioned sexual harassment, but Greg spoke about the problems with significant detail, emotion, and insight. It is clear to me from both how he spoke and how Jordan spoke about him that he listens deeply to people who have different experiences than he does. Because of this listening, Jordan and others deeply trust him, and he had the opportunity to provide important support to her when she was in need. I hope that men reading this will follow his example in deeply listening to and believing women, and offering support when they need it.

Jordan's story is emblematic of an important theme in my interviewees' stories about what helped them stay in the discipline: proactive, caring mentorship. Jordan told me that she expected her adviser to respond to her assault by saying, "well, that's just part of fieldwork. You just got to go through it." She was pleasantly surprised when, instead, he told her, "You know what, if you don't feel safe, just come home and we'll figure out a new project. We'll transfer the grant money. It will be okay." By believing her about the significance of her experience and valuing her safety and personhood over her graduation schedule, Jordan's adviser helped her succeed in the field despite her co-director's violence.

To further illustrate the importance of proactive mentorship, I will share the story of Taylor, a white queer genderfluid person. Taylor was an undergraduate student at a public college in a rural, conservative area, and began taking the few anthropology courses that were offered at their college. Their anthropology professor saw that they were interested and motivated and told them,

> "You need to get out of [small, local public university]. You need to do something else. Why don't I introduce you to my friend [adviser], or my friend [professor], or my friend over here? [at a nearby, larger research university]" And I was like, "Okay. I have no idea who these people are." She actually drove me up one weekend and I stayed with her, and she set up interviews for me with a lot of people to get a feel of the department. It was entirely out of the

way, and the best thing that's happened to me to get into this career.

This mentor set up meetings with faculty at a research university, and supported Taylor in transferring to that university, where they could focus on anthropology and pursue a career as an archaeologist. Furthermore, the research university is located in a town that is more welcoming to queer people than the town where they lived at the time, so this mentor facilitated Taylor's move to a safer and more comfortable place to live. Through their respect and active support, Jordan and Taylor's mentors went above the basic requirements of advising, and Jordan's friends went above and beyond a basic friendship. These colleagues and mentors, while they were not queer themselves, made it possible for these two queer archaeologists to continue to pursue archaeological careers despite hostile circumstances.

POSSIBLE SOLUTIONS

As safety and respect for all members of our professional communities becomes a more widely-held principle of archaeological ethics, we must take proactive steps to build a culture of inclusivity. Currently, marginalized people are less likely to enter archaeological careers, and are less likely to have long-term success in them, than their more privileged colleagues, due to the barriers they face. These patterns repeat themselves in each generation of archaeologists, maintaining the straight-, white-, male-, and middle-class-domination of the discipline over time. In order to interrupt these cycles, archaeologists must proactively work to recruit and retain talented marginalized archaeologists.

Funding for both research and educational experiences is of paramount significance for recruiting and retaining marginalized people in archaeology. Directors of research projects and field schools should make their programs as inexpensive as possible, ideally making them free or even paying students for their labor.

Although many archaeologists may be loath to forgo the funding provided by student tuition payments, there are some funding streams that make this possible. For example, the National Science Foundation offers Research Opportunities for Undergraduates grants (National Science Foundation n.d.), and some universities provide funding to pay students for research labor, as in the case of Boston University's Undergraduate Research Opportunities Program (Boston University n.d.). Projects on or near campuses and that take place during the semester can be more accessible, since they do not interfere with summer jobs and can be supported by financial aid packages (e.g., Dufton et al. 2019; Moreno 2017; Stubbs et al. 2010). Archaeologists leading research projects have an unparalleled opportunity to recruit diverse students into archaeology, given the power of fieldwork to clinch student interests in the discipline: proactively inviting talented students to join the project, making sure they are able to afford it, and giving them opportunities to succeed can make a difference in those students' careers. Directors should also ensure that their projects have anti-harassment policies and that those policies are communicated to all participants and are enforced.

Archaeologists who teach in colleges and universities also serve essential roles in recruiting diverse aspiring archaeologists into the discipline. While university systems often undervalue undergraduate teaching, general education and introductory courses are essential to many archaeologists' decisions to pursue their careers. These courses should therefore be prioritized and should include diverse global case studies in order to appeal to a broad range of students. Professors also have the ability to guide and nurture the professional trajectories of marginalized students, as Taylor's mentor did when she helped them transfer to a more cosmopolitan and prestigious university with a larger anthropology program.

Not all archaeologists are in the position to change policies or provide mentorship, but there are many other actions we can take to build a more inclusive discipline. We can do broad outreach to under-resourced public schools, perhaps following the model set by Dr. Alexandra Jones of Archaeology in the Community, which has educated thousands of children about archaeology (Jones n.d.). This can even be done virtually, through programs like Skype a Scientist, which connects scientists (including archaeologists) with school classrooms across the country by videoconference. Even before the COVID-19 pandemic made online learning ubiquitous, Skype a Scientist connected 4638 scientists to 9384 classes in 2019 (Skype a Scientist 2019), and the organization works from a position of inclusivity and anti-racism (McAnulty n.d.). These outreach efforts allow a broader range of students to be exposed to archaeology, so that not only the most privileged children aspire to become archaeologists, and contribute to recruitment of a more diverse next generation.

All archaeologists can contribute to building a disciplinary culture that retains talented scholars of all identities. Sometimes, this is as simple as listening to and believing colleagues when they say they have been mistreated. We can also advocate for the creation and enforcement of anti-harassment policies in our departments, programs, firms, museums, labs, and field projects. This work does not need to be done by sexual assault survivors alone, and allies can do important advocacy work to end endemic harassment in the discipline. Similarly, fundraising for and management of scholarships for archaeological fieldwork are essential, and can be done by any archaeologist, not only those who relied on scholarships to enter the field themselves.

All archaeologists should be safe and respected in their workplaces and all professional settings: building a community where this is the case is a part of ethical practice in the discipline. Although there is much work to do in order to realize this vision, if all archaeologists take action in their own communities, we can build a discipline that is diverse, inclusive, and ethical.

Acknowledgments

Thank you to Sarah Kielt Costello and Sarah Lepinski for inviting me to participate in this volume, for organizing a workshop at the 2019 ASOR meeting to discuss the chapter drafts, and for your thoughtful comments on my work in progress. Thank you also to Morag Kersel for introducing me to Sarah Kielt Costello in the first place. This chapter was also improved by the suggestions of two anonymous reviewers. Many of the ideas presented in this chapter were first developed in Chapters 9 and 10 of my dissertation (Heath-Stout 2019). Thank you to my dissertation committee members—David Carballo, Mary Beaudry, Catherine Connell, and Chris Schmidt—for your support throughout the research and writing of the project. The project was approved by the Boston University Institutional Review Board (protocol number 4381X). Finally, thank you to my interviewees for sharing your stories with me.

References

Adler, K. W.
2017 Female Scientists Report a Horrifying Culture of Sexual Assault. *Marie Claire*, December 11, 2017. https://www.marieclaire.com/career-advice/a14104684/sexual-harassment-assault-in-science-field/

Ahmed, S.
2012 *On Being Included: Racism and Diversity in Institutional Life.* Durham, NC: Duke University.
2017 *Living a Feminist Life.* Durham, NC: Duke University.

American School of Oriental Research
n.d. ASOR Code of Conduct for Fieldwork Projects."American School of Oriental Research. Accessed November 5, 2019. http://www.asor.org/about-asor/policies/code-of-conduct-for-fieldwork-projects

Boston University
n.d. Turning Students Into Researchers. Undergraduate Research Opportunities Program. Accessed June 29, 2021. https://www.bu.edu/urop/

Charmaz, K.
2014   *Constructing Grounded Theory.* 2nd ed. London: Sage.

Childress, H.
2019   *The Adjunct Underclass: How America's Colleges Betrayed Their Faculty, Their Students, and Their Mission.* Chicago: University of Chicago Press.

Clancy, K. B. H.
2013. I Had No Power to Say That's Not Okay: Reports of Harassment and Abuse in the Field. *Scientific American: Context and Variation* (blog). April 13, 2013. https://www.scientificamerican.com/blog/context-and-variation/safe13-field-site-chilly-climate-and-abuse/

Clancy, K. B. H.; Lee, K. M.; Rodgers, E. M.; and Richey, C.
2017   Double Jeopardy in Astronomy and Planetary Science: Women of Color Face Greater Risks of Gendered and Racial Harassment. *Journal of Geophysical Research: Planets* 122.7. https://agupubs.onlinelibrary.wiley.com/doi/full/10.1002/2017JE005256

Clancy, K. B. H.; Nelson, R. G.; Rutherford, J. N.; and Hinde, K.
2014   Survey of Academic Field Experiences (SAFE): Trainees Report Harassment and Assault. *PLoS ONE* 9.7: e102172.

Colannino, C. E.; Lambert, S. P.; Beahm, E. L.; and Drexler, C. G.
2020   Creating and Supporting a Harassment and Assault Free Field School. *Advances in Archaeological Practice.* https://doi.org/10.1017/aap.2020.8

Dufton, J. A.; Gosner, L. R.; Knodell, A. R.; and Steidl, C.
2019   Archaeology Underfoot: On-Campus Approaches to Education, Outreach, and Historical Archaeology at Brown University." *Journal of Field Archaeology* 44.5: 304–18. https://doi.org/10.1080/00934690.2019.1605123

Gentry, R., and Stokes, D.
2015   Strategies for Professors Who Service the University to Earn Tenure and Promotion. *Research in Higher Education Journal* 29 (September). https://eric.ed.gov/?id=EJ1077941

Gifford-Gonzalez, D.
2016   SAA Ethics Principle No. 9, December 9, 2016.

Gnecco, C., and Lippert, D. (eds.)
2016   *Ethics and Archaeological Praxis.* Ethical Archaeologies 1. New York: Springer.

Green, E. L.
1984   *Ethics and Values in Archaeology.* New York: Free.

Hays-Gilpin, K.; Thies-Sauder, M.; Jalbert, C.; Heath-Stout, L. E.; and Thakar, H.
2019   Changing Our Professional Culture of Apathy and Creating Safety in Archaeology: Progress Report from the SAA Task Force on Sexual and Anti-Harassment Policies and Procedures." *SAA Archaeological Record* 19.4: 9–11.

Heath-Stout, L. E.
2019   Diversity, Identity, and Oppression in the Production of Archaeological Knowledge. PhD dissertation, Boston, MA: Boston University.

Heath-Stout, L. E., and Hannigan, E. M.
2020   Affording Archaeology: How Field School Costs Promote Exclusivity. *Advances in Archaeological Practice* 8.2: 123–33. https://doi.org/10.1017/aap.2020.7

Ireland, T., and Schofield, J.
2015   The Ethics of Cultural Heritage. *Ethical Archaeologies* 4. New York: Springer.

Jones, A.
n.d.   About AITC. *Archaeology in the Community.* Accessed May 9, 2019. http://www.archaeologyincommunity.com/about-aitc/

Kelsky, K.
2017   A Crowdsourced Survey of Sexual Harassment in the Academy. *The Professor Is In*

(blog). December 1, 2017. https://theprofes
sorisin.com/2017/12/01/a-crowdsourced-
survey-of-sexual-harassment-in-the-
academy/

Kloß, S. T.
2017   Sexual(ized) Harassment and Ethnographic
Fieldwork: A Silenced Aspect of Social Research. *Ethnography* 18.3: 396–414. https://
doi.org/10.1177/1466138116641958

Lilienfeld, S.
2017   The Science of Microaggressions: It's Complicated. *Scientific American Blog Network*
(blog). June 23, 2017. https://blogs.scientific
american.com/observations/the-science-
of-microaggressions-its-complicated/

Long, J. S.; Allison, P. D.; and McGinnis, R.
1993   Rank Advancement in Academic Careers:
Sex Differences and the Effects of Productivity. *American Sociological Review* 58.5:
703–22. https://doi.org/10.2307/2096282

Lynott, M. J., and Wylie, A.
2000   *Ethics in American Archaeology.* Washington, D.C.: Society for American Archaeology.

Marshall, B. W., and Rothgeb, J. M.
2011   So You Want Tenure? Factors Affecting Tenure Decisions in Political Science Departments. *PS: Political Science & Politics* 44.3:
571–77. https://doi.org/10.1017/S10490
96511000680

McAnulty, S.
n.d.   Anti-Racism in Science. *Skype a Scientist.*
Accessed June 29, 2021. https://www.skype
ascientist.com/anti-racism-in-science.html

Meyers, M. S.; Horton, E. T.; Boudreaux, E. A.;
Carmody, S. B.; Wright, A. P.; and Dekle, V. G.
2018   The Context and Consequences of Sexual
Harassment in Southeastern Archaeology.
Advances in Archaeological Practice 6.4:
275–87. https://doi.org/10.1017/aap.2018.23

Moosa, I. A.
2018   *Publish or Perish: Perceived Benefits versus
Unintended Consequences.* Cheltenham:
Elgar.

Moreno, J. E.
2017   UTRGV-Hidalgo County Project Working
to Restore Dignity, Identify Burial Plots at
Abandoned Pauper Cemetery. *University of
Texas Rio Grande Valley,* December 21, 2017.
https://www.utrgv.edu/en-us/about-utrgv/
news/press-releases/2017/december-
21-utrgv-hidalgo-county-project-working-
to-restore-dignity-identify-burial-plots-at-
abandoned-pauper-cemetery/index.htm

National Science Foundation.
n.d.   Research Experiences for Undergraduates. Accessed June 29, 2021. https://www.
nsf.gov/funding/pgm_summ.jsp?pims_
id=5517

Nelson, R. G.; Rutherford, J. N.; Hinde, K.;
and Clancy, K. B. H.
2017   Signaling Safety: Characterizing Fieldwork
Experiences and Their Implications for Career Trajectories. *American Anthropologist*
119.4: 710–22.

Scarre, C., and Scarre, G. (eds.)
2006   *The Ethics of Archaeology: Philosophical
Perspectives on Archaeological Practice.* Cambridge, UK: Cambridge University.

Skype a Scientist
2019   Impact Report. https://www.dropbox.com/
s/ck5nf8azr74c6fm/Annual_Report_2019.
pdf?dl=0

Smith, L.; Comstock, B.; Davis, R.; Clancy, K. B.
H.; McEntee, C.; and Larsen, K.
2018   *A Review of Sexual Harassment and Misconduct in Science.* 2318 Rayburn House
Office Building. https://science.house.
gov/legislation/hearings/subcommittee-
research-and-technology-hearing-review-
sexual-harassment-and, https://uofi.app.
box.com/s/otynwiz0cz13vb4wxkovxpo3q-
t6exzei

Smith, M. E.
2016   Why I Voted NO on SAA Ethics Principle
9. *Publishing Archaeology* (blog). September 19, 2016. http://publishingarchaeology.
blogspot.com/2016/09/why-i-voted-no-on-
saa-ethics-principle-9.html

Society for American Archaeology
n.d.   Principles of Archaeological Ethics. Society for American Archaeology: Career and Practice. Accessed November 5, 2019. https://www.skypeascientist.com.

Stubbs, J. D.; Patricia Capone, P.; Hodge, C.; and Loren, D. D.
2010   Campus Archaeology/Public Archaeology at Harvard University, Cambridge, Massachusetts. In *Beneath the Ivory Tower: The Archaeology of Academia*, ed. R. K. Skowronek and K. E. Lewis. Gainesville, FL: University Press of Florida. https://muse.jhu.edu/chapter/619662

Sue, D. W.
2010   *Microaggressions in Everyday Life: Race, Gender, and Sexual Orientation.* Hoboken, NJ: Wiley.

Vitelli, K. D., and Colwell, C.
2006   *Archaeological Ethics.* Lanham, MD: Altamira.

Wright, R. P.
2002   COSWA Committee Article: Gender Equity, Sexual Harassment, and Professional Ethics. *SAA Archaeological Record* 2.4: 18–19.
2008   Sexual Harassment and Professional Ethics. *SAA Archaeological Record* 8.4: 27–30.

Zimmerman, L. J.; Vitelli, K. D.; and Hollowell-Zimmer, J. (eds.)
2003   *Ethical Issues in Archaeology.* Walnut Creek, CA: AltaMira.

Chapter 3

Gender and Power in the Practice of Mediterranean Archaeology

Grace Erny and Dimitri Nakassis

Abstract

Sexism and gender-based harassment pervade archaeological research in the Mediterranean and the Near East. These issues affect the demographics of the field and shape archaeological knowledge production. Although recent efforts to develop codes of conduct for archeological projects and professional conferences are important, any plan to end gender harassment in archaeology must confront structural issues of sexism and power in academic settings in order to be truly effective. Furthermore, the burden of addressing sexism cannot fall primarily upon its victims. This chapter outlines the scope of the problem and proposes concrete steps towards building a more ethical future for archaeology and the academy.

Introduction

In November of 2019, Dani Bradford received the Marsh Archaeology Award for Early Career Research in Archaeology from the Council of British Archaeology (CBA). As the CBA's executive director Mike Heyworth introduced the subject of Bradford's work—sexual harassment and assault in archaeological fieldwork—a group of older men in the audience laughed audibly, to the point where Heyworth reprimanded them. As Bradford wrote on her Twitter account (@danihpayne) after the event: "I managed to go up and get my certificate, but as soon as I sat back down I burst into tears. In front of a hall full of people. It was humiliating."[1]

Just a few months before, during the spring Annual Meeting of the Society for American Archaeology (SAA) in Albuquerque, NM, the problem of sexual harassment in archaeology was likewise made suddenly and painfully visible. David Yesner, a former professor at the University of Alaska Anchorage who was found by a Title IX investigation to have harassed at least nine women, was allowed to register for the confer-

---

1 https://twitter.com/danihpayne/status/11979719547 22103297. For the results of Bradford's research, see Bradford and Crema 2022.

ence on site. This caused intense distress for other attendees, some of whom were former targets of Yesner's and Title IX claimants (Wade 2019). Another conference attendee attempted to physically escort Yesner from the meeting and was subsequently ejected from the conference by SAA leadership, while Yesner was allowed to remain. Several prominent SAA members who criticized the organization for its slow response and lack of transparency regarding the situation were blocked by the SAA on social media (Flaherty 2019a; 2019b; Awesome Small Working Group 2019). In the wake of the incident, the SAA formed a Task Force on Sexual and Anti-Harassment Policies and Procedures and subsequently created a Meeting Safety Policy and Code of Conduct for use at all SAA events.[2] The pervasive sense among many members that the SAA leadership sorely mishandled the Yesner incident and its aftermath, however, has been slow to fade.

These two anecdotes exemplify the current state of archaeology's disciplinary reckoning with sexism, harassment, and assault (Voss 2021a; 2021b). In the case of the 2019 SAA meetings, a professional organization proved unable to prevent a scholar who had been found guilty of harassment in a formal investigation and sanctioned by his own university from attending a major conference, a failure that harmed survivors of Yesner's abuse. The fact that much harassment is never reported or sanctioned makes the incident even more troubling: if the reaction to such a clear-cut example of misconduct is paralysis and institutional fumbling, how could harassers in more ambiguous, less well-documented cases ever be expected to suffer real consequences? Bradford's award ceremony at the CBA also reveals the gap between institutional rhetoric and reality. While it is encouraging that research on harassment and gender equity is being publicly recognized and rewarded by professional organizations, it is disturbing that a powerful contingent of archaeologists is comfortable with publicly de-

meaning a young colleague's work. This episode also highlights the chilling effect of institutional hierarchy and sexism on archaeological knowledge production. Whether they realized it or not, the senior men in the audience who mocked Bradford's research were exerting their power, attempting to police the boundaries of "real" archaeological work, and issuing a reminder that they, not she, were the authorities in the room.

These examples remind us that while public-facing support for gender equity in archaeology is a well-meaning and important first step, it remains inadequate if we do not address the structural issues of sexism and power that undergird harassment and abuse, both in academia more broadly and in archaeology in particular. Since the 1980s, archaeologists working in anthropological archaeology have addressed the effects of sexism on the trajectory of archaeological research and the career experiences of archaeologists (Conkey and Spector 1984; Gero 1983; 1985; see Wylie 1997). Our chapter builds on these insights to discuss how structural sexism influences archaeological fieldwork and publication in the Mediterranean and Near East, a topic which has been understudied until recently (though see Nixon 1995; Nakhai 2018 and this volume; Erny and Godsey 2022; Heath-Stout et al. 2023).

Although the archaeology of these regions faces many of the same issues discussed in the pioneering work of Gero, Conkey, and Spector, it has also developed in distinctive ways, with important ramifications for the gender dynamics of the discipline. As a first step towards understanding these regionally-specific traditions and mechanisms, we present below an original journal authorship study of six years of publications (2015–2020) in two flagship journals for Mediterranean and Near Eastern archaeology: the *American Journal of Archaeology* (*AJA*) and the *Bulletin of ASOR* (*BASOR*). We demonstrate that that the topic and methodology of published articles correlate significantly with author gender. Our results suggest that structural sexism influences not only who directs archaeological fieldwork in the Mediterranean, but also what topics of study scholars of different genders

2 The most recent version of this policy at the time of publication was posted on the 2025 SAA Annual Meeting website (https://www.saa.org/annual-meeting/meeting-policies/meeting-safety-policy).

pursue. Analysis of citation metrics for different categories of articles by topic reveals that this phenomenon may have ramifications for hiring and promotion.

Though the connection between sexual and gender-based harassment and gendered knowledge production may not be immediately apparent, we understand them as interconnected issues. As Voss (2021a: 14) has observed, harassment has "shaped our discipline at a fundamental level, affecting who can practice archaeology, how archaeologists are trained, what research topics are investigated and how archaeological data is interpreted, published, and cited." Sexual harassment can thus be seen as both a manifestation of and a reinforcing mechanism for structural sexism. Nelson and colleagues, for example, found that fieldwork projects without clear codes of conduct had (1) higher rates of harassment and assault and (2) a greater prevalence of alienating behaviors, unnecessary physical tests, and gendered divisions of labor (Nelson et al. 2017: 714). This same suite of behaviors is often replicated in non-fieldwork contexts, with direct effects on career trajectories (Wylie 1994). Although the gendered division of published research is only one proxy for the effects of sexism in archaeology, it is an easily measurable one with important consequences for archaeological careers.

Our discussion is limited in scope. We largely discuss sexism and sexual harassment within university departments in the U.S. and Canada and on archaeological projects where faculty and students based at these departments work. We focus mostly on the power dynamics between two groups of people: (1) tenured professors, project directors, or PIs (principal investigators) and (2) the graduate students who work under their supervision.[3] We are thereby emphasizing two salient components of identity: gender and institutional power. We recognize that these two identities intersect in complex ways both with

each other and with identities and experiences related to race, class, nationality, sexual orientation, and disability. Our chapter does not interrogate the impact of these other identities, although they are critically important: women of color, queer women, and gender minorities experience sexual and gender harassment at higher rates than white women, heterosexual women, and cisgender women (National Academies of Sciences, Engineering, and Medicine 2018: 171). Heath-Stout (this volume) provides a more detailed discussion of gender and power dynamics in archaeology involving other groups such as undergraduates, as well as how race and sexual orientation intersect with gender identity in the archaeological workplace; Sneed and Shrader (this volume) focus on the experience of archaeological fieldwork for people with disabilities. A few studies to date have focused on the intersection of class and gender in the academic workplace (see the contributions in Gutiérrez y Muhs et al. 2012) and in archaeology specifically (Leighton 2020); this is an important topic that merits more attention.[4]

Many of our conclusions are applicable beyond a U.S. or Canadian university setting, but we chose to focus on this narrow slice of a complex issue partly because of our own identities and experiences. At the time of writing, Grace Erny was a PhD student in a Classics department conducting archaeological fieldwork and dissertation research in the Mediterranean. Dimitri Nakassis is a tenured professor in Classics who has directed field projects in the Mediterranean. We see sexism and harassment in archaeological fieldwork and in the academy as part of a wider problem of gender discrimination and sexual harassment in the workplace in general. We argue that structural features of academia allow sexual harassment and gender-based discrimination to flourish and that,

3 Though our focus on tenured professors and graduate students risks leaving out both undergraduates and contingent, non-tenure track, early-career, or otherwise vulnerable faculty, we believe that similar pressures obtain for these groups as for graduate students.

4 The high cost of archaeological field schools, as well as the income that students lose from participating in an archaeological field school instead of working a summer job, pose significant barriers for first-generation students or students from low-income backgrounds who want to become archaeologists (Heath-Stout and Hannigan 2020). For students based in the U.S., field schools located in the Mediterranean or Near East, which require an expensive round-trip plane ticket, are even less accessible.

as in other workplaces, a "chilly climate" poses significant obstacles to gender equity in the field of archaeology (Sandler 1986; Wylie 2011).

Harassment, discrimination, and sexism are ethical problems for our field in at least two respects. First, as many professional archaeological associations have recognized, archaeologists have an ethical responsibility to maintain safe teaching and working environments that are free from discrimination, harassment, and violence of all types.[5] Second, sexism shapes archaeological knowledge production in a variety of subtler ways, such as creating gendered hierarchies of archaeological work (e.g., men in the field, women in the lab) and valuing "men's work" more highly. Both types of discrimination are unethical because they disrespect classes of persons, treat them unfairly, and do them harm (Thomsen 2017). Unconscious bias or assumptions about gender can also harm archaeological interpretation when archaeologists uncritically reconstruct such gendered hierarchies in their study of past societies. We therefore argue that it is an ethical responsibility to strive to make academic archaeology more equitable and inclusive. This process must involve (1) profound change within the universities, professional societies, and granting institutions that fund archaeological research and (2) solidarity and coalition-building among archaeologists with different levels of institutional power.

DEFINING THE PROBLEM

Specifying definitions for sexual and gender-based harassment is complicated, and varying definitions can lead to large discrepancies in recorded rates of abuse. Two recent studies have focused on issues of sexual and gender-based harassment in academic settings, and we will draw on their language and definitions here. The most recent iteration of the Campus Climate Survey on Sexual Assault, conducted in 2019 by the Association of American Universities (AAU), was the largest of its kind ever performed: more than 180,000 undergraduate and graduate respondents across 33 universities completed the survey (Cantor et al. 2019). The National Academies of Sciences, Medicine, and Engineering (NASEM) published a comprehensive report in 2018 on harassment in science, medicine, and engineering, which synthesized previous research and formulated policy recommendations.

The 2019 Campus Climate Survey defined sexual harassment as "behaviors with sexual connotations that interfered with an individual's academic or professional performance, limited the individual's ability to participate in an academic program, or created an intimidating, hostile, or offensive social, academic, or work environment" (Cantor et al. 2019: v). "Gender-based harassment" encompasses a broader set of actions and was defined by the NASEM report as "verbal and nonverbal behaviors that convey hostility, objectification, exclusion, or second-class status about members of one gender," most commonly women and gender minorities (NASEM 2018: 48). Sexual and gender-based harassment can be perpetrated by people of any gender against people of any gender, and perpetrators may be unconscious of their actions, though this makes the behavior no less pernicious.

An expansive view of sexism in an academic setting includes not only unwanted sexual contact or overtly misogynistic statements, but a pervasive culture that systematically underestimates women's competence and derides their achievements. The inaugural study of the "chilly climate" for women faculty, administrators, and graduate

---

5   Statements that understand the imperative against gender-based discrimination and harassment as ethical in nature have been made by the Archaeological Institute of America (https://www.archaeological.org/wp-content/uploads/2019/05/Code-of-Professional-Standards.pdf), ASOR (https://www.asor.org/about-asor/policies/code-of-conduct-for-fieldwork-projects), the Register of Professional Archaeologists (https://rpanet.org/resources/Documents/Register-Code.pdf), the Society for American Archaeology (https://www.saa.org/career-practice/ethics-in-professional-archaeology), and the Society for Historical Archaeology (https://sha.org/about-us/ethics-statement/) in the United States; the European Association of Archaeologists has also revised its code of conduct to incorporate more such language (https://www.e-a-a.org/EAACodes).

students in academia presents a litany of behaviors that are as familiar today as they were more than thirty years ago: devaluation of women's abilities, commenting on women's personalities and appearance rather than their achievements, low representation of women among tenured full faculty, social isolation and "outsider" status in mostly male peer groups, and a particularly toxic environment for women of color (Sandler 1986). We would add to this list: less compensation for the same work, expectations that women should perform certain kinds of work in their male colleagues' stead, lack of professional respect or esteem, sexist comments or "jokes," and exclusion from opportunities (in academic archaeology, often fieldwork or publication-related opportunities) based on gender. Few women in academia do not harbor memories of being spoken over by a male colleague, having their ideas attributed to a male peer or mentor, or having their intelligence or expertise unwarrantedly called into question. Rebecca Solnit gives an eloquent account of these behaviors and their effects in her 2014 essay *Men Explain Things to Me*, as she reflects on encountering a man who insisted on lecturing her about her own book. "Every woman knows what I'm talking about. It's the presumption that makes it hard, at times, for any woman in any field; that keeps women from speaking up and from being heard when they dare; that crushes young women into silence by indicating, the way harassment on the street does, that this is not their world. It trains us in self-doubt and self-limitation just as it exercises men's unsupported overconfidence... This syndrome is a war that nearly every woman faces every day, a war within herself too, a belief in her superfluity, an invitation to silence" (Solnit 2014: 45).

Since sexism in academia extends far beyond sexism in archaeology, or sexism in Mediterranean and Near Eastern archaeology in particular, we feel that it is critical to ground our discussion in the broader literature on the gender sociology of academia. For many archaeologists based in universities, fieldwork occupies only several months out of the year. The majority of their time is spent in a more traditional academic setting, teaching and researching on university campuses. A holistic approach to the ethics of archaeological practice requires that we consider sexism, harassment, and discrimination in its many different professional manifestations, of which conduct during archaeological fieldwork is only one aspect.

Academia's "Chilly Climate"

Since Sandler's (1986) early work on the chilly academic climate, myriad psychology and sociology studies have documented institutionalized sexism in the academy across the three domains of work expected from university faculty: service, teaching, and research. Women perform significantly more academic service than men, controlling for race, field or department, and rank, and this service load often increases as women move up the ranks of academia (Guarino and Borden 2017). The lower status of service in the value hierarchy of academia is exacerbated by a process of "gender devaluation," whereby positions that once conferred respect (department chair, dean) lose their prestige once women occupy them (Monroe et al. 2008). Female instructors receive poorer teaching evaluations than their male peers for the same online courses (MacNell et al. 2015), and they receive more requests for special favors from their students (El-Alayli et al. 2018). The language in teaching evaluations is so clearly biased against women and people of color that it has been argued that it should be illegal to use teaching evaluations in employment and promotion decisions (Mitchell and Martin 2018: 652).[6]

Sexism harms women's career prospects in other ways as well. Academic hiring commit-

---

6 For a fascinating visualization of the problem, see the online tool at https://benschmidt.org/profGender/#, which allows users to see the words used in 14 million reviews of teachers on RateMyProfessor.com filtered by gender and discipline (for a discussion of the website, see Schmidt 2015). The tool reveals that while female instructors tend to be praised or condemned for their interpersonal behavior (they are "helpful" or "kind"), male instructors tend to be discussed in terms of their intelligence and are much more likely to be described as "brilliant" or a "genius" than their female peers.

tees penalize women (but not men) for having an opposite-sex partner who is an academic or high-status professional (Rivera 2017; Jaschik 2017). Decades of research have documented in painstaking detail how the decision to start a family hurts women's academic careers while helping men's. Men who have a spouse and children are seen as mature, whereas women with families are viewed as distracted from their academic work (Mason et al. 2013). Graduate students of all genders share many concerns about starting families, including the financial cost of having children and balancing family life with the heavy time investment required for a PhD. However, women are 2.5 times more likely than men to fear their advisor will take their work less seriously if they have children and almost 4 times more likely to say that future employers will take them less seriously (Mason et al. 2013: 12, Table 1.1). The PhD and postdoctoral years are the "leaky pipeline," when many women (and some men) leave academia because it seems incompatible with family life. Providing benefits like parental leave, spousal health insurance, and affordable childcare only to tenure-track faculty is insufficient to stop the flow of early-career scholars, disproportionately women, who leave academia because of lack of access to these basic needs. Unfortunately, in many institutions of higher education in the U.S., these benefits may not be extended even to tenure-track faculty.

Harassment and gender-based discrimination thrive in academia in part because of academia's hierarchical structure and increasing reliance on a contingent and precarious labor force (Hall 2016). In most departments, faculty members, and particularly committee members or doctoral supervisors, have immense power over their graduate students through both formal channels (letters of recommendation, passing grades on qualifying exams, approval for admission to candidacy, opportunities for co-authorship) and informal channels (promotion of students to colleagues, quality and level of feedback on dissertation work). This makes graduate students particularly vulnerable to abuse. PhD students in archaeology are often "trapped" in their position for six to eight years

working with a very small network of faculty. A supervisor's expertise may be highly specialized, meaning that a student cannot viably switch to a different advisor within the same department if their own advisor becomes dismissive or abusive. In the current academic ecosystem, faculty members' influence over their students does not end at the dissertation defense. Most recent PhDs who pursue a career in academia must work multiple temporary positions before finding a permanent job. These individuals will require positive letters of recommendation from their degree-granting institutions for years after they obtain their degree, meaning that securing faculty goodwill is even more crucial.

Given these power imbalances, it is not surprising that recent studies have demonstrated high levels of sexual harassment of graduate students by faculty. Faculty members and instructors were responsible for nearly one quarter (24%) of incidents of sexual harassment reported by women graduate and professional students in the AAU Campus Climate Survey (Cantor et al. 2019: 49, 79). In another recent survey of graduate students at the University of Oregon, more than one-third of female graduate students and almost one-quarter of male students reported that they had been sexually harassed by faculty or staff (Rosenthal et al. 2016). This rate is comparable to those recorded in the late 1980s by some of the first studies of sexual harassment in academia (McKinney et al. 1988; Fitzgerald et al. 1988).[7] A recent study of hundreds of legal cases, Title IX investigations, and media reports documenting sexual harassment of graduate students by faculty reveals disturbing trends. The majority (53%) of

---

7 McKinney et al. found that out of 149 female graduate students contacted by a mail-in survey, 35% reported being sexually harassed, and the perpetrator was most often identified as a male professor (McKinney et al. 1988: 321–22). However, participants were allowed to define "sexual harassment" on their own terms, meaning that some respondents classified sexist, but not explicitly sexual, comments as sexual harassment. Fitzgerald et al.'s study found that nearly 30% of graduate women surveyed had been the target of "unwelcome seductive behavior" from a professor, though they often hesitated to label such behavior as sexual harassment (Fitzgerald et al. 1988: 162–63, 171).

faculty perpetrators in these cases were repeat offenders, and a worryingly high proportion of cases involved not only verbal harassment but also physical contact and controlling behavior reminiscent of domestic abuse (Cantalupo and Kidder 2018). These two findings suggest that (1) faculty harassers tend to retain their positions, giving them access to more students, and (2) many instances of academic harassment are likely to cause intense fear for survivors. In many cases, other faculty may not be aware of their colleagues' abuses. Even if these faculty observe or suspect harassment of students, there are strong disincentives to intervene. Many faculty will prioritize long-term relationships with powerful colleagues over short-term relationships with powerless graduate students, safeguarding their personal comfort and institutional prestige.[8] It is easier for faculty to characterize graduate students as "problematic," "troublemakers," "whiny," or even "disturbed" than to confront the abuses of powerful colleagues (Amienne 2017).

The psychological and professional effects of sexual and gender-based harassment, as well as the hostile climate of academia more broadly, are profound and far-reaching. Sexual harassment of female graduates by faculty and staff has been shown to result in female students feeling less safe on campus than male students, making them less able to do their work (Rosenthal et al. 2016). In academic settings, the trauma of sexual harassment is often compounded for survivors by institutional betrayal, defined as "institutional action and inaction that exacerbate the impact of traumatic experiences" or "when an institution causes harm to an individual who trusts or depends upon that institution" (Smith and Freyd 2014: 577–78). Institutional betrayal can occur passively (failure of the institution to adequately protect its members or respond to abuses) or through commission (cover-up of abuses or retaliation for reporting) (Smith and Freyd 2014: 579). Experiencing institutional betrayal compounds the negative effects that harassment and sexism have on mental health and research productivity, ultimately posing a further barrier to advancement in the academy.

Sexism and Archaeology

Since the 1980s, scholars have documented sexism and gender bias within academic archaeology, though these studies have most often focused on American archaeology (traditionally housed in Anthropology departments) rather than Mediterranean or Near Eastern archaeology (usually found in Classics, Art History, or Near Eastern Studies departments). Past work has explored topics like the "sexual division of labor" in archaeology, where fieldwork is gendered male and post-collection data analysis female (Gero 1983; 1985), disparities in the number of research grants sought by and awarded to women (Goldstein et al. 2018), and gender imbalances in submission and authorship in major archaeological journals (see further discussion below).

Harassment and sexism are especially pronounced on archaeological field projects. In a survey of 666 respondents in field-based sciences (abbreviated as SAFE, or the Survey of Academic Field Experiences), 64% said they had personally experienced sexual harassment in the field, and 22% reported that they had been sexually assaulted (Clancy et al. 2014). Furthermore, survey results suggested that the types of harassment experienced by men and women were different: harassment aimed at men was primarily horizontal (coming from peers) while harassment aimed at women was primarily vertical (coming from superiors) and was more likely to lead to significant impacts on career and mental health. Nearly a quarter of the SAFE respondents were archaeologists, and the work of Clancy and her colleagues inspired several other surveys that sought to measure the frequency and nature of sexual harassment and assault among various subcommunities of archae-

---

8 One recent and high-profile example of this behavior occurred in February 2022, when 38 Harvard faculty members signed a letter protesting sanctions imposed by Harvard against Anthropology Professor John Comaroff after an investigation into alleged gender-based and sexual harassment of graduate students (Cho and Kim 2022a). Thirty-five of them retracted their signatures a week later after three graduate students filed a lawsuit against the university (Cho and Kim 2022b).

ologists (see Meyers et al. 2018 for Southeastern archaeology; Radde 2018 for California archaeology; Nakhai 2018 for the Near East, North Africa, and the Mediterranean; Hodgetts et al. 2020 for CRM and academic archaeology in Canada; Voss 2021a provides a recent review of research on this topic). Though the full results of Nakhai's survey have not yet been published, her preliminary findings suggest that fieldwork in the Mediterranean and Near East has similar harassment problems as fieldwork in other regions, with physical assault or violence reported at 22% of projects and gender discrimination in fieldwork or post-fieldwork opportunities reported at almost one-third (Nakhai 2017; 2018; this volume).

The high prevalence of sexual harassment and assault in archaeological fieldwork is largely the result of a system where powerful hierarchies operate in an environment of social informality. As Leighton (2020) has recently shown, informal socializing, which often includes boisterous parties and group drinking, is a common feature of archaeological projects. These practices can be positive, encouraging group solidarity that cuts across age, gender, and rank, but they can also create an environment that promotes unwelcome sexual advances, harassing comments disguised as "jokes," or other unwanted acts. Even in the absence of sexual harassment, this "performative informality" (Leighton 2020: 2) serves to mask significant hierarchies and encourages the conflation of personal and professional relationships. Since directors typically retain total control over the right to publish field reports or archaeological material and can withhold or dispense these opportunities at will, maintaining good personal relationships with directors and other project staff is crucial to securing professional opportunities. Structural and logistical features of many field projects can contribute to a potentially unsafe environment. In a communal living situation, participants may reside in close proximity to perpetrators of harassment and have little ability to avoid them. Many projects are also conducted in isolated settings where fieldworkers have limited access to their normal support networks, such as family, friends, and mental health services.

These dynamics make graduate students and early career researchers vulnerable to abuse. In a recent survey of Canadian archaeologists in CRM and academia, graduate students reported experiencing physical violence, unwanted sexual touching, and sexual violence or assault at higher rates than undergraduates or faculty (Hodgetts et al. 2020: 34). These same power imbalances also disincentivize those in precarious positions, such as graduate students, contingent faculty, or pre-tenure faculty, from reporting harassment and abuse. Reporting is further dampened by the fact that reporters are unlikely to feel that faculty, especially tenured faculty, will suffer any real consequences for their behavior.[9] Sadly, this is borne out by survey results. SAFE found that of 131 women who experienced unwanted physical contact in the field, only 36 reported the contact, and only seven were satisfied by the outcome of reporting (Clancy et al. 2014). Given these barriers and pressures, graduate students who are harassed are often (and understandably) unwilling to report offensive behavior, especially if the harasser is a superior who has control over their research materials, fieldwork opportunities, or professional future.

In addition to the harm that sexual harassment and discrimination causes for victims/survivors, structural sexism has real ramifications for archaeological knowledge production. Androcentric biases can cause researchers to discount some archaeological interpretations without justification while elevating others (Conkey and Spector 1984; Gero and Conkey 1991; Murray et al. 2020). In addition to negatively affecting the creation of archaeological knowledge, sexism and discrimination in the academy are also unethical because they commit what archaeologist and philosopher of science Alison Wylie, drawing on Miranda Fricker's work, has called "epistemic injustice." Epistemic injustice occurs when certain groups of people are viewed

---

9 Changes to Title IX announced in May 2020 limited the application of Title IX regulations to the United States, which will reduce the already minimal effectiveness of Title IX legislation in international fieldwork settings (Anderson 2020).

as incompetent and subjected to higher scrutiny, despite their credentials or demonstrated abilities; these groups are thus deprived of the interpretive tools to communicate their experience (Fricker 2007; Wylie 2011: 7). Epistemic injustice thus threatens the interpretive work that lies at the core of archaeology and the humanistic social sciences more broadly. Our next section explores the intersection of gender and knowledge production in Mediterranean and Near Eastern archaeology specifically through an authorship study of two of the discipline's journals.

Authorship and Gender in *BASOR* and the *AJA*

In order to better understand the effects of sexism on knowledge production in the archaeology of the Mediterranean and the Near East, we carried out a small pilot study on the six most recent years (2015–2020) of publications in two flagship journals: the *American Journal of Archaeology* (*AJA*), published quarterly by the Archaeological Institute of America (AIA), and the *Bulletin of ASOR* (*BASOR*), published biannually by the American Society of Overseas Research.[10] Studies on various aspects of gender and authorship have been conducted for several archaeological journals that focus primarily on anthropological or historical archaeology, including *American Antiquity, Latin American Antiquity, Journal of Archaeological Method and Theory, Journal of Archaeological Research, Historical Archaeology, Journal of Field Archaeology*, and others (Beaudry and White 1994; Rautman 2012; Bardolph 2014; Tushingham et al. 2017; Heath-Stout 2020a; 2020b). Other recent work has explored correlations between gender and the topic of conference presentations at the Society for American Archaeology, the European Association of Archaeologists, and the Computer Applications and Quantitative Methods in Archaeology annual meetings (Chen and Marwick 2023). However, journals or conferences focused specifically on the archaeology of the Mediterranean and the

Near East have received less attention (though see Heath-Stout et al. 2023). Unlike in New World archaeology, where many dissertations and much early-career research involve new fieldwork, a large proportion of such work in Mediterranean and Near Eastern archaeology consists of synthetic studies of previously published data or artifact-based projects that analyze archaeological collections or ancient art in new ways. This is probably due in part to the difficulty junior scholars face in obtaining archaeological permits in many Mediterranean countries.

We hypothesized that structural inequities within the discipline would manifest themselves in the types of articles published in each of these journals, with men more likely to take the prestigious first-author position on field reports that present new archaeological data and women tending to be first authors on art-historical or object-based studies.[11] There are several mechanisms through which this might take place. Since men tend to dominate the upper ranks of the academic hierarchy, including tenured full professorships in archaeology, they might find it easier to get permits and establish themselves as directors of archaeological projects, making them first authors on the publications that issue from such projects (see Overholtzer and Jabert 2021 for recent data on the underrepresentation of women among full professors of archaeology in Canada). The prevalence of sexual harassment and assault in archaeological fieldwork, as well as structures that make fieldwork disproportionately unwelcome to women (such as lack of childcare or male-dominated hierarchies), might discourage some women from working on field projects. Finally, stereotypes about female scholars' interests and capabilities might nudge more women towards art historical or object-based research projects. If men were disproportionately expected

---

10 Our data are available at https://core.tdar.org/dataset/489111/.

11 We recognize that much archaeological work and publication is inherently collaborative, but we chose to focus on first authorship for this study due to the increased weight that first or single-authored publications hold for hiring and promotion in humanities departments such as Classics or Near Eastern Studies. These differences are clearly present, if somewhat less pronounced, when taking all authors into account (see below).

or encouraged to think about the "big picture," while women were considered to be more detail-oriented and visually acute, these biases might influence their choice of research topics.

To test whether gender was correlated with article topic in these two journals, we created a database recording year, volume, issue, title, authors, author gender(s), and a topic code for every article in the 2015–2020 issues of the *AJA* and *BASOR*.[12] For *AJA*, we included pieces with the heading "article," "field report," or "forum," but not museum reviews, book reviews, or short "archaeological notes." For *BASOR*, we included articles only, excluding book reviews. Our preferred method of determining gender was from the pronouns used in author biographies published by an academic journal (e.g., the *AJA* website) or institutional homepages. If no biography was readily available, we performed a Google search to find an online biography, profile, or press release using pronouns, which we assumed would have been approved by the person under question. If this turned up nothing, gender was listed as "U" for "unknown." All of the *AJA* authors for whom we could locate pronouns used "he" or "she" mutually exclusively. One *BASOR* author's profile used the pronoun "they," and this author was coded "N" for nonbinary. We recognize that we may have inadvertently misgendered some authors during this analysis and that it would have been preferable to reach out to scholars directly to ask them about their gender identity (see Heath-Stout 2020b). However, this was not logistically feasible for this study, and we are confident that our coding captures major trends in gender and authorship in these two journals.

We assigned articles to one of four categories based on the primary focus of the article (Table 3.1). Category 1 was reserved for articles publishing the results of new fieldwork. Category 2 was used if the article synthesized previously published archaeological data, inscriptions, and/or literary sources. Category 3 denotes art historical studies (sculpture, painting) or articles that chiefly analyzed artifacts or small finds (ceram-

TABLE 3.1 Categories used to assign topics to *AJA* and *BASOR* articles, 2015–2020.

Category 1	Results of new fieldwork
Category 2	Synthesis of previously published data
Category 3	Art historical or artifact-based studies
Category 4	Epigraphy

ics, glass, figurines, etc.). Traditional epigraphic studies that focused closely on textual analysis and interpretation rather than archaeological context were assigned to Category 4. We coded articles by reading the abstract and keywords and, if necessary, looking more closely at the main text. Though these categories are necessarily crude and do not represent the full diversity of topics covered by *AJA* or *BASOR* articles, they suffice for our research question. In some cases, categories overlapped slightly. We assigned any paper that presented newly-excavated material to Category 1. For example, a newly excavated relief sculpture published by the excavation director would be coded as a 1, even though the object of analysis is art historical. Any art-historical or object-based analyses that were synthetic in nature, such as a discussion of stirrup jars across the eastern Mediterranean during the Bronze Age, were coded as a 3 because the primary focus of the study was material culture or art.

To test our hypothesis that field reports (Category 1) might accrue more prestige or professional advantages for their author(s) than other types of articles, we determined the number of times each article was cited (Table 3.2).[13] Indeed, Category 1 articles in *AJA* and *BASOR* are the most cited, followed by Category 2 articles. Somewhat surprisingly, Category 3 articles

---

12 We thank Amelia Chouinard for assisting us with data collection.

13 We used Google Scholar to determine the number of citations per year for each article, since we found that it provided the most robust figures. Other studies of citation databases have reached similar conclusions, especially for the humanities; see Martín-Martín et al. 2021. These calculations were undertaken well after our initial analysis, in response to a reviewer's comment, and thus did not affect our categorization of the articles.

TABLE 3.2 Number of articles and average number of citations per year by article category.

Article category	Number of articles, *AJA*	Average citations per year, *AJA*	Number of articles, *BASOR*	Average citations per year, *BASOR*
1	26	2.96	31	2.69
2	41	2.12*	37	1.72
3	47	1.52	30	0.97
4	1	0.75	12	1.54

* This figure omits a single outlier which significantly inflated the average (to 2.86). This outlier, an article by Knapp and Manning (2016), had 32.4 citations per year, a full nine standard deviations above the mean number of citations for all *AJA* articles in the sample. No other article in our database reached double-digit citations per year.

(art historical and artifact-based studies) were the least-cited in both journals (disregarding Category 4 in the *AJA* due to its small sample size). A one-way ANOVA test of equal means showed that there was a statistically significant difference in average citations per year between at least two categories of articles in both publications (for *AJA*: $F(2, 110)= 6.400$, $p = 0.0023$; for *BASOR*: $F(3, 106) = 6.264$, $p = 0.0005$).[14] A Tukey's pairwise test for multiple comparisons showed that the difference in average citations per year between Category 1 and Category 3 articles was statistically significant for both publications (for *AJA*, $p = 0.0015$; for *BASOR*, $p = 0.0002$). The differences between Category 1 and Category 2 articles were not significant at the $p = 0.05$ level (for *AJA*, $p = 0.1101$; for *BASOR*, $p = 0.0584$). However, these *p*-values are still fairly low, meaning that there is a low probability that the differences in average citations between Category 1 and Category 2 are the result of random chance.

Of the 115 articles published by the *AJA* between 2015 and mid-2020, first authorship is split roughly evenly between men and women, with 60 female first authors and 55 male first authors (fig. 3.1). Category 2 and 3 articles outnumber Category 1 articles, which is consistent with our expectation that research in Mediterranean archaeology often

involves synthetic or object-based studies of previously collected data rather than new fieldwork (fig. 3.2). Only one *AJA* article was categorized as a 4, perhaps because other Classics-oriented journals, some of which focus specifically on Greek and Latin epigraphy, are more likely venues for the publication of inscriptions (*Hesperia, Zeitschrift für Papyrologie und Epigraphik,* etc.). *BASOR* authorship is more male-dominated than *AJA*: men make up roughly 60% of first authors and total authors since 2015 (fig. 3.1). The breakdown of articles by topic also differs between *BASOR* and *AJA*: over the past six years, *BASOR* has published more field reports (28% versus 23%), fewer art historical or artifact-based studies (27% versus 40%), and many more epigraphy-focused articles (11% versus < 0.1%) than *AJA* (fig. 3.2).

In both *AJA* and *BASOR*, however, authors of different genders are not distributed evenly across categories. Women are far less likely to be first author on Category 1 articles: 21 men to five women in *AJA* and 26 men to five women in *BASOR*. Conversely, women were far more likely to be first authors on art historical or object-focused studies in *AJA* (12 men to 34 women), though this is not true for *BASOR*. First authorship on Category 2 articles was exactly even between men and women in *AJA* and close to even in *BASOR*. This difference is both pronounced (men are first authors of field reports four to five times as often as women) and highly statistically significant: X^2 (3, N = 115), $p = 0.0001$ for *AJA*; X^2 (3, N = 107), $p = 0.0083$ for

14 An ANOVA (Analysis of Variance) test can be used to compare the means of more than two populations (thereby generalizing the more familiar t-test, which is used to compare the means of two populations).

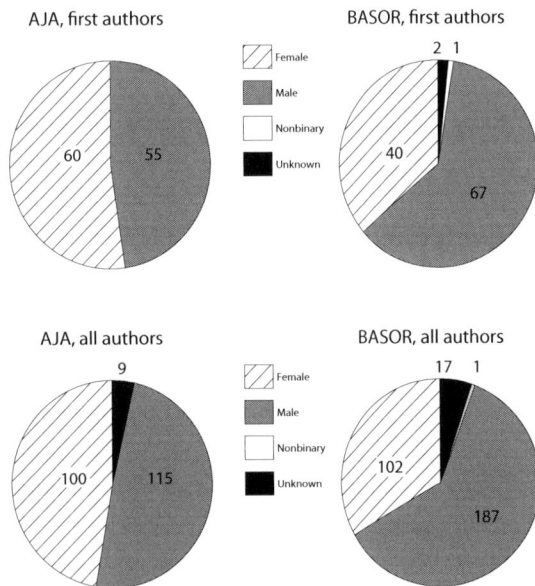

FIG. 3.1 *Gender of authors for AJA (issues 119.1–124.2) and BASOR articles (issues 373–383).*

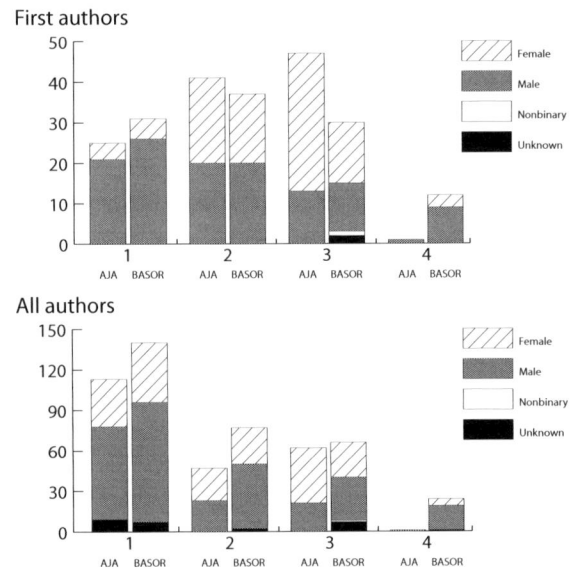

FIG. 3.2 *Number of articles by category published in AJA (issues 119.1–124.2) and BASOR (issues 373–383).*

BASOR. If we consider all authors on Category 1 articles, not just first authors, the balance improves, but men still dominate: 61% in *AJA,* 63% in *BASOR.*

These results suggest that gender plays an important role in shaping archaeological knowledge production and publication. To us, the most probable explanation for the observed pattern is that men are more likely to be project directors and therefore first authors on Category 1 articles. To explore this hypothesis, we identified the directors of the projects that published their results in Category 1 articles within our sample. We then determined their gender using the same methods described above for article authors. More than three quarters of these directors are men (fig. 3.3). Indeed, in Greece, where both authors of this article conduct most of their fieldwork, 18 out of 25 U.S.-based directors of archaeological projects affiliated with the American School of Classical Studies at Athens (ASCSA) since 2005 are men (fig. 3.3).[15] Even though many of these

projects employ female staff, women are still underrepresented as authors on publications of new fieldwork. This could reflect a fieldwork culture that is less welcoming, on average, to women than it is to men, pushing women to focus on other areas of study where they are more rewarded for their work or confront less resistance. For women who wish to have children, an expectation that directing a fieldwork project is incompatible with pregnancy, nursing, and caring for small children, as well as hurdles to securing affordable childcare in the field, may further discourage them from taking on a directorial role.[16] The disproportionate representation of women as first authors of Category 3 articles may also result from gender

---

15   The ratio is even more male-dominated if years of direction are taken into account, since men tend to direct projects that are in the field for longer. Co-directors of ASCSA projects were not counted if they were not based in the U.S., since these individuals reflect different national archaeological traditions. Greek co-directors of ASCSA collaborative projects (*synergasíes*) are overwhelmingly

female, but this is because most Greek archaeologists are women. A 2011 survey found that 76% of all Greek archaeologists and 80% of the archaeologists who work for the Greek Ministry of Culture and Athletics were women (Initiative for Heritage Conservancy 2014).

16   In their study of gender and presentation topics at the SAA, EAA, and CAA meetings, Chen and Marwick found that both GIS and isotope analysis were associated with women. They suggest that these subfields may be more convenient to pursue as a caregiver than subfields that require frequent travel and physical presence in the field (Chen and Marwick 2023: 6). It is possible that object-based or art historical studies fulfill a similar role in Mediterranean and Near Eastern archaeology.

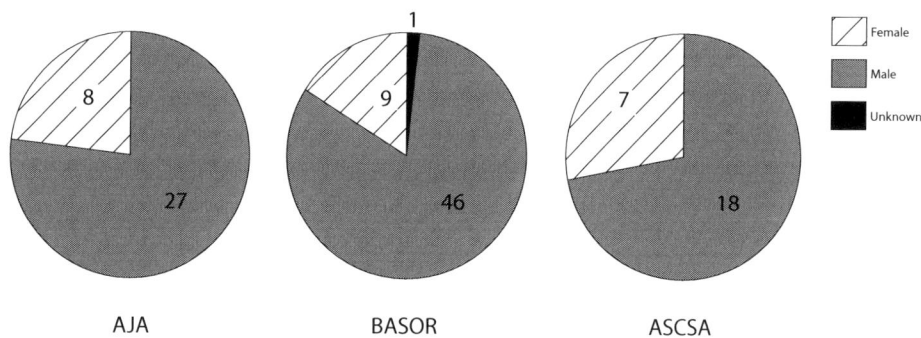

FIG. 3.3 *Gender of the directors of archaeological projects from Category 1 articles in the AJA and BASOR from 2015 to mid-2020, and, for comparison, the gender composition of the project directors issued permits by the American School of Classical Studies at Athens from 2005 to 2019.*

stereotyping—the idea that art historical or object-focused studies are more appropriate for women. Since *AJA* and *BASOR* submissions are all subject to blind review, this is likely *not* due to bias on the part of reviewers, but rather to internalized bias and institutional pressures on the authors. While we did not track class, race, or ethnicity of authors in this study, recent work reveals that authors of all genders in *AJA* from 2000 to 2020 were overwhelmingly white and from privileged socioeconomic backgrounds, as measured by parental educational attainment (Heath-Stout et al. 2023); no comparable data were available for *BASOR*. This demonstrates that, even though women are authoring an increasing proportion of articles in archaeological journals, much more work is required to make Mediterranean archaeology equitable.

These patterns are especially concerning because of the tendency, noted above, for field reports to be cited with much greater frequency than other types of articles. Excluding epigraphy (Category 4), there is a general correlation between a category of article's average citations per year and the percentage of male authors: field reports are the most male (61.72% of all authors) and most cited (2.81 citations per year), synthetic studies are less male (56.35% of all authors) and less cited (1.93 citations per year), and object-oriented studies are the least male (41.54% of all authors) and least cited (1.31 citations per year).

These differences in average citations between different categories of publication may contribute to the fact that articles authored by men or

majority-male authorial teams are more frequently cited on average (2.04 citations per year, n=113) than articles authored by women or majority-female authorial teams (1.77 citations per year, n=79). A *t*-test for equal means found that this difference is not statistically significant, however (t = 1.0682, p = 0.2868). In Categories 1, 2 and 3, publications authored by women or majority-female authorial teams are cited *more* often than their male and majority-male counterparts, but women are underrepresented among authors of the most-cited type of articles (field reports) and overrepresented among authors of the least-cited type of articles (object-oriented studies). Thus, although Category 1 articles authored by men or majority-male authorial teams are *less* frequently cited than articles authored by women or majority-female authorial teams (2.99 versus 3.76 average citations per year), there are many fewer of the latter (5) than the former (38). Similarly, Category 3 articles authored by women and majority-female authorial teams are cited slightly more frequently (1.37, n=43) than their counterparts authored by men and majority-male authorial teams (1.24, n=24), and although the former are more numerous than the latter, Category 3 publications are much less frequently cited overall.[17] These findings suggest that article category has a more pronounced effect on citation frequency than author gender. In other words, women are not cited less than men because they are women, but rather because men

---

17 These figures omit a single outlier in our Category 2 (see above, Table 3.2).

disproportionately author prestigious publications (in this case, field reports).

We also note another pattern (though the sample size is admittedly small) related to articles that focus specifically on women, gender, or gender identity in the ancient world. Six such articles appeared in *AJA* between 2015 and 2020, and two in *BASOR*. In the *AJA*, all authors of these six articles are women, and three of the articles focus on women specifically (the word "women" appears in the title of these three, while the other three discuss "gender" or derivatives like "gendered," "gendering"). Both *BASOR* articles are written by men, and they focused on gender or gendered identities more broadly. It appears from this sample that, in Mediterranean archaeology, studying gender is largely the domain of female scholars. That half of these articles focus specifically on women rather than "gender" more broadly may suggest the persistence of a second-wave feminist approach to gender scholarship in Classics, rather than a third-wave approach that treats gender as a negotiated and constructed category.

In conclusion, our journal study clearly indicates significant gender disparities in who directs field projects and publishes the results of those projects in the Mediterranean and Near East. These discrepancies are even more pronounced than those in archaeology generally (Heath-Stout 2020): 81% (21 of 26) of first authors of new fieldwork in *AJA* are male and 84% (26 of 31) in *BASOR*; these correspond fairly closely to the percentages of male directors of field projects published in those journals: 77% (27 of 35) and 82% (46 of 56) respectively. Women are far more likely to author publications that are synthetic or object-oriented, corresponding to Gero's observation that women do the archaeological housekeeping, cooking the raw data collected by their male counterparts (Gero 1983: 51). What is more, publication types associated with and dominated by men (field reports) are most likely to be cited, whereas publications associated with and dominated by women (object-based studies) are least likely to be cited. It is also worth considering, however, whether some women publish in these areas as part of a strategy designed to avoid the hazards of the male-dominated world of fieldwork that we described above: harassment and sexism, including the tendency for male directors to promote and give publication opportunities to their male students. In the Mediterranean, avoiding fieldwork and publishing synthetic or art historical work is a feasible path to a successful career, unlike in other archaeological traditions where original fieldwork is more central. We suggest that this distinctive aspect of Mediterranean archaeology is responsible in part for the heightened disparities we see in our data.

TOWARDS SOLUTIONS

Mitigating the damage caused by sexism necessarily involves a combination of changes to individual behavior, targeted anti-harassment policies, and broader shifts in the way archaeological fieldwork and academic culture function (see Voss 2021b: 5–13 for a similar multi-level model drawn from public health paradigms). Below, we evaluate some of the steps that have been taken so far to protect students from sexual harassment and gender-based discrimination in academic settings. We also propose far-reaching policies that can make archaeology and academia safer and more inclusive, emphasizing the importance of substantive and costly (in terms of both time and money) changes to the structures that bolster sexism in the academy.

Codes of conduct for archaeological field projects and anti-harassment policies for professional conferences are becoming increasingly popular. The major professional archaeological societies in the U.S. (the Society for American Archaeology, Archaeological Institute of America, ASOR, and the Society for Historical Archaeology) have all decried harassment in fieldwork settings, though the degree of specificity in their policies ranges.[18] The documents from ASOR and the AIA make

---

18 ASOR: http://www.asor.org/about-asor/policies/code-of-conduct-for-fieldwork-projects. SHA: https://sha.org/about-us/sha-sexual-harassment-discrimination-policy/. AIA: https://www.archaeological.org/about/governance/policies/. SAA: https://www.saa.org/career-practice/saa-statements-guidelines/statement-details/2015/11/01/saa-statement-on-sexual-harassment-and-violence

archaeology-specific policy recommendations for project directors, while the shorter SAA statement largely encourages compliance with Title IX and other federal or institutional guidelines. Similar harassment policies have been put in place for professional archaeological conferences, and the SAA and AIA have instituted ombudspeople who can serve as a confidential source of support for conference attendees.[19] Some policies are even further-reaching: for instance, the AIA and the SCS (Society for Classical Studies), which share a joint conference and job placement service, emphasize that candidates should not be asked about sexual preferences, marital status, or children during any stage of the job interview process.[20]

These policies are well-intentioned and valuable in that they publicly signal a lack of tolerance for harassment in professional settings. Enforcement, however, is much more difficult than policy-making. One wonders, for example, how the AIA/SCS will follow up on its promise to bar "individuals who are currently or have been sanctioned for assault or harassment by an adjudicating institution" from annual meetings. Ombudspeople are, by definition, sworn to preserve confidentiality and cannot register formal complaints with disciplinary bodies. The anecdote from SAA 2019 referenced at the beginning of this chapter clearly demonstrates that the mere existence of policies without detailed procedures and robust enforcement is insufficient. Should plenary speakers, presenters, and attendees of professional conferences be vetted in advance to make sure that they have not been "sanctioned for assault or harassment by an adjudicating institution," and how would that work? Clearly the onus to report the presence of abusers at conferences should not fall on survivors of abuse, who might be retraumatized by speaking up, or on vulnerable junior scholars whose reputations and careers could be jeopardized. What about the myriad examples of harassment and abuse that have flown under

the radar for years or decades? Given that many victims do not report sexual harassment, even in the era of #MeToo, and indeed have good reason to fear that reporting will harm their future prospects in archaeology, banning only individuals who have been formally sanctioned will surely leave large gaps. How can these cases be most fairly adjudicated and addressed in professional settings? There are no easy answers to these questions, but these are the kinds of discussions that need to be taking place at the highest levels of the discipline. One option that has yet to be explored by professional archaeological organizations is an online tool like Callisto, which allows survivors of sexual assault to submit time-stamped reports that document their experiences.[21] If a named perpetrator "matches" between two or more reports, all survivors are put in touch with legal counsel who can help them decide how to proceed. Although not without shortcomings, such an approach is valuable because it can help to flag serial offenders without forcing survivors into the limelight. Conference organizers and university departments could thus be alerted to predatory individuals in advance, and prior conduct could be taken into consideration when deciding whether to allow these individuals to register for conferences or lead field schools.

While curtailing harassment is important, establishing systems of positive mentorship can also help to create inclusive environments. Professional institutions can host chapters and organizations that mentor women and gender minorities (the Women's Classical Caucus, affiliated with the Society for Classical Studies, is one example). Informal networks like these are an important stopgap and can greatly improve the experiences of those who have experienced sexual and gender harassment, possibly even preventing them from leaving the field in discouragement and disgust. Supportive faculty and graduate students can help spread informal knowledge about which graduate programs and field projects are toxic, unsafe, or discriminatory. Good mentorship could also help to shift some of the demographic trends in archaeological journal

19 AIA: https://classicalstudies.org/annual-meeting/2020/joint-harassment-policy. SAA: https://www.saa.org/annual-meeting/submissions/anti-harassment-policy

20 https://classicalstudies.org/placement/placement-service-guidelines

21 https://mycallisto.org/

publication that we discuss above without under-mining the blind peer review process. In many cases, disparities in journal publication are due to disparities in submission. As Rautman puts it, "if an author does not submit a manuscript, there is zero chance of getting it published!" (Rautman 2012: 26). Mentoring of early-career scholars can build their confidence and may encourage them to submit manuscripts at higher rates (Heath-Stout 2020b).

Structural changes to academic programs can undermine the power imbalances in academia that allow many abusers to act with near impu-nity. Currently, most PhD programs in archaeo-logy are designed as a "one-on-one" mentorship experience, similar to an apprenticeship, where a student works closely with one advisor in their area of expertise (and often works on their field project as well). While this can work very well if the advisor is supportive, it can be a disaster if the advisor and student are unable to develop and maintain a healthy working relationship. A shift in expectations away from single-advisor models towards a committee-based approach or a "mentoring network" could help to improve this situation, and an arrangement like this has already been instituted in the History department at the University of Michigan.[22] This structure makes it easier for students to change advisors and escape abusers, and, on a more positive note, allows students to develop a broader set of intel-lectual connections.

In archaeological fieldwork, this could trans-late into having a group of diverse co-directors rather than a single director. Hiring diverse faculty and promoting female faculty are routes to this same end, since male-dominated gender ratios have been shown to be linked to higher rates of sexual harassment in academic settings (National Academies of Sciences, Engineering, and Medicine 2018: 171). In archaeology, the lack of female project directors in a field where graduate and undergraduate students are disproportionally women is clearly a symptom of structural prob-lems. Increasing the representation of women in

directorial roles should absolutely be a goal for the field moving forward (see also Nakhai 2018), and granting agencies might consider gender parity between directors as one line along which to evaluate research proposals for new fieldwork. However, as with the other solutions we have proposed, simply adding female directors and supervisors to archaeological projects is hardly sufficient in the absence of wider cultural changes. Not only is more work needed to determine whether harassment is less frequent on projects with female supervisors, but it is also important to ensure that women in the field are not pressured into disproportionately performing stereotypical-ly feminine roles such as logistical arrangements or caretaking of students (cf. our discussion above about the gendering of university service).[23] As we have repeatedly stressed, the problem is not representation *per se*, but equity and inclusion.

Supporting archaeologists who wish to start a family is another area where there is room for substantial improvements. As discussed above, sexism creates disproportionately severe profes-sional consequences for women in academia who have partners and children. Many PhD students in archaeology are likely to finish their degrees in their early to mid-thirties. If students are expected to be in the field every summer to work towards their dissertations or other scholarly publications, it can be difficult to know when pregnancy and the early months of parenthood can be accom-modated, especially if there is little support on projects for people with children. A lack of role models for female project directors, pregnant archaeologists, and parents with children in the field is harmful. Projects that welcome the pres-ence of children and help to subsidize childcare for their students and staff can play an important role in shifting the culture around families in archaeological research. Granting organizations should allow applicants to ask for funds to cover

23 In their study of Southeastern archaeological field schools, Meyers et al. found that the rate of harassment was about the same on projects with female and male supervisors, though the rate of assault was higher on male-supervised projects (Meyers et al. 2018: 282).

childcare, and professional organizations can provide on-site childcare at conferences.

An intersectional feminist approach to these issues would be incomplete without policies that make academia more inclusive and accessible in general. We reject a feminism that seeks only to establish what has been called "equal-opportunity domination": "where the task of managing exploitation in the workplace and oppression in the social whole is shared equally" between genders (Arruzza et al. 2019: 2). We maintain that a living wage and full benefits for all employees of the university, including contingent faculty, graduate students, and administrative and custodial staff, is essential for curtailing sexual harassment and gender discrimination. Free healthcare for university workers and their families, paid maternity and paternity leave, and affordable childcare are both human rights and gender equity issues. Unfortunately, these benefits are rarely available to graduate students and contingent faculty. Graduate student and contingent faculty unions are powerful tools for securing living wages and benefits for their members and for negotiating workplace abuses, including sexual harassment-related ones. Many unions have grievance procedures that provide formal channels through which advisor abuse or exploitation can be reported. Despite the argument often propagated by anti-union administrators that graduate student unionization harms faculty–student relationships, there is no evidence that faculty feel that unionization hinders their ability to advise and teach graduate students (Hewitt 2000). In fact, collective bargaining can improve relationships between faculty and students by clarifying expectations (Julius and Gumport 2003: 201–2), and graduate students who are unionized report higher levels of personal and professional support from their faculty mentors (Rogers et al. 2013: 500). So long as advising on campus and directing in the field remain black boxes where those with power can act with near impunity, we are skeptical that the dynamics driving sexism, harassment, and abuse will change. The empowerment of students and contingent faculty is central to any solution.

People in positions of institutional power or security, like tenured professors and project directors, must be willing to reprimand abusers and assist victims, even if it places them in a socially uncomfortable position. A recent study has suggested that, when a "bystander" reports sexual harassment, it can help to mitigate the negative stereotyping and career-harming repercussions that self-reporting of harassment incurs for targets (Hart 2019). The burden for changing the culture around sexism and gender harassment cannot fall primarily on its victims. Men, especially tenured men, have an important role to play in discussions about sexual harassment, doctoral training reform, and graduate student or contingent faculty unionization. In addition to advocating for far-reaching structural reforms, tenured faculty can also use their platform to support graduate students who require parental leave, increased time to degree, extra financial support for childcare, or other family-related accommodations.

Conclusions

This chapter really began in the summer of 2014, when the authors started working together on the Western Argolid Regional Project (WARP). One of us was a graduate student who served as a supervisor and team leader (Erny) and the other was a recently-tenured professor who served as co-director (Nakassis). Our project typified the general pattern sketched in this chapter, in that men outnumbered women three to one among the senior staff, but virtually all of our graduate student staff and most of our undergraduate field school students were women or non-binary. Conversations between the two co-authors about how our project could have done better, sparked initially by the work of Nelson et al. (2017) on fieldwork policies, resulted in two written pieces: an essay by Nakassis on his personal blog[24] and an interview of the two of us and Stephanie Steinke (like Erny, a team leader on WARP) in the

---

24 https://englianos.wordpress.com/2017/10/25/field-archaeology-sexual-harassment/

online journal *Eidolon*.[25] These discussions were revealing in multiple respects. First, while we all agreed that formal policies for field projects and professional organizations were a positive step, their limitations in the absence of broader changes to the systems of power that structure archaeological practice were all too clear. While we appreciate recent efforts to create committees and policies to combat discrimination and harassment, we would now emphasize even more strongly that these must be accompanied by real expenditures of time and material resources to be effective.

In particular, it is imperative for those with institutional power to advocate for an equitable field. This observation puts senior men in a difficult position: on the one hand, they are better positioned to advocate for equity. On the other hand, they may risk dominating the conversation and replicating (even inadvertently) the systems that amplify certain voices and silence others. We feel that it is the ethical responsibility of senior men to listen to and amplify the voices of women and gender minorities, junior colleagues, and graduate students advocating for structural change. Most importantly, these people must make an effort to do the difficult work that their positions (as tenured professors, project directors, or members of granting committees) allow, even if this does not earn them formal recognition or draws censure from their peers. This is essential for the well-being of the field and its practitioners. Without the intervention of those in positions of institutional power, the current system will continue to replicate itself.

The story with which we began this chapter serves as an instructive example: although the discipline's institutions publicly recognized Bradford's work, her award was derided by some of its senior members. We do not see the laughter of these men as merely an individual moral failure (although it is also that!). Rather, it is the product of a system that continues to marginalize and disparage women and their contribution to archaeological knowledge. This system manifests itself in diverse and interconnected ways, from sexual harassment and discrimination to the valorization of subfields dominated by men. So long as this mismatch exists between official and informal discourse and action, we cannot envision real progress.

REFERENCES

Amienne, K. A.
2017   Abusers and Enablers in Faculty Culture. *The Chronicle of Higher Education.* https://www.chronicle.com/article/AbusersEnablers-in/241648 (accessed 25 April 2020).

Anderson, G.
2020   Location-Based Protection. *Inside Higher Ed.* https://www.insidehighered.com/news/2020/05/12/new-title-ix-regulation-sets-location-based-boundaries-sexual-harassment-enforcement (accessed 5 June 2020).

Arruzza, C.; Bhattacharya, T.; and Fraser, N.
2019   *Feminism for the 99%: A Manifesto.* London: Verso.

Awesome Small Working Group
2019   Take Back the SAA. *The SAA Archaeological Record* 19.4: 16–21.

Bardolph, D. N.
2014   A Critical Evaluation of Recent Gendered Publishing Trends in American Archaeology. *American Antiquity* 79.3: 522–40.

Beaudry, M. C., and White, J.
1994   Cowgirls with the Blues? A Study of Women's Publication and the Citation of Women's Work in Historical Archaeology. Pp. 138–58 in *Women in Archaeology*, ed. C. Claassen. Philadelphia: University of Pennsylvania.

Bradford, D. J., and Crema, E. R.
2022   Risk Factors for the Occurrence of Sexual Misconduct during Archaeological and Anthropological Fieldwork. *American Anthropologist* 124.3: 548–59

---

25 https://eidolon.pub/cleaning-up-the-field-f7c4c15a2f08

Cantalupo, N. C., and Kidder, W. C.
2018   A Systematic Look at a Serial Problem: Sexual Harassment of Students by University Faculty. *Utah Law Review* 2018.3: 673–786.

Cantor, D.; Fisher, B.; Chibnall, S.; Harps, S.; Townsend, R.; Thomas, G.; Lee, H.; Kranz, V.; Herbison, R.; and Madden, K.
2019   *Report on the AAU Campus Climate Survey on Sexual Assault and Misconduct.* Association of American Universities. https://www.aau.edu/key-issues/campus-climate-and-safety/aau-campus-climate-survey-2019

Chen, Y., and Marwick, B.
2023   Women in the Lab, Men in the Field? Correlations between Gender and Research Topics at Three Major Archaeology Conferences. *Journal of Field Archaeology.* https://doi.org/10.1080/00934690.2023.2261083

Cho, I. B., and Kim, A. H.
2022a 38 Harvard Faculty Sign Open Letter Questioning Results of Misconduct Investigations into Prof. John Comaroff. *The Harvard Crimson.* 4 February. https://www.thecrimson.com/article/2022/2/4/comaroff-sanctions-open-letter/ (accessed 14 March 2022).
2022b Lawsuit Alleges Harvard Ignored Sexual Harassment Complaints Against Prof. John Comaroff for Years. *The Harvard Crimson.* 9 February. https://www.thecrimson.com/article/2022/2/9/comaroff-lawsuit/ (accessed 14 March 2022).

Clancy, K.; Nelson, R.; Rutherford, J.; and Hinde, K.
2014   Survey of Academic Field Experiences (SAFE): Trainees Report Harassment and Assault. *PLoS ONE* 9.7: e102172. https://doi.org/10.1371/journal.pone.0102172

Conkey, M., and Spector, J.
1984   Archaeology and the Study of Gender. *Advances in Archaeological Method and Theory* 7: 1–38.

El-Alayli, A.; Hansen-Brown, A. A.; and Ceynar, M.
2018   Dancing Backwards in High Heels: Female Professors Experience More Work Demands and Special Favor Requests, Particularly from Academically Entitled Students. *Sex Roles* 79: 136–50.

Erny, G., and Godsey, M.
2022   Forum: Scholarly Networks, Gender Sociology and Knowledge Production in Aegean Survey and Eastern Mediterranean Archaeology. *Journal of Eastern Mediterranean Archaeology and Heritage Studies* 10.3–4: 343–55.

Fitzgerald, L. F.; Shullman, S. L.; Bailey, N.; Richards, M.; Swecker, J.; Gold, Y.; Ormerod, M.; and Weitzman, L.
1988   The Incidence and Dimensions of Sexual Harassment in Academia and the Workplace. *Journal of Vocational Behavior* 32: 152–75.

Flaherty, C.
2019a Unwanted Attendee. *Inside Higher Ed.* https://www.insidehighered.com/news/2019/04/15/archaeology-group-faces-backlash-over-how-it-handled-known-harassers-attendance (accessed 23 April 2020).
2019b Scholarly Society in 'Crisis.' *Inside Higher Ed.* https://www.insidehighered.com/news/2019/04/30/how-not-handle-me-too-related-public-relations-crisis (accessed 23 April 2020).
2019c Graduate Education Reform, Starting with Advising. *Inside Higher Ed.* https://www.insidehighered.com/news/2019/01/10/historians-and-language-professors-discuss-advising-recent-conferences (accessed 3 June 2020).

Fricker, M.
2007   *Epistemic Injustice: Power and the Ethics of Knowing.* Oxford: Oxford University.

Gero, J.
1983   Gender Bias in Archaeology: A Cross-Cultural Perspective. Pp. 51–57 in *The Socio-Politics of Archaeology,* ed. J. M. Gero,

D. M. Lacy, and M. L. Blakey. Research Reports Number 23. Amherst: Department of Anthropology, University of Massachusetts Amherst.

1985   Socio-Politics at the Woman-at-Home Ideology. *American Antiquity* 50.2: 342–50.

Gero, J., and Conkey, M. (eds.)
1991   *Engendering Archaeology: Women and Prehistory.* Oxford: Blackwell.

Goldstein, L.; Mills, B. J.; Herr, S.; Burkholder, J.; Aiello, E. L.; and Thornton, C.
2018   Why Do Fewer Women Than Men Apply for Grants After Their PhDs? *American Antiquity* 83.3: 367–86.

Guarino, C. M., and Borden, V. M. H.
2017   Faculty Service Loads and Gender: Are Women Taking Care of the Academic Family? *Research in Higher Education* 58: 672–94.

Gutiérrez y Muhs, G.; Niemann, Y. F.; González, C. G.; and Harris, A. P. (eds.)
2012   *Presumed Incompetent: The Intersections of Race and Class for Women in Academia.* Boulder, CO: University of Colorado.

Hall, G.
2016   *The Uberfication of the University.* Minneapolis: University of Minnesota.

Hart, C. G.
2019   The Penalties for Self-Reporting Sexual Harassment. *Gender and Society* 33.4: 534–59.

Heath-Stout, L. E.
2020a   Guest Editorial Introduction: Gender, Equity, and the Peer Review Process at the *Journal of Field Archaeology. Journal of Field Archaeology* 45.3: 135–39.
2020b   Who Writes about Archaeology? An Intersectional Study of Authorship in Archaeological Journals. *American Antiquity* 85.2: 1–20.

Heath-Stout, L. E.; Erny, G.; and Nakassis, D.
2023   Demographic Dynamics of Publishing in the *American Journal of Archaeology. American Journal of Archaeology* 127.2: 151–63.

Heath-Stout, L. E., and Hannigan, L.
2020   Affording Archaeology: How Field School Costs Promote Exclusivity. *Advances in Archaeological Practice* 8.2: 123–33.

Hewitt, G. J.
2000   Graduate student employee collective bargaining and the educational relationship between faculty and graduate students. *Journal of Collective Negotiations* 29: 153–66.

Hodgetts, L. M.; Supernant, K.; Lyons, N.; and Welch, J. R.
2020   Broadening #MeToo: Tracking Dynamics in Canadian Archaeology Through a Survey on Experiences Within the Discipline. *Canadian Journal of Archaeology* 44: 20–47.

Initiative for Heritage Conservancy
2014   Ανακαλύπτοντας τους αρχαιολόγους της Ελλάδας 2012–14. Athens: Initiative for Heritage Conservancy.

Jaschik, S.
2017   But Will Her Husband Move? *Inside Higher Ed.* https://www.insidehighered.com/news/2017/10/27/hiring-junior-faculty-positions-study-finds-bias-against-female-candidates-who-have (accessed 4 June 2020).

Julius, D. J., and Gumport, P. J.
2003   Graduate Student Unionization: Catalysts and Consequences. *The Review of Higher Education,* 26.2: 187–216.

Knapp, A. B., and Manning, S. W.
2016   Crisis in Context: The End of the Late Bronze Age in the Eastern Mediterranean. *American Journal of Archaeology* 120: 99–149. https://doi.org/10.3764/aja.120.1.0099

Leighton, M.
2020   Myths of Meritocracy, Friendship, and Fun Work: Class and Gender in North American Academic Communities. *American Anthropologist.* https://doi.org/10.1111/aman.13455

MacNell, L.; Driscoll, A.; and Hunt, A. N.
2015   What's in a Name: Exposing Gender Bias

in Student Ratings of Teaching. *Innovative Higher Education* 40: 291–303.

Martín-Martín, A.; Thelwall, M.; Orduna-Malea, E.; and Delgado López-Cózar, R.
2021 Google Scholar, Microsoft Academic, Scopus, Dimensions, Web of Science, and OpenCitations' COCI: A multidisciplinary comparison of coverage via citations. *Scientometrics* 126: 871–906.

Mason, M. A.; Wolfinger, N.; and Goulden, M.
2013 *Do Babies Matter? Gender and Family in the Ivory Tower.* New Brunswick: Rutgers University.

McKinney, K.; Olson, C. V.; and Satterfield, A.
1988 Graduate Students' Experiences With and Responses to Sexual Harassment: A Research Note. *Journal of Interpersonal Violence* 3: 319–25.

Meyers, M. S.; Horton, E. T.; Boudreaux, E. A.; Carmody, S. B.; Wright, A. P.; and Dekle, V. G.
2018 The Concept and Consequences of Sexual Harassment in Southeastern Archaeology. *Advances in Archaeological Practice* 6.4: 275–87.

Mitchell, K. M. W., and Martin, J.
2018 Gender Bias in Student Evaluations. *PS: Political Science & Politics* 51.3: 648–52.

Murray, S.; Chorgay, I.; and MacPherson, J.
2020 The Dipylon Mistress: Social and Economic Complexity, the Gendering of Craft Production, and Early Greek Ceramic Material Culture. *American Journal of Archaeology* 124.2: 215–44.

Monroe, K.; Ozyurt, S.; Wrigley, T.; and Alexander, A.
2008 Gender Equality in Academia: Bad News from the Trenches, and Some Possible Solutions. *Perspectives on Politics* 6.2: 215–33.

Nakhai, B. A.
2017 Keeping Archaeological Field Work Safe from Sexual Harassment and Physical Violence. *Mar Shiprim: Newsletter of the International Association for Assyriology.* https://iaassyriology.com/field-work-safe/

2018 How to Avoid Gender-Based Hostility During Fieldwork. *The Chronicle of Higher Education.* https://www.chronicle.com/article/How-to-Avoid-Gender-Based/243912

National Academies of Sciences, Engineering, and Medicine.
2018 *Sexual Harassment of Women: Climate, Culture, and Consequences in Academic Sciences, Engineering, and Medicine.* Washington, DC: The National Academies. https://doi.org/10.17226/24994

Nelson, R. G.; Rutherford, J. N.; Hinde, K.; and Clancy, K. B. H.
2017 Signaling Safety: Characterizing Fieldwork Experiences and Their Implications for Career Trajectories. *American Anthroplogist* 119.4: 710–22.

Nixon, L.
1995 Gender Bias in Archaeology. Pp. 1–23 in *Women in Ancient Societies,* ed. L. J. Archer, S. Fischler, and M. Wyke. London: Palgrave Macmillan.

Overholtzer, L., and Jabert, C. L.
2021 A "Leaky" Pipeline and Chilly Climate in Archaeology in Canada. *American Antiquity* 86.2: 261–82. https://doi.org/10.1017/aaq.2020.107

Radde, H.
2018 Sexual Harassment Among California Archaeologists: Results of the Gender Equity and Sexual Harassment Survey. *California Archaeology* 10.2: 231–55.

Rautman, A. E.
2012 Who Gets Published in American Antiquity? *SAA Archaeological Record* 12.2: 25–26, 30.

Rivera, L.
2017 When Two Bodies Are (Not) a Problem: Gender and Relationship Status Discrimination in Academic Hiring. *American Sociological Review* 82.6: 1111–38.

Rogers, S. E.; Eaton, A. E.; and Voos, P. B.
2013 Effects of Unionization on Graduate Student Employees: Faculty-Student Relations,

Academic Freedom, and Pay. *ILR Review* 66.2: 487–510.

Rosenthal, M. N.; Smidt, A. M.; and Freyd, J. J.
2016   Still Second Class: Sexual Harassment of Graduate Students. *Psychology of Women Quarterly* 40.3: 364–77.

Sandler, B.
1986   "The Campus Climate Revisited: Chilly for Women Faculty, Administrators, and Graduate Students." Pp. 3–30 in *Project on the Status and Education of Women*, ed. B. R. Sandler. Washington, DC: Association of American Colleges.

Schmidt, B.
2015   Gender Bias Exists in Professor Evaluations. *New York Times*, 16 December 2015.

Solnit, R.
2014   *Men Explain Things to Me.* Chicago: Haymarket.

Smith, C. P. and Freyd, J. J.
2014   Institutional Betrayal. *American Psychologist* 69.6: 575–87.

Thomsen, F. K.
2017   Discrimination. In *Oxford Research Encyclopedia of Politics*, ed. W. R. Thompson. Oxford: Oxford University. https://doi.org/10.1093/acrefore/9780190228637.013.202

Tushingham S.; Fulkerson, T.; and Hill, K.
2017   The peer review gap: A longitudinal case study of gendered publishing and occupational patterns in a female-rich discipline, Western North America (1974–2016). *PLoS ONE* 12(11): e0188403. https://doi.org/10.1371/journal.pone.0188403

Voss, B.
2021a   Documenting Cultures of Harassment in Archaeology: A Review and Analysis of Quantitative and Qualitative Research Studies. *American Antiquity* 86.2: 244–60. https://doi.org/10.1017/aaq.2020.118
2021b   Disrupting Cultures of Harassment in Archaeology: Social-Environmental and Trauma-Informed Approaches to Disciplinary Transformation. *American Antiquity* 86.3: 447–64. https://doi.org/10.1017/aaq.2021.19

Wade, L.
2019   #MeToo Controversy Erupts at Archaeology Meeting. *Science.* https://doi.org/10.1126/science.aax7037 (accessed 23 April 2020).

Wylie, A.
1994   The Trouble with Numbers: Workplace Climate Issues in Archeology. Abstracted from *Women in Archaeology: A Feminist Critique*, ed. H. du Cros and L. Smith, Australian National University, 1993. Pp 65–71 in *Equity Issues for Women in Archaeology*, ed. S. M. Nelson, M. C. Nelson, and A. Wylie. Archaeological Papers 5. Washington, DC: American Anthropological Association.
1997   The Engendering of Archaeology: Refiguring Feminist Science Studies. *Osiris* 12: 80–99.
2011   What Knowers Know Well: Women, Work, and the Academy. Pp. 157–79 in *Feminist Epistemology and Philosophy of Science*, ed. H. Grasswick. Dordrecht: Springer.

Chapter 4

Digging While Impaired

Promoting the Accessibility of Archaeology as a Discipline

Debby Sneed and Mason Shrader

ABSTRACT

In this chapter, we argue that the ethical practice of archaeology involves the active recruitment and inclusion of disabled people in archaeological fieldwork. While archaeology as a discipline is not reducible to fieldwork, fieldwork is nevertheless privileged and must be performed to earn undergraduate and graduate degrees in the field and be considered a legitimate practitioner. By discouraging or actively preventing disabled students from participating in field schools—that is, by gatekeeping these professionalizing experiences—we restrict their access to the discipline as a whole. We begin this article by establishing that disabled people are, indeed, discriminated against in archaeological fieldwork situations. We attribute this discrimination to a disciplinary embrace of the medical model of disability, which locates the problem within the body of the individual, as opposed to the social model of disability, which argues that it is structures, not people, that are the problem. We demonstrate how archaeologists already accommodate their nondisabled colleagues, thereby throwing into stark relief the discrimination disabled people experience. We then provide a blueprint for how we can expand our preexisting commitment to accommodation to our disabled students and colleagues. Far from being a prescriptive list of right and wrong behaviors, the key to this ethical approach is open and honest dialogue that not only includes but is led by the disabled person, who has the best understanding of their body, their disabilities, and their abilities.

INTRODUCTION

I always experience slight trepidation whenever someone asks me what I do for a living. It is a scenario familiar to many archaeologists: you take your seat on a plane and begin small talk with your neighbor. They ask what you do, you say you are an archaeologist and brace yourself for the seemingly inevitable Indiana Jones joke or worse, "So what is your favorite type of dinosaur?" Yes, these responses are part of why I am often less than enthused to admit my occupation, but they do not account for the entirety of my apprehension. Because for me, before the quips about lost arks and paleontological confusion, the conversation goes like this: my neighbor asks what I do, I say I am an *archaeologist, and then they confusedly look me up and down for a brief moment. Then, if they are polite, they ask shyly something to the effect of, "I hope this isn't rude, but how exactly do you do archaeology?" or in the case of a comically boisterous interlocutor, "You? You do archaeology with everything you have going on?"*[1]

The diversity of modern researchers is critical for expanding our field of vision, and this is especially true of archaeology and anthropology, disciplines charged with illuminating the role of humans and humanity in the past. But the discipline has a problem with diversity: in a 2020 survey by the Society for American Archaeology (SAA), 83.5% of respondents identified as "White or Caucasian" (up from 77.7% in 2015), while only 0.5% identified as Black or African American (Association Research, Inc. 2020). William White and Catherine Draycott (2020) poignantly demonstrated that "a lack of diversity is especially problematic in archaeology because archaeologists help shape humanity's understanding of the past. Who archaeologists are—our backgrounds, experiences, and mental models—can shape which questions we ask and how we interpret archaeological evidence." Whitney Battle-Baptiste (2016: 21) personalized the call for diversity when she highlighted "that my identity often urges me to ask different questions, see from different perspectives, and maintain an ongoing and honest dialogue with my colleagues and various stakeholders." These statements about the value of and need for diversity are relevant—for different reasons and with necessarily different implications—in the present context, as we call for the active recruitment and inclusion of disabled people in archaeology. We want to confront the oft-begged question of *who belongs* in archaeology.

Our argument, however, does not directly address the epistemic value of inclusion, that is, the increase in valuable insights that we gain from disabled people participating on our research teams. We suspect that readers of this volume are already convinced by the general and specific benefits of diversity and inclusion, at least in theory. Rather, we aim to lay bare the unethical structures that facilitate the exclusion of disabled people in archaeological fieldwork. We demonstrate that it is often not the embodied reality of disability that prevents interested individuals from pursuing archaeology vocationally or avocationally: not only are disabled people competent and capable of engaging in archaeological fieldwork, but most necessary accommodations are *already* being selectively granted to nondisabled people. Disability accommodation is often framed as a positive right, "an obligation by others to provide some benefit to the rights holder" (Foldvary 2011). Indeed, accommodation can be understood as a positive right, but, importantly, it is a right that is already being exercised by nondisabled archaeologists on field projects, as we explain below. The exclusion of disabled people in archaeology, then, represents not an inability to accommodate, but an erroneous adherence to ableist assumptions about disabled people. Furthermore, it reflects a lack of disability ethics in the organization and application of archaeological practice.

We begin our chapter by justifying our focus on fieldwork over other necessary components of the discipline. We then discuss the sources of the data we use to make our subsequent arguments: first, that disabled people are, in fact, excluded from fieldwork despite demonstrated competence and skill, and second, that the division between disabled and nondisabled is not quite as secure as many believe. We argue that discrimination against disabled people is the result of a disciplinary adherence to the medical model of disability and show how the framing of disability accommodations as unreasonable in fieldwork situations is fallacious. Having established that accommodations already exist on projects, we argue that it is unethical to withhold the right to accommodation from one category of person. We move then to present a more ethical model for archaeological practice, one that prioritizes access over accommodation. There is no single answer to the question of how best to accomplish our goal of

---

1   Unless otherwise attributed, personal narratives reflect the experiences, perspectives, and voice of author Mason Shrader.

recruiting and including disabled archaeologists on our projects. Rather, we emphasize, as others have, that "archaeological ethics are flexible rules, negotiated as part of daily practice, and largely dependent upon the context in which conflict and resolution reside" (Dissard, Rosenzweig, and Matney 2011: 60).

Fieldwork as a Legitimating Performance

Because fieldwork can be both physically and emotionally demanding, it is often coded in such a way to exclude people with physical and/or mental disabilities, echoing ways that the field has historically been coded "male" and "white" (White and Draycott 2020; Cobb and Croucher 2016; Battle-Baptiste 2016; Moser 2007; Woodall and Perricone 1981). The exclusion of disabled people from archaeology is clearly part of a larger cultural narrative that expects bodies to conform to a "standard model of human form and function that is called normal in medical-scientific discourses, average in consumer capitalism, and ordinary in colloquial parlance" (Garland-Thomson 2007: 114) and rejects any that do not. Legislation like the Americans with Disabilities Act (ADA) of 1990 and the United Kingdom's Disability Discrimination Act (DDA) of 1995 mandate inclusion in a variety of contexts, including higher education. Still, however, archaeology and other disciplines that incorporate fieldwork, such as geography, maintain their earned reputations for exclusion (Hall, Healey, and Harrison 2002).

We recognize, of course, that as a discipline, archaeology is not reducible to fieldwork and that, in fact, the false equation of archaeology with fieldwork presents problems for the discipline and its practitioners. At least one of us is not even convinced of the ethics of continued archaeological fieldwork at a time when projects and museums often do not have adequate funding for the storage and conservation of a wide range of inorganic and especially organic archaeological materials. What is more, we acknowledge that no aspect of the discipline is particularly inclusive and that we may have an easier case if we argued for the inclusion of disabled people in less physi-

cally demanding and travel-dependent projects in libraries, archives, or labs. Nevertheless, the explicit focus on fieldwork here is justified. Even leaving aside popular perceptions of archaeology-as-fieldwork (Brosman 2019; Johnson 2014; Holtorf 2007), archaeologists themselves privilege fieldwork (i.e., data collection) over conservation and analysis. In many ways, fieldwork is a legitimating performance, something that *must be done* for one to be considered a valid practitioner of the discipline (see, e.g., Fraser 2007: 17–18; Moser 2007; Gero 1994). And, of course, undergraduate and graduate students at many colleges and universities are required to participate in fieldwork in order to complete archaeology degree programs (Colaninno et al. 2020; Phillips and Gilchrist 2005: 17–18). A recent profile of archaeologists in the United Kingdom revealed that 93% of practicing archaeologists had at least a bachelor's degree (Aitchison and Rocks-Macqueen 2013), demonstrating the necessity of completing this coursework, with its required fieldwork, to become employed in the field. Whether we personally like it or not, then, fieldwork remains a critical component of becoming and being an archaeologist. Fieldwork operates as a gate, and by controlling access to it—gatekeeping—we control access to the discipline as a whole.

On another level, it is the adventure of fieldwork that attracts many students to our projects, independent of any intention they have to complete a degree in archaeology or become professional archaeologists. We argue, too, that disabled people should be encouraged to pursue even single experiences with fieldwork, as these can confer practical and transferrable skills and instill lifelong interests in archaeology, history, and conservation (see, e.g., Colannino et al. 2020; Cartrette and Melroe-Lehrman 2012; Sheppard and Huckleberry 2010). It is not just exceptional disabled students who exhibit a preternatural aptitude for archaeology whom we should accommodate, but any disabled student who wishes to participate. That is, any investment in the accessibility of our discipline as a whole and on individual projects is worthwhile for all students with either a casual or dedicated interest in archaeology.

"Nothing About Us Without Us"

Throughout this chapter, we make extensive use of the data collected by the Inclusive, Accessible, Archaeology (IAA) project (Phillips and Gilchrist 2015; Phillips et al. 2007; The IAA Project Team 2007) and its successor, the Disability and the Archaeological Profession (DAP) project (Phillips and Creighton 2010). These projects worked to promote the "integration of disabled students into archaeological fieldwork and related activities" and were specifically organized with reference to disability legislation in the United Kingdom (Phillips and Gilchrist 2005: 5). Researchers conducted extensive surveys of both nondisabled and disabled archaeologists to quantify and qualify issues related to inclusion and exclusion in archaeology. Based on these surveys and their research, project members then provided a series of guidelines for how archaeology can adhere to the mandates for inclusion stipulated in the DDA (Phillips and Creighton 2010: 2). We engage, too, with the *Enabled Archaeology Guide 41* created by Theresa O'Mahony (2015) to provide examples of adjustments or accommodations that can easily be effected in a variety of archaeological contexts. In all these projects, the reproduction of survey responses in published reports, as well as the active and continuous involvement of disabled people reinforce the notion that disabled people must be key participants if we want to be successful in our efforts to enable broader participation on archaeological field projects. This is true at the disciplinary level, as well as at the level of individual projects: the key is direct and open communication with disabled people.

At the end of this chapter, we provide some suggestions to help guide archaeologists toward a more practical understanding of what resources are available and what inclusion requires of them. Throughout, we present an interdisciplinary argument for archaeologists that is nevertheless valid for any discipline that incorporates fieldwork. We want to show that "fieldwork which is accessible for all participants no matter their current physical or mental circumstances can be achieved with only a few minor adjustments and often at little

or no financial cost to the organizer or contractor" (O'Mahony 2015: 2).

Archaeologists of all ages—from undergraduate students to tenured professors—have experienced confusion in my presence, all due to a narrative of perceived conflict between my disability and archaeological fieldwork. It is a narrative stemming from a lack of education about the reality of disability and the possibilities of adaptive technology. It is a narrative stemming from a lack of imagination for creative solutions to accessibility issues in the field. Often, it is a narrative stemming from an abundance of fear. The goal of this chapter, then, is to serve as a first step to educate. The goal is to inspire imagination and to dispel fears. The goal is to ensure that inclusive fieldwork for people with disabilities is the reality.

A note is necessary regarding the structure of our contribution, as well as its authors. Dr. Debby Sneed is (at present) a nondisabled archaeologist. Her work is largely informed by Disability Studies, a field aimed at "replacing narrow and deficit-based understandings of disability with alternative knowledge claims grounded in disabled people's subjective and situated experience" (Ferri 2011: 2271; see also Couser 2009). In the field of Disability Studies, memoirs are critical because disabled people "have been spoken about, or spoken for, but rarely listened to" (Sherry 2005: 165). For these reasons, we combine familiar research-based academic prose with the first-person narratives of Mason Shrader, a disabled archaeologist. As a student, Mason worked on two archaeological field projects and in his narratives, he reflects on his relationship with archaeology as both a discipline and a practice. These narratives "do cultural work. They frame our understandings of raw, unorganized experience, giving it coherent meaning and making it accessible to us through story" (Garland-Thomson 2007: 122). Mason's narratives are an integral part of our chapter because they move our arguments beyond the theoretical, emphasize that the disability politic is embodied, and illuminate for readers one archaeologist's reality of digging while impaired. Both authors are responsible for the final product of this entire article. Throughout, however, first-person singular pronouns in the narratives refer to Mason.

Disability as Excludable

In responses provided to the IAA and the DAP, as well as in informal conversations with colleagues, two factors recur as justifications for the continued exclusion of disabled people from archaeological excavations: money and time. Field school directors and operators often cite (what they assume is) the prohibitively high cost of accommodation, especially for insurance and potential injury lawsuits, which seems impossible to manage on the shoestring budgets of many projects. One DAP respondent said that they "suppose it's fear of me getting damaged on site and them getting sued" (Phillips and Creighton 2010: 40). Additionally, project directors complain that they are too busy during a project to devote additional time—and with it, mental and emotional energies—to what they deem are the special needs of individual students. These justifications are what Tanya Titchkosky refers to as "say-able," commonplace statements that "make inaccessibility sensible under contemporary conditions" (Titchkosky 2011: 74). "Sayable" statements make exclusion "seem part of a rational project" and they rely on and sustain "the common-sense understanding of *disability as excludable*" (Titchkosky 2011: 77, emphasis original; see also Titchkosky 2003). These statements allow those saying them to find comfort in their very sensibility and rationality.

The IAA survey reported "mixed reactions to the employment of disabled staff in archaeology" (Phillips and Gilchrist 2005: 90). Some employers responded positively to the idea of working with disabled people or provided positive reflections on their experiences doing so. Unfortunately, many reactions reported in the IAA survey were negative, and one respondent went so far as to say that the "concept of anyone who is physi-

cally or mentally impaired being involved with field archaeology, particularly excavation, is absurd" (Phillips and Gilchrist 2005: 86). Such discrimination exists in academic archaeology, as well. Theresa O'Mahony, a strong advocate for disabled archaeologists and founder of the Enabled Archaeology Foundation, recounted how when she was an undergraduate student of archaeology in London, she disclosed her disabilities in her applications to 38 field training schools, museums, and archives (O'Mahony 2018; see also Rocks-Macqueen 2019). She had previous field experience and high grades in her university field-training course, yet 36 (95%) of her applications were rejected.

What I "have going on" is a reference to the fact that I have a neuromuscular condition known as Cerebral Palsy (CP). My CP presents itself in fairly apparent ways: my gait is substantially affected, causing me to ambulate primarily with cuff-arm crutches, and my voice is noticeably affected, as well. The oft-confused response I get from inquirers comes from them noting these identifiers and immediately assuming incompetence in my profession.

The justifications of cost and time may be "sayable," but they are not grounded in reality, as we will show. Negative and ambivalent reactions to the very idea of disabled people as archaeologists seem to be rooted in two things: a failure to recognize the presence of disabled people already in the field and nondisabled archaeologists' ignorance of the realities of digging while impaired. We will not address the first point in depth here, except to say that "people with experiences of (dis/)ability *already do archaeology*" (Fraser 2007: viii, emphasis original). It is not always possible to identify a disabled person: while some disabilities are visible, others are nonvisible (Heath-Stout 2022; Disabled World 2019; Samuels 2013), including, for example, mental illness, chronic illness or pain, sleep disorders, asthma, celiac disease, and epilepsy. An IAA survey reported that as many as 14% of undergraduate archaeology students in the United Kingdom declared that they had a disability, with dyslexia disproportionately represented, and indeed the author of a popular and highly visible blog, "Doug's Archaeology," has dyslexia (Rocks-Macqueen 2014). Significantly, this statistic is likely too low because many disabilities "go undeclared, or even undiagnosed, especially unseen disabilities" (Phillips and Gilchrist 2005: 91).

In addition to those who enter the field with disabilities, it is generally true that every body is contingent and, as it were, only temporarily nondisabled. In a field like archaeology, workplace injury and the accumulated strain on bones and joints (Phillips and Creighton 2010: 16), drug and alcohol abuse (Colannino et al. 2020; Miller 2018; Rathbone 2013), illness and exposure (Flanagan 1995), and old age are all potentially disabling in either temporary or permanent ways. As Morag Cross (2007: 191) put it, "[S]ome archaeologists will become disabled; some disabled people are archaeologists. 'The disabled' are 'us,' not 'them over there.'"

> *A few months ago, I was having a chat over drinks with a friend in archaeology and our conversation eventually turned to the topic all archaeologist grad school conversations seem to reach: fieldwork. When we had satisfactorily discussed their field plans for the summer, they in turn asked me if I had any plans. After hearing mine, they, with the same shyness as those plane passengers, asked, "I hope you don't mind me asking, but how do you ... you know, do field work?"*

Having established that, yes, there are disabled archaeologists, nondisabled archaeologists who will become disabled, and disabled people who want to become archaeologists, we focus on our second point, that the ignorance of nondisabled archaeologists about the embodied realities of disability contributes significantly to the continued exclusion of disabled people from the field. One revelation of the DAP survey was that the "biggest single difficulty that was cited as being experienced by archaeologists with a dis-

ability was a lack of understanding and awareness of the condition" (Philips and Creighton 2010: 34). Nondisabled and neurotypical archaeologists' reticence to include visibly and openly disabled students seems rooted in their inability to imagine a variety of *how* questions: how can an archaeological excavation, with its deep trenches and concomitant hazards, be accessible to someone who uses a wheelchair? How can a blind student participate in a field school with a significant travel component? How can disabled people perform the tasks essential to archaeological fieldwork? As Mason's colleague asked, how can disabled people *do* archaeology?

Models of Disability: The Medical and the Social

Fear, confusion, or reticence to include disabled students on our projects is at least partially explained by a common, but flawed, understanding of where the problem with disability is located. Two prominent views of disability are the medical model and the social model. The medical model of disability, sometimes referred to as the individual model, is underpinned by the idea of personal tragedy. In this model, disability is located in a person's body, or simply *is* their body. The disabled person is therefore responsible for correcting the problem—*their* problem—and making their body conform to the established or accepted norm as far as possible (Cross 2007: 181). On the other hand, the social model of disability relocates the problem within disabling environments, barriers, and cultures (Oliver 1981; UPIAS 1976: 3). At its theoretical base, the social model distinguishes between impairment and disability in much the same way that early feminist scholarship divided sex from gender: one is biological, the other social and cultural (Barnes 2012; Oliver 1981; UPIAS 1976: 14). Impairment, then, is "a form of biological, cognitive, sensory or psychiatric difference that is defined within a medical context, and disability is the negative social reaction to those differences" (Sherry 2007: 11). In this way, impairment is only assigned meaning, positive or negative, in a social context (Hevey 1993: 19). Of these two, the social model of disability is preferred among disabled people, Disability Studies scholars, and activists. The social model is not, however, free from critique (e.g., Levitt 2017; Shakespeare 2013; Oliver 2013), most notably because of its lack of engagement with the lived realities of impairment (O'Mahony 2016: 13). As Fraser (2007: 13) notes in her research on the barriers for disabled people in archaeology, the "social model's division between mind/body and environment ultimately leaves interconnections between those experiences unacknowledged and unexplored." Moreover, many scholars now prefer the more intersectional methodologies and modes of analysis provided by critical disability theory (Bell 2006; Minich 2016; Schalk 2017). Still, the distinction here between the medical and social models remains relevant.

ACCOMMODATING PRACTICE

While the medical model has been supplanted by the social model in many contexts, it nevertheless persists in others, including in archaeology. When discussing the subject of disability and archaeology with colleagues, the *how* questions abound. In one conversation, a colleague described why they could not accommodate disabled students: excavators had to take a boat to an island, but the boat could not be pulled to shore, and everyone had to wade from the boat to the shore. "How," he asked, "would a disabled person be able to do this?" Questions like this ignore the heterogeneity of the disability community, as well as spectrums of experience. More importantly, though, they reflect that, when pushed, archaeologists expect that in order for disabled students to be successful in archaeology and not to hinder progress on an excavation, they must be able to fulfill all the demands of fieldwork with little or no accommodation (O'Mahony 2016: 43). The problem with this mindset is twofold. First, it fails to acknowledge the reality of fieldwork, which *already supports accommodation* on a regular basis. Second, it requires that disabled people be able to perform archaeology in the same ways as their nondisabled colleagues, that is, to hold a trowel or process information identically.

I wish I could say the hyper-able narrative of archaeology was weightless rhetoric and misrepresentation which did little to affect the opportunities of archaeologists with disabilities, but this has not held true in my experience. In fact, the very first time I attempted to do fieldwork, I was rejected on the basis of my disability. I was in my third year of college, and I had already spent the prior summer doing extensive lab work for my advisor's project in the Yucatán, Mexico. I decided I should apply to field schools that would provide me with the work in the field I was thus far lacking. I found a reputable project that suited my interests and sent in my application along with the requisite medical forms. I received an email back from the head of the project saying how my academic credentials were sufficient, but he had "concern" over the specifics of my medical forms and asked for my primary care physician's contact information. I was never contacted by the project again, and what happened after I only know because my primary care physician and advisor told me: the project head contacted my physician and expressed his worries about me being able to function in the field. After he had explained the specifics of what the field school would entail, my physician assured him that my ability level was, in fact, up to the task. The field director was still concerned about the "dangers" of me being on the project and so he contacted my advisor, who also tried to convince him of my capability. After this, neither my advisor nor my physician heard from the director again.

The truth of the matter is that even in the most rigorous fieldwork situations, archaeologists make accommodations of all kinds, and accommodations are generally not difficult to enact. As one respondent to the DAP survey suggested, "[I]f we think in terms of the fact that we all work

with disabilities, and that we adjust to some disabilities in other people without thinking, then
it is easier to adjust to all disabilities because
adjustment is part of life" (Phillips and Creighton
2010: 46). On every project that both authors of
this chapter have worked on, active and passive
accommodations were made for team members
on a daily basis, without question or reservation.
Each project hired local people to perform or
assist with certain tasks, including (depending
on the project) construction, big picking, heavy
lifting, sifting, and pottery washing, that is, more
physically demanding tasks, as well as those
tasks that are less appealing to American university students. What work was performed by
students and other staff was not shared equally.
Rather, tasks were assigned and performed according to individuals' demonstrated or pro-
fessed abilities or even preferences. When team
members could not push a full wheelbarrow or
carry heavy buckets of soil, we reduced the size
of loads and in some cases the weight was moved
by others. On a project in Greece, accommodations were also made according to workers' mobility, strength, and comfort within tight spaces.
One trench was accessible only by descending
and ascending three aluminum ladders, weaving
one's body through and around a maze of steel
shoring supports. Soil, rocks, and archaeological materials were removed from the bottom by
means of a pulley system, which required a certain amount of upper body mobility and strength
for those at the bottom who raised the buckets,
as well as for those at the top who transferred
the buckets from the pulley to the wheelbarrow.
The only team members assigned to this area
were those who were comfortable navigating
the ladder, descending to the depth of the trench,
working within the spatial constraints, and lifting
the full buckets.

> *Since that first field application, I have
> experienced slightly improved variations
> on this story. Some directors prefer I only
> work in the lab and not in the field, while
> others have suggested that I do fieldwork on
> a "trial" basis, with the caveat that I would*

> *exclusively work in the lab if the director
> deemed me incapable of fieldwork. Regard-
> less, all of these project directors considered
> their evaluations of my capability to be more
> trustworthy than my own. I understand the
> reasons these directors felt uncertain about
> my ability: for many, I am the first disabled
> archaeologist they have encountered, and
> their reticent attitude stems from a lack of
> education and fear of what they do not know.
> What they should have done, however, was
> trust me. I think it is safe to say that I am the
> one with the most hands-on experience being
> me. As such, I have the best grasp of what I
> am capable and not capable of. The phrase
> "nothing about us, without us" originated in
> disability activist circles to express the need
> to include those with disabilities in the legal
> and political conversation surrounding dis-
> ability (Charlton 1998). The same principle
> applies to inclusive archaeological fieldwork.
> If the conversation around the participation
> of an individual with disabilities in field-
> work does not include that individual, it
> should not happen. True inclusivity means
> involvement at every level of the process.*

Team members were also regularly accommo-
dated for less physical aspects of fieldwork. On
surveys, team members who had difficulty reading maps or keeping consistent and accurate
artifact counts were assigned to other necessary
tasks, like labeling or recording. Team members
assisted colleagues who could not easily or always
distinguish soil colors or who requested help
translating live measurements to the appropriate
scale for drawings. Trench edges and protruding
rebar were flagged with bright tape to increase
their visibility, and team members concerned with
balance worked away from edges. Shorter team
members and those whose dexterity was affected
by disability, injury, pain, or just cold weather
shoveled away the previous day's spoil piles while
others hung shade tarps high up by thin ropes.

Bodies are not identical, and this anecdotal
survey should make it abundantly clear that we
already create and support a wide range of ac-

commodations on our projects. We are confident that readers can reflect on their own experiences and construct a long list of similar adaptations and modifications on their own projects. We accommodate our nondisabled colleagues. We accommodate colleagues who were once young and hale but who experience changes in their mobility, dexterity, vision, or hearing after long years in the field. We make temporary accommodations, too, for team members who become ill or injured during the excavation season. Disability is a devalued form of difference, and we only consider accommodation an inconvenience or insurmountable obstacle when the person who needs it identifies as disabled. But by insisting that disabled people cannot participate in fieldwork if they require accommodations—that is, by insisting that they overcome their bodies—we hold them to a standard that no archaeologist achieves. And by refusing to acknowledge the fact of accommodation on our projects, we perpetuate a false narrative that serves primarily, if not exclusively, to exclude disabled people.

Framework of Access

The medical model of disability locates the "problem" within the bodies of disabled people and insists that these bodies be altered or adjusted so that they conform as closely as possible to the "norm" (Davis 2013). The implicit and explicit embrace of this model in archaeology is problematic (O'Mahony 2016: 23), not least because it is supported by a fiction that all people share equally in all work on our projects. Instead, we should shift our mode to something more akin to the social model of disability, recognizing that it is the field of archaeology itself, not disabled archaeologists, that should be the target of our modifications. To do this, we must embrace the accessibility that already characterizes archaeological excavation. Likewise, we must critically evaluate where and how archaeology can be modified to facilitate even greater inclusion (Phillips et al. 2007: 6).

After my first rejection, I was accepted into the next field school I applied to. However,

when I arrived at the project that summer, the director sized me up, saw the reality of my impairment, and began to express concern about me operating in the field. Despite my objections, he insisted that my time in the field had to be shortened and I would be bussed back early each day. I was incredibly frustrated. Not only would this imposition make me a less efficient contributor than my colleagues, implicitly affirming to them that people with disabilities contribute less, but it would also force someone else to contribute less because they had to drive me back early. I began to fear that my experience in the field would always be dictated by others' evaluation of my ability.

I am glad to say that this story does not end there. I was assigned to the site's necropolis, which was overseen not by the director, but by another archaeologist. This archaeologist pulled me aside and assured me that if I wanted to work the full time, I could do so and that he would talk to the director about it. He asked me which burial I thought would be the most accessible and assigned me to the one I selected. The burial was still difficult for me to reach, as I had to use my crutches and simultaneously haul my excavation equipment. Trowels and dental picks may not seem like much of a burden, but when one is trying to walk with crutches without falling into other burials, the little things become quite troublesome. Since we excavated each burial in teams, my partners carried my equipment each day while I made my way to our burial. Inside the burial, my partners and I lined the sides with foam mats (which many on the project already used for knee protection), which allowed me to lay down and excavate. This was how I excavated for the field season. The director occasionally tried to tell me to leave early, but the overseeing archaeologist and my team members advocated for my continued inclusion in the fieldwork. It was indeed a team effort, but then again, when is an excavation not one?

We need to accept the reality of our workflow and admit that "the actual process of doing archaeology is flexible and lends itself to including people with disabilities" and that "you can accommodate almost anyone on an archaeological project" (Phillips and Creighton 2010: 46). This is a part of the ethical practice of archaeology. As a DAP respondent articulated, "you pick the most appropriate person for a particular job, whether it's drawing, excavation, or whatever. It's all part of the job of running a site, getting the right people to do a particular job" (Philips and Creighton 2010: 15). A team is successful when we acknowledge and support everyone's strengths and "[J]ust as every excavation member makes a valuable contribution to a dig, disabled archaeologists/people are no different" (O'Mahony 2015: 2).

Nondisabled archaeologists assume that making field projects accessible will be costly, in terms of time and money. Even in cases where it is, we support our same argument for inclusion, believing as we do that the value of inclusion cannot be reduced to its costs. As it is, however, the process of accommodation is often relatively straightforward. A number of examples were listed above and included things like flagging hazards with bright tape for increased visibility, shifting duties among team members, and assisting team members with certain tasks. The DAP survey revealed that the "most successful 'adjustment' cited by respondents was achieved simply by employers being flexible" (Phillips and Creighton 2010: 42). Significantly, "the only examples of using special equipment related to office work and recording, rather than anything specifically for the physical side of archaeology" (Phillips and Creighton 2010: 42). In Mason's case, he was able to work effectively alongside his colleagues by using mats that others on the project were similarly using to accommodate their own bodies in different ways. A DAP survey respondent with restricted mobility recounted that their "Director would come to me and say, 'What are you doing it that way for? I'm intrigued.' So I would explain why. He would say as long as I was doing it right, it was fine" (Phillips and Creighton 2010: 42).

At the core of accessibility in archaeology are two related points. First, there should be an emphasis on ability. Second, accessibility—including any necessary adjustments and accommodations—must take the form of a dialogue *with the disabled person*. The reality is, "[D]isabled students have successfully participated in archaeological fieldwork training when there has been an understanding and knowledge of their potential abilities and possible limitations" (Phillips et al. 2007: 6). This "understanding and knowledge" must be developed with everyone regardless of the "type" of their disability (Phillips and Creighton 2010: 17). What is more, this dialogue must be ongoing, as an "individual's abilities are not static, they change and develop with experience...Any method of self-evaluation must reflect this dynamic aspect and provide a means by which changes and developments can be tracked" (Phillips et al. 2007: 6). Additionally, nondisabled archaeologists must be flexible enough to recognize that tasks can be performed in different ways and still be done correctly. Familiarity and tradition are not acceptable reasons for persisting in modes or methods that exclude people who want to participate, including disabled people, when alternatives are readily available. Why, after all, should foam pads be restricted to providing relief only to knees?

I recognize that my story here is not the perfect blueprint for complete inclusion of individuals with any disability on any project. The burial I was excavating did not represent the upper limit of physical activity in archaeology and I have just one example of one type of impairment. Still, the basics of what I have recounted here—the need for inclusion at every level and the interconnectivity of accessibility and teamwork—can, I think, serve as good starting points for just about any conversation surrounding inclusive field work.

Disability is not the problem and successful inclusion can be achieved by committing to (Phillips et al. 2007: 19):

- An attitude of acceptance and understanding
- Communication
- Flexibility
- Common sense
- Regular reviews or appraisals of the situation and of any adjustments

The social model of disability, which properly locates the problem outside of the body of the individual, can provide a productive framework for our commitments, with the caveat that the body is not irrelevant. It is likely impossible "to provide environments or develop activities where everybody can do everything, and this will certainly be the case with some tasks undertaken in archaeology. People, both disabled and nondisabled, will have different levels of ability to undertake tasks" (Phillips et al. 2007: 6). In some cases, individuals, disabled and nondisabled alike, may be able to perform some tasks but unable to perform others, regardless of accommodation. A respondent to the DAP cautioned that it is "no good pretending that you can do everything. You have to look at your capabilities and practical abilities and work with what you've got" (Phillips and Creighton 2010: 11). As above, however, it is critical that the disabled person be empowered to determine which tasks they can and cannot perform and that they are "enabled through being totally involved with all choices for their participation" (O'Mahony 2015: 2). This is, above all, because "[N]o one can discover their own potential ability and limitations better than the individual concerned" (Phillips et al. 2007: 6).

Blueprint for Inclusion?

Nondisabled archaeologists may be open to the idea of accommodating disabled students but confused or uncertain about the practicalities. What does this kind of inclusion look like? Can I ask a student about their disability? There is no single blueprint. Every situation will be different, as no two projects or individuals are the same. Even two people with the same diagnosis will have different experiences of their disability. As we have emphasized throughout, the key is com-

munication that is both open and ongoing and, most importantly, the conversation must include and be led by the disabled person. Mason's is not the only story of field school directors calling their nondisabled peers and physicians to ask about the capabilities of a disabled student while neglecting to ask the disabled person themselves. In many cases, the disabled person will require no more accommodation than their nondisabled peers. In all cases, they will have a better understanding of their bodies—including their abilities and limitations—than literally anyone else.

The first and perhaps biggest obstacle for a disabled person considering whether to apply to work on a project is predicting if and what additional accommodations may be required. As is the case for anyone participating in a field school for the first time or working on a new project, there is a gap between expectation and reality. Fortunately, however, there are ways that everyone, including disabled people, can anticipate where they may need accommodation. In advertisements and orientations for the project, the director and other experienced team members can present the realities of fieldwork on the site. This includes simple things like detailing typical daily schedules with breaks, weather, bathroom access, sleeping arrangements, and meal components. It should also include other details, such as what the terrain is like and whether excavators hike or drive to the site, how students typically spend their leisure time, what kinds of tools are used on site (e.g., trowels, hand picks, big picks, hand brooms, shovels), qualities of the earth and environs (e.g., clayey vs. sandy, wet vs. dry), potential outdoor allergens, proximity of pharmacies and hospitals, and so on. These details will benefit all students evaluating their potential participation on a project, disabled and nondisabled alike. This approach should not be aimed at discouraging disabled people, but at providing information that allows people to make useful comparisons between what they already know from their daily lives and what life will be like on the project. If necessary, schedule individual appointments with students so that they can ask questions and brainstorm what kinds of additional materials the project or student can pack to facilitate their participation. It is imperative that students know that disability and the need for accommodation are not, in and of themselves, disqualifying.

Fortunately, there is also a tool available to help all students anticipate their needs on field projects. In the last phase of the IAA, researchers developed the Archaeological Skills Self-Evaluation Tool kit (ASSET) (Phillips et al. 2007: 12). This tool kit was designed to assist students with little or no experience with archaeological fieldwork. By taking a questionnaire, field school neophytes can forecast which typical tasks they would be able to complete without accommodation and which they may need adjustments or accommodations for by making analogies between everyday tasks and tasks performed on excavations. The tool kit was intended to enable students, not limit them, by allowing them to forecast their experience on an archaeological project while warning that, as always, the reality for many would be different than the projection. The IAA then developed guidelines—not set rules—for making archaeological fieldwork inclusive (Phillips et al. 2007: 16–37). Their packet includes a discussion of "reasonable adjustments," as well as information about and general guidelines for including students with several specific disabilities, such as dyslexia and other nonvisible disabilities, visual and hearing impairments, mobility impairments, mental health issues, and Autism. Examples of both minor and major adjustments help ground the guidelines in practical ways and a series of case studies online (The IAA Project Team 2007) concretize their recommendations further. These guidelines and case studies can be used to help in brainstorming the kinds of accommodations and adjustments that might be useful, and it will be up to the disabled person to determine whether such adjustments would, in fact, benefit them.

The DAP, which succeeded the IAA, expanded on these first guidelines and published a pamphlet on "Employing People with Disabilities: Good Practice Guidance for Archaeologists" (Phillips and Creighton 2010). This pamphlet discusses the British legal perspective and provides not just general guidance, but also more targeted sug-

gestions for employing people with specific disabilities. Examples of specific conditions and disabilities, the challenges that could arise therefrom, and potential adjustments (Phillips and Creighton 2010: 13), as well as action points and sources for more information related to specific disabilities help readers think through the realities of accommodation, while the inclusion of personal narratives grounds the necessity of inclusion in the lives of practicing archaeologists. The guidelines provided by the DAP emphasize that disability "is not just about theoretical frameworks, nor legislative definitions, it is fundamentally about people and sets of 'attitudes': how people with disabilities see themselves, and how others see them" (Phillips and Creighton 2010: 9).

The Enabled Archaeology Foundation also created a guide for increasing inclusivity in both the actual practice of fieldwork and in the advertisement of jobs or fieldwork vacancies, surveying, and recordkeeping (O'Mahony 2015). This guide provides examples of accommodations that can assist some disabled people, from plans for a wheelchair-accessible trench and tips for using cushions as props, to links for easy-grip trowels with compatible support cuffs. With regard to specific tools and practices, Fraser (2007) discusses the specific ways that embracing Universal Design (UD) and Inclusive Design (ID) frameworks can remove barriers to inclusion in archaeology while simultaneously fulfilling the desired outcomes of fieldwork.

These kinds of guides and pamphlets exist because, as noted above, there are already disabled people doing archaeology. It is important to remember, however, that guidelines are not rules. Not everyone will benefit from the same adjustments or accommodations. Disabled people must be directly involved in determining what will and will not work for them. As one DAP respondent described, "[P]eople kept trying to persuade me to use a prosthetic arm, but I rejected it. I haven't worn one, apart from driving...It was almost like a thing to protect me from heavy work" (Phillips and Creighton 2010: 44). It is inappropriate for anyone to make decisions for disabled people, from whether they participate in the first place to what accommodations or adjustments they need. Rather, the role of the director or other team members is to be open and flexible and, based on their experience in the field, to suggest potential adjustments. What is necessary, from the beginning, is for nondisabled archaeologists to embrace a different idea of what archaeology looks like and, more importantly, who is an archaeologist.

Conclusion

Our call for inclusion is not about charity. Nor is it about the very real legal requirement to make reasonable accommodations for disabled people. Rather, it is about our responsibility to make archaeology, as a whole, available to disabled people *as it is* for nondisabled people. We have an affirmative responsibility to act ethically by supporting people who are "skilled and qualified and capable of doing a job in archaeology, but for whom adjustments may have to be made in the way that job is done" (Phillips and Creighton 2010: 3). This includes not just disabled students who apply to work on our projects, but also archaeologists who become disabled by injury, illness, or age. This is about providing disabled people with the same considerations that we give to nondisabled people on our projects, including the freedom to engage and contribute to the field in their own ways. The benefits of inclusion rebound not just to the disabled person, but also to the discipline as a whole, as we all learn new methods, processes, and practices.

A few years ago, I had the great fortune to go to Pompeii for the first time. I, of course, knew of the layout of the city and had seen the cobblestone laden streets in textbooks, but to walk on the stones myself was quite the stunning experience. One might think that I am referring to the awe enthusiasts of the ancient world often feel standing amidst its material remains, and while I certainly did feel such awe, the "stunning" I am referring to is much more physical than some nebulous gut feeling about the past. Indeed, as I took my very first step onto the ancient

street, I found myself physically startled as the rubber tip of my crutch slid off the large cobblestone and into a crevasse, knocking my footing out of balance and threatening to send me to the ground. What followed was a clumsy ballet of me desperately trying to walk the streets of Pompeii without falling, each cobblestone seeming like some peak which I, the comically inexperienced climber, had to summit to proceed down the road.

At long last and with minimal falls, I reached the Forum. As I stood there, tired but too excited and proud to turn back, I heard various tour guides proclaiming how "strikingly modern" so many of the ancient amenities seemed to be. Their larger message was that, in ruins which often seem alien to modern viewers, much familiarity can be found if one knows where to look. This is a message that academics often champion as well, as is evidenced by the common quip used in anthropological circles of "making the strange familiar and the familiar strange." In some sense, it is the duty of scholars of the past to make the strange past familiar by shedding light on those life experiences that can relate to present circumstances. As I, a person with a physical disability, stood exhausted in the ruins of Pompeii, I was struck with the thought that this was the type of physical space that a person with mobility impairments would have navigated constantly. For such a person, the careful precision I needed to navigate the cobblestones for only brief hours might very well have been the daily mindset required to simply walk down the street in their neighborhood. Suddenly and for the first time, the strangeness of the distant past seemed as though it could be very familiar to me personally.

I share this final story not as a plea for pity, but rather as an example which is symptomatic of the ableist notions of exclusion we have discussed above. My embodied experience in Pompeii gave me a newfound realization of the unique contribution my disabled perspective could bring to the study of the ancient past, and yet, that realization should not have been so novel. The novelty came from the fact that I had been continually told that I cannot contribute anything to archaeology. Thus, my experience was so transformative precisely because it was a direct contradiction to the ableist narrative which I had internalized. While such an overt message of discrimination may not be the intentions of those who exclude disabled archaeologists from their projects, make no mistake, this is the message that is communicated to us.

REFERENCES

Aitchison, K., and Rocks-Macqueen, D.
2013   *Archaeology Labor Market Intelligence: Profiling the Profession 2012–13*. Sheffield, UK: Landward Research.

Association Research, Inc.
2020   SAA 2020 Member Needs Assessment. https://ecommerce.saa.org/saa/SAAMember/Members_Only/2020_Needs_Assessment.aspx

Barnes, C.
2012   Understanding the Social Model of Disability: Past, Present and Future. Pp. 12–29 in *Routledge Handbook of Disability Studies*, ed. N. Watson, A. Roulstone, and C. Thomas. New York: Routledge.

Battle-Baptiste, W.
2016   *Black Feminist Archaeology*. New York: Routledge.

Bell, C.
2006   Introducing White Disability Studies: A Modest Proposal. Pp. 275–82 in *The Disability Studies Reader*, 2nd ed., ed. L. J. Davis. New York: Routledge.

Brosman, E.
2019   You call this archaeology?! Archaeologists in the Netherlands according to the Dutch public. M.A. Thesis. University of Leiden.

Cartrette, D. P., and Melroe-Lehrman, B. M.
2012   Describing Changes in Undergraduate Students' Preconceptions of Research Activities. *Research in Science Education* 42: 1073–1100.

Charlton, J. I.
1998   *Nothing About Us Without Us: Disability Oppression and Empowerment*. Berkeley, CA: University of California.

Cobb, H., and Croucher, K.
2016   Personal, Political, Pedagogic: Challenging the Binary Bind in Archaeological Teaching, Learning and Fieldwork. *Journal of Archaeological Method and Theory* 23: 949–69.

Colaninno, C. E.; Lambert, S. P.; Beahm, E. L.; and Drexler, C. G.
2020   Creating and Supporting a Harassment- and Assault-Free Field School. *Advances in Archaeological Practices* 8.2: 111–22.

Couser, G. T.
2009   *Signifying Bodies: Disability in Contemporary Life Writing*. Ann Arbor, MI: University of Michigan.

Cross, M.
2007   Accessing the Inaccessible: Disability and Archaeology. Pp. 179–94 in *The Archaeology of Identities: A Reader*, ed. T. Insoll. New York: Routledge.

Davis, L. J.
2013   Introduction: Disability, Normality, and Power. Pp. 1–16 in *The Disability Studies Reader*, 4th edition, ed. L. J. Davis. New York: Routledge.

Disabled World
2019   Invisible Disabilities: List and General Information. *Disabled World*. November 8. https://www.disabled-world.com/disability/types/invisible/

Dissard, L.; Rosenzweig, M.; and Matney, T.
2011 Beyond Ethics: Considerations in Problematizing Community Involvement and Outreach in Archaeological Practice. *Archaeological Review from Cambridge* 26.2: 59–70.

Ferri, B. A.
2011 Disability Life Writing and the Politics of Knowing. *Teachers College Record* 113: 2267–82.

Flanagan, J.
1995 What You Don't Know *Can* Hurt You. *Field Archaeology.* 8.2: 10–13.

Foldvary, F. E.
2011 Positive Rights. In *Encyclopedia of Global Justice*, ed. D. K. Chatterjee. Dordrecht: Springer. https://doi.org/10.1007/978-1-4020 -9160-5_359

Fraser, M. A.
2007 Dis/Abling Exclusion, En/Abling Access: Identifying and Removing Barriers in Archaeological Practice for Persons with (Dis/)Abilities. PhD Dissertation. American University.

Garland-Thomson, R.
2007 Shape Structures Story: Fresh and Feisty Stories about Disability. *Narrative* 15.1: 113–23.

Gero, J. M.
1994 Excavation Bias and the Woman at Home Ideology. Pp. 37–42 in *Equity Issues for Women in Archaeology*, ed. M. C. Nelson, S. M. Nelson, and A. Wylie. Archaeological Papers of the American Anthropological Association 5. Washington, DC: American Anthropological Association.

Hall, T.; Healey, M.; and Harrison, M.
2002 Fieldwork and Disabled Students: Discourses of Exclusion and Inclusion. *Transactions of the Institute of British Geographers* 27.2: 213–31.

Heath-Stout, L.
2022 The Invisibly Disabled Archaeologist. *International Journal of Historical Archaeology.* https://doi.org/10.1007/s10761-022-00653- 8

Hevey, D.
1993 The Tragedy Principle: Strategies for Change in the Cultural Representation of Disabled People. Pp. 116–21 in *Disabling Barriers, Enabling Environments*, ed. J. Swain. London: Open University.

Holtorf, C.
2007 *Archaeology is a Brand! The Meaning of Archaeology in Contemporary Popular Culture.* Walnut Creek, CA: Left Coast.

Johnson, M.
2014 *Lives in Ruins: Archeologists and the Seductive Lure of Human Rubble.* New York: Harper Perennial.

Levitt, J. M.
2017 Exploring how the social model of disability can be re-invigorated: In response to Mike Oliver. *Disability & Society* 32.4: 589–94.

Miller, A.
2018 In some disciplines, heavy drinking is part of the culture. That can be a problem. *Science* (Dec. 6). https://www.science.org/ content/article/some-disciplines-heavy- drinking-part-culture-can-be-problem

Minich, J. A.
2016 Enabling Whom? Critical Disability Studies Now. *Lateral* 5.1. https://doi.org/10.25158/ L5.1.9

Moser, S.
2007 On Disciplinary Culture: Archaeology as Fieldwork and Its Gendered Associations. *Journal of Archaeological Method and Theory.* 14.3: 235–63.

Oliver, M.
1981 A New Model on the Social Work Role in Relation to Disability. In *The Handicapped*

Person: a New Perspective for Social Workers? London: RADAR. https://disability-studies.leeds.ac.uk/wp-content/uploads/sites/40/library/Campling-handicppaed.pdf

2013 The Social model of disability: Thirty years on. *Disability & Society* 28: 1024–26.

O'Mahony, T.
2015 *Enabled Archaeology Guide 41.* Pp. 1–14 in British Archaeology Jobs and Resources. Retrieved 15 May 2020 from World Wide Web: http://www.bajr.org/BAJRGuides/41_Enabled_Archaeology/41EnabledArchaeology.pdf

2016 Empowering Archaeology: What Model of Disability Do People with Dyslexia in University Archaeology Courses Experience? M.A. Thesis. University College London.

2018 Reflections in UK Archaeology – A personal journey in academic life. *Journal of Community Archaeology & Heritage* 5.3: 216–18.

Phillips, T., and Creighton, J.
2010 *DAP: Disability and the Archaeological Profession. Employing People with Disabilities: Good Practice Guidance for Archaeologists.* Institute for Archaeologists Professional Practice Paper 9. Reading: Institute for Archaeologists.

Phillips, T., and Gilchrist, R.
2005 *Inclusive, Accessible, Archaeology (HEFCE FDTL5) Phase 1. Disability and Archaeological Fieldwork: Summary of a report based on a questionnaire survey of Archaeology Subject Providers, Disability Support Services in HEIs and Archaeological Employers.* https://archaeologydataservice.ac.uk/archives/view/iaa_hefce_2006/downloads.cfm

Phillips, T; Gilchrist, R.; Hewitt, I.; Le Scouiller, S.; Booy, D.; and Cook, G.
2007 *Guides for Teaching and Learning in Archaeology. Number 5. Inclusive, Accessible, Archaeology: Good practice guidelines for including disabled students and self-evaluation in archaeological fieldwork training.* London: Higher Education Funding Council for England.

Rathbone, S.
2013 The four and a half inch pointing trowel… and the damage done. Robert M Chapple, *Archaeologist* (blog), Blogspot. (Sept. 5), http://rmchapple.blogspot.com/2013/09/the-four-and-half-inch-pointing-trowel.html

Rocks-Macqueen, D.
2014 My Disabilities, My Archaeology. *Doug's Archaeology: Investigating the Profession and Research* (blog). Blogspot. (August 13). https://dougsarchaeology.wordpress.com/2014/08/13/my-disabilities-my-archaeology/

2019 RIP Theresa O'Mahony. *Doug's Archaeology: Investigating the Profession and Research* (blog). Blogspot. (September 24). https://dougsarchaeology.wordpress.com/2019/09/24/rip-theresa-omahony/

Samuels, E.
2013 My Body, My Closet: Invisible Disability and the Limits of Coming Out. Pp. 316–32 in *The Disability Studies Reader*, 4th edition, ed. L. J. Davis. New York: Routledge.

Schalk, S.
2017 Critical Disability Studies as Methodology. *Lateral* 6.1. https://doi.org/10.25158/L6.1.13

Shakespeare, T.
2013 The Social Model of Disability. Pp. 214–21 in *The Disability Studies Reader*, 4th ed., ed. L. J. Davis. New York: Routledge.

Sheppard, P. R., and Huckleberry, G.
2010 Quantitative assessment of a field-based course on integrative geology, ecology and cultural history. *International Research in Geographical and Environmental Education* 19.4: 295–313.

Sherry, M.
2005 Reading Me/Me Reading Disability. *Prose Studies* 27.1–2: 163–75.

2007   (Post)colonising Disability. *Intersecting Gender and Disability Perspectives in Rethinking Postcolonial Identities. Wagadu* 4: 10–22.

The IAA Project Team

2007   Case studies. *Inclusive, Accessible, Archaeology project.* May 9. https://archaeology dataservice.ac.uk/archives/view/iaa_hefce _2006/downloads.cfm?phase=5

Titchkosky, T.

2003   Governing Embodiment: Technologies of Constituting Citizens with Disabilities. *The Canadian Journal of Sociology/Cahiers canadiens de sociologie* 28.4: 517–42.

2011   *The Question of Access: Disability, Space, Meaning.* Toronto: University of Toronto.

UPIAS

1976   *Fundamental Principles of Disability.* London: Union of the Physically Impaired Against Segregation.

White, W., and Draycott, C.

2020   Why the Whiteness of Archaeology Is a Problem." *Sapiens* (July 7). https://www.sapiens. org/archaeology/archaeology-diversity/

Woodall, J. N., and Perricone, P. J.

1981   The Archaeologist As Cowboy: The Consequence of Professional Stereotype. *Journal of Field Archaeology* 8: 506–9.

II. Ethical Practices Across the Discipline

Chapter 5

Teaching an Antiracist Archaeology of the Ancient Mediterranean

Nadhira Hill and Maggie Beeler

ABSTRACT

This chapter discusses issues of equity and inclusion in archaeological instruction and offers some guidance for teaching an antiracist archaeology of the ancient Mediterranean. Archaeologists working in the ancient Mediterranean and adjacent regions have a professional duty to undertake antiracist work in our field because of our discipline's entrenched colonial methodologies and theoretical orientation. Teaching an antiracist archaeology of the ancient Mediterranean is an ethical imperative today because of the prominent role the field continues to play in the maintenance of supremacist narratives of "western civilization" and "classical" antiquity. We argue that integrating explicitly antiracist pedagogies (ARP) and insights from critical race theory (CRT) is one way for instructors to combat these harmful historical narratives and to create more inclusive learning environments that promote equity in the academy as a matter of professional ethics.

INTRODUCTION

In these times of global protest against intensifying anti-Black racism, American universities struggle to respond effectively to calls from the Black Lives Matter (BLM) movement to promote racial justice and equity in higher education. Diversity initiatives in higher education generally include statements of solidarity, diversity training sessions, and student support services, all of which have failed to recruit and promote students and faculty of color in academia (Ash et al. 2020). This failure is nowhere more clearly seen than in the persistently low affiliation of Black archaeologists with professional organizations (Franklin 1997; Zender 1997). The approaches to diversity and inclusion in archaeology lack awareness of—and serious reflection on—how systems of oppression affect whether individuals from historically excluded backgrounds choose to join or remain in the field (Agbe-Davies 2002: 27). As archaeologist Kathleen Sterling observes, "[d]iversity is seen as a social good but not necessarily a disciplinary good" (Sterling 2015: 98–99).

The paucity of Black archaeologists is a longstanding question for historical archaeologists working in North America, who have developed antiracist archaeologies that are instructive for practitioners in all periods (Franklin 1997; Orser 2004; Sterling 2015; Blakey 2020). For those working in the ancient Mediterranean and Near East, however, until recently antiracism was perhaps less familiar than other critical approaches such as postcolonialism (Dietler 2015; Porter 2010; Hamilakis 2012). Archaeologists focusing on prehistory are specifically called out as "not invested in creating change in the discipline—because it is not seen as relevant to their work" (SBA et al. 2020: 21) in the "'Archaeology in the Time of Black Lives Matter' Resources List" created by the Society for Black Archaeologists (SBA). But directly addressing race is both possible and necessary for all archaeologists, regardless of their area of expertise (Sterling 2015).

Race is remarkably undertheorized in so-called Old World archaeology (the term itself a product of archaeology's colonial history), considering its centrality in early archaeological theory. V. Gordon Childe, for instance, explicitly equated race with ancient people in his influential definition of archaeological culture, which is often quoted but rarely in full because it associates race with skeletal remains (Childe 1929: v–vi). Like many of his 19th- and early 20th-century contemporaries, Childe promoted scientific racism to assign racial identities to the human remains they excavated using craniometry (Gould 2006; Siapkas 2016; Challis 2013). Archaeology was thus in direct dialogue with race pseudoscience and contributed to the creation and maintenance of racial hierarchy and notions of racial determinism in constructing historical narratives in racialized terms. Ethnicity replaced race in archaeological discourse in the mid-20th century, when race was reconceptualized beyond biology as a social construct in response to the atrocities of World War II, notably in UNESCO's Statement on Race in 1951 (Jones 1997: 40–55). Biological anthropologists abandoned race as a tool for analyzing human variation, focusing more narrowly on population genetics and the evolution of specific traits within geographically-situated communities, such as skin color as an adaptive trait and the influence of equatorial locations and greater UV exposure (Relethford 2017: 161–62). Ethnicity provided more neutral ground for the analysis of past peoples, since shared group ancestry and cultural practices are identifiable in the archaeological record through the spatial and temporal distribution of shared material culture. Although both race and ethnicity are today understood to be social constructs, the idea of race as biological determinism and ethnicity as self-determined cultural groups still persists in part because scientists legitimized it, including archaeologists (Sussman 2014). Scholars focused nearly exclusively on ethnicity and avoided the subject of race altogether, rather than working to reconcile archaeology's racist past through critical investigations of how modern racial ideologies have shaped archaeological theory and practice. In avoiding the issue of race in favor of ethnicity to discuss ancient social difference, however, archaeologists advance uncritically supremacist narratives of "western civilization" and "classical" Greece and Rome. Like the infantilizing notion of Mesopotamia as the "cradle of civilization," this framing privileges European over global histories and reflects deeply entrenched colonial interpretive paradigms (see Hitchcock, this volume). How we teach archaeology—especially what we don't teach when we avoid the subject of race—runs the risk of alienating a broad cross-section of our diverse students.

Archaeologists bear an ethical responsibility to their students, as outlined in the codes of professional ethics by major archaeological institutes in North America, including the American Society of Overseas Research (ASOR)'s *Policy on Professional Conduct* (ASOR 2019), the Archaeological Institute of America (AIA)'s *Code of Ethics* and *Code of Professional Conduct* (AIA 2016), and the Society for American Archaeology (SAA)'s *Principles of Archaeological Ethics* (SAA 2018). Antiracist teaching, however, is not included in these policies, all of which describe the ethical responsibilities of teaching in terms of public education and stewardship while ethical duties to students are discussed more in terms of non-discrimination. The onus is nevertheless on individual instructors to integrate antiracism into our teaching. This conscious and critical inclusion contributes to creating more inclusive learning environments and potentially provides opportunities to recruit more diverse undergraduate and graduate students into our faculty ranks. This is especially true for white instructors, although some report facing challenges when trying to integrate antiracist pedagogy (ARP) into their teaching, from personal barriers such as struggling with their own white privilege to perceived professional barriers, to tenure and promotion (Phillips et al. 2019). Yet when white instructors fail to lead the conversation on race in the classroom, they place the burden on students identifying as Black, Indigenous, or people of color (BIPOC) to address the systems that oppress them. White instructors in particular, then, must educate themselves on ARP as a matter of professional ethics.

In the space between higher education's diversity initiatives and the institutional reforms needed to address systemic racism, archaeologists face increasingly urgent calls to diversify and decolonize our classrooms (Flewellen et al. 2021; Franklin et al. 2020). How can archaeologists working in the ancient Mediterranean and adjacent areas promote racial justice and equity in our field? The appetite for this conversation and training is reflected in the proliferation of well-attended antiracist pedagogy workshops, panels, and webinars for archaeologists. The authors of this chapter were both panelists for the AIA's "Critical Conversations on Race, Teaching, and Antiquity" webinar series (AIA 2020), where we discussed our respective experiences with teaching race and archaeology. This chapter marks a collaborative effort to share our collective insights on teaching an antiracist archaeology of the ancient Mediterranean, drawing attention to how our different positionalities informed our engagements: Nadhira as a Black female graduate student and instructor and Maggie as a white female instructor. Our aim is to provide practical recommendations for integrating critical race theory (CRT) and antiracist pedagogy (ARP) into everyday teaching practice to promote more inclusive learning environments. The first half of

the chapter provides a necessarily brief overview of race and archaeology to establish discussion of CRT and ARP as an ethical issue, followed by reflections on our respective teaching and learning experiences and some successful strategies and guidelines for teaching an antiracist archaeology of the ancient Mediterranean.

We argue that CRT and ARP are necessary for archaeological instruction because teaching the archaeology of the ancient Mediterranean without these frameworks runs the risk of privileging perspectives of white individuals and groups. Omitting the personal narratives of historically excluded groups also leads to painting the ancient world in a rosier light than existed and flattening out the diversity of ancient populations. These critical frameworks therefore require us, and by extension our students, to confront race and racism, to interrogate how these concepts have shaped and continue to shape archaeological interpretation, and to provide our students with the necessary tools to act on our racialized world.

RACE AND ARCHAEOLOGY

The history of race as a concept and archaeology as a discipline are inextricably linked and their intersection is a subject that archaeologists have avoided for too long. We argue that in failing to counter historical narratives of "western civilization" that press archaeological data into the service of (white) nationalist ideology, archaeologists' silence on the topic of race serves to reinforce institutionalized white supremacy. A brief discussion of archaeology's role in the creation of racial hierarchy provides context for the limitations of a narrow focus on ethnicity in investigations of past personhood.

Today's racial categories were formulated and ranked by early race pseudoscientists, who sought to justify the existing social order of European colonialism and trans-Atlantic slavery using now debunked methodologies such as craniometry (Challis 2013). Craniometry, the study of skull shape and size, was used by early race scientists to legitimize Enlightenment ideas of European superiority. The use of human remains—and especially skullsacquired illicitly for the purposes of "scientific inquiry" has a long history (see Smiles 2021 for a summary of the uses of human remains from Indigenous communities). A notable example of the unethical acquisition of human remains that has recently been in the spotlight is the collection of physician and naturalist Samuel G. Morton (Crimmins 2021). His collection of skulls, including those belonging to Native Americans, amounted to more than one thousand at the time of his death in 1851 and formed the basis of his own research which used craniometry to promote white supremacist ideals. The ideals of European physical and cultural superiority which originated in the Enlightenment were embodied in the Greek statue of the Apollo Belvedere, which Johann Joachim Winckelmann (the German art historian and so-called "father of art history") elevated to the status of the "classical ideal" (Bindman 2002). The Apollo Belvedere was the standard by which human variety was judged by 18th-century Dutch anatomist Petrus Camper, who ranked human skulls in a hierarchy surmounted by the ancient marble statue of a Greek god with a primate skull at the bottom, comparing European skulls to the idealized statue and African skulls to the primate (Evans 2012: 23–25). Craniometry presented a veneer of scientific objectivity because it generated quantified data that were used to argue that Europeans were not only more beautiful but also more intelligent and therefore racially and culturally superior.

Archaeological cultures have been defined in racial or ethnic terms since the culture-historical archaeology of the late 19th- and early 20th century (Trigger 2006: 232–48; Jones 1997: 15–25), even if the equation of artifacts with ethnic groups remains an "often unstated working assumption" in archaeological practice (Bahrani 2006: 53). In addition to the methodological limitations of equating pots with people, ethical concerns attend the uncritical identification of ethnic groups from archaeological assemblages. The ultimate cautionary tale is Gustaf Kossina's work on the archaeology of German prehistory, which the Nazi regime invoked to construct a nationalist narrative of German superiority used

to scientifically justify the genocide of its Jewish population (Arnold 2002). We might also look to the treatment of Great Zimbabwe, a medieval fortress discovered in the early 16th century by Portuguese settlers, and whose interpretation has since been "characterised by severe racism" (Duesterberg 2015: 144). Upon encountering Great Zimbabwe, 19th-century German explorer Karl Mauch cast doubt on the idea that the fortress could have been built by indigenous Africans, since, to him, it closely resembled the Queen of Sheba's palace in Jerusalem. From this comparison, Mauch assumed that "only a 'civilised nation must...have lived there'" (Koutonin 2016). Mauch's racist assumptions were shared by other European writers of the time, who alternatively suggested that "it was built by Portuguese travellers, Arabs, Chinese or Persians" based on the discovery of artifacts which betrayed contact with those populations (Koutonin 2016). In search of evidence that confirmed these ideas, the site was partially destroyed in investigations led by James Bent, funded by Cecil Rhodes in 1890, and especially by British journalist and curator of Great Zimbabwe Richard Hall in 1902. The evidence which suggested a Black origin for Great Zimbabwe was often ignored in order to justify the colonization of the region.

More subtle racist metanarratives are involved in interpretations that attribute the accomplishments of ancient peoples not to white individuals, but to extraterrestrial beings. These approaches are unethical because they perpetuate racist ideas about the capabilities of ancient peoples which originated in the 18th and 19th centuries. Most prevalent are conspiracy theories surrounding the achievements of African civilizations—such as claims that aliens built the pyramids at Giza popularized by History Channel programming— but there seems to be no continent that has remained untouched by these racist ideas. The assumed intellectual and cultural inferiority of Indigenous peoples prompted early colonial settlers who encountered the great Moundbuilders' monuments in North America to attribute their construction to a variety of groups from outside the continent, since they argued that Native

Americans were incapable of such architectural feats (Orser 2004: 40–49; Trigger 2006: 181–89). Similarly, misinformation gleaned from the writings of European colonizers who visited Easter Island in the 18th and 19th centuries, including that there were no trees on the island, that there was not enough food to support a large enough workforce to produce and transport the statues, and that trade with the island would have been unlikely in antiquity, led Erich von Däniken to argue that it would have been impossible for humans to have created and transported the Moai on Easter Island (von Däniken 1971). Instead, he suggested that their construction by extraterrestrial beings was more likely. Recent advances in technology, which has shown us that the island was densely forested until at least 1200 CE (Flenley 1984; Bowdery 2015), and experimental archaeology, which has been used to test transportation methods for the Moai (Van Tilburg 1996; Hunt and Lipo 2012), have since proven von Däniken's theory wrong.

Although race played a formative role in the invention of racial hierarchy, explicit interest in race as an avenue of archaeological inquiry is a relatively new development, with the focus having generally been on ethnicity (cf. summaries and bibliographies in Orser 2004; 2014; Agbe-Davies 2020; Gosden 2006; Emberling 1997; Jones 1997). Ethnicity is still widely used in archaeological investigations of the diverse peoples in the ancient Mediterranean, Near East, and Egypt. Scholars working on Greece and Rome use ethnicity to describe the multiple, overlapping, and diverse collective identities in the ancient Mediterranean, where difference was described primarily in terms of geographic location and social practice (McInerney 2014; Siapkas 2014; Malkin 2001; Hall 1997; Jones 1997). Scholars working on Egypt use ethnicity to describe a similar conceptualization of identity in geographic and cultural terms that distinguished Nile-dwellers (*remetj* 'people') from foreigners based on location, religion, and burial practices (Leahy 1995; Smith 2018; Matić 2020). Representations of foreigners in Egyptian art and literature as either tribute-bearers or conquered foes were expressions of an ideology of divine kingship in which foreigners were dominated as a matter of cosmic maintenance to illustrate the king's power and reach. Libyan, Nubian, Asiatic, and other foreigners were represented with distinctive dress, physical attributes, and carrying goods and animals from their homelands to visually emphasize their difference as distance and bolster the pharaoh's image as an all-powerful ruler (Moreno García 2018). Similarly, ethnicity is used to describe social difference in Mesopotamia, where the evidence suggests that geographic location and social practices were used to distinguish between urban/civilized and nomadic/uncivilized beginning in the third millennium BCE, with alterity represented as evil only in the Neo-Assyrian period to legitimize imperial invention (Van Soldt 2005; Bahrani 2006; Emberling 2014). As in Egypt, Neo-Assyrian and Achaemenid Persian imperial art depicted foreign tribute-bearers with distinctive clothes, objects, and animals to illustrate the geographic extent of the king's authority. In addition, ethnicity has been used to describe the diverse peoples of Hittite Anatolia (Bryce 2014) and shifting definitions in antiquity for *hapiru* in the Levant (Killebrew 2014).

Ancient ethnicity studies yield important insights that can be expanded by integrating critical discussions of race. Although the terms race and ethnicity have been used interchangeably, they are distinct concepts with different histories and interpretive potential (see the debate between Howard Winant and Andreas Wimmer in *Ethnic and Racial Studies* 38.13). Whereas ethnicity is a more neutral designation for "other," race invokes the oppressive systems of colonialism, imperialism, and slavery it was invented to legitimize. Race provides a critical framework for investigating past personhood because it introduces an analysis of power. Power dynamics, both past and present, are important considerations because ancient ideas and identities are modern reconstructions, filtered through and subject to the racial ideologies of modern scholars. Examples of such racialized receptions of ancient ideas in modern Europe and North America are the use of Tacitus' ideas of Germanic purity by the Nazis party and Aristotle's "natural slavery" by anti-abolitionists

(Arnold 2002; Krebs 2009; Monoson 2011; Isaac 2004). Ethnicity and race are therefore complementary frameworks for archaeological investigations of past social difference but a concerted effort must be made to address race because of the previous emphasis on ethnicity.

Recent work draws attention to the ways that race and racism have informed archaeological practice and its resulting historical narratives, especially the impact of scientific racism on Egyptian, Near Eastern, and Mediterranean archaeology (Smith 2020; Moreno García 2018; Matić 2018; Challis 2013; Evans 2012). These current approaches reflect individual scholars' efforts to promote racial reconciliation, but a wider reorientation of the field is suggested by the recent efforts of professional societies and academic institutes to reconcile the field's problematic past. For example, the Penn Museum is repatriating part of the Samuel G. Morton collection, described above, hundreds of skulls (some from enslaved people) that Morton used to develop and popularize craniometry and legitimize white supremacy, has apologized for their stewardship of the unethical collection (DeSanto 2021), and is moving to bury the skulls of enslaved Black Philadelphians that were part of Morton's collection (Tumin 2022). In addition, the decision by ASOR to change its name from the "American Society of Oriental Research" to the "American Society of Overseas Research" marks a concerted effort at accountability (Herbert 2020), as does the recent creation of diversity, equity, and inclusion subcommittees by ASOR and the AIA. These conciliatory gestures by major U.S. archaeological institutions and societies demonstrate that archaeology's race problem has always been a matter of professional ethics. Archaeologists thus bear an ethical responsibility to undertake antiracist work to acknowledge and reconcile our discipline's historical contributions to early race pseudoscience, entrenched colonial theories and methods, and continued contributions to (white) nationalist discourses (Blakey 2001). In order to effectively take up this work, archaeologists must center race in their teaching and look to critical race theory and antiracist pedagogy for best practices.

CRITICAL RACE THEORY (CRT) AND ANTIRACIST PEDAGOGY (ARP)

Instructors of archaeology in the ancient Mediterranean must be both cognizant of how deeply entrenched archaeology is in racist metanarratives and informed about the appropriate ethical frameworks and strategies for discussing race and racism in the classroom, including critical race theory (CRT) and antiracist pedagogy (ARP). Critical race theory examines the role of race and racism in perpetuating social inequalities among dominant and marginalized racial groups and provides a framework for addressing and dismantling white supremacy (Delgado and Stefancic 2012; 2013). CRT was initially developed by legal scholars to attribute the historic exclusion especially of Black Americans, but also of Native Americans, Latinos/-as/-xs, Hispanics, and Asian Americans, in our legal system to systemic racism. The tenets of CRT include: counter-storytelling or counter-narrative (amplifying marginalized voices to challenge dominant narratives); the permanence of racism (recognizing that systemic racism structures all social institutions); whiteness as property (acknowledging that legal privileges are afforded to white people at the expense of marginalized groups); interest convergence (recognizing that white people are the primary beneficiaries of civil rights legislation and diversity initiatives); and the critique of liberalism (highlighting the limitations of colorblindness and assumptions of equal rights under the law for marginalized groups within a system of white supremacy) (DeCuir and Dixson 2004). This framework has been adapted by scholars in various disciplines and has been used to examine racial disparities in higher education (Ladson-Billing and Tate 1995; Hiraldo 2010; Ash et al. 2020).

The recent controversy surrounding CRT in education can be linked to the rising tide of white nationalism under the Trump administration. Published in August 2019, the 1619 Project, conceived of by journalist Nikole Hannah-Jones, sparked controversy because it focused on the lasting impact of slavery in the U.S. (Serwer

2019). More than a year later, Former President Donald Trump issued the "Executive Order on Combating Race and Sex Stereotyping" which particularly prohibited claims that "consciously or unconsciously, and by virtue of his or her race or sex, members of any race are inherently racist…or that members of a sex are inherently sexist" (Exec. Order No. 13950, 2020). More directly in response to Hannah-Jones' work, Trump formed the 1776 Commission, which "offered what it claimed to be a non-partisan review of American history" (Evelyn 2021). As more and more Republican lawmakers have followed Trump's ideological lead, a wedge has been driven between the proponents and critics of CRT, leaving Americans divided over how K-12 schools should approach the history of race and racism in the U.S. By August 2021, in at least 27 states Republican lawmakers have successfully passed bills dictating what teachers can and can't say about racism in the classroom, including prohibiting the teaching of CRT. Texas joined these states on September 1st, passing a law "aimed at teaching complex subjects such as slavery and racism without making white children feel guilty" (DeBenedetto 2021). The law banning critical race theory was just one of several conservative Texas laws, including ones which prohibit abortion "once cardiac activity is detected in an embryo" and which allow protesters who block roads and hospitals to be charged with felonies, that went into effect on that day (DeBenedetto 2021). Strauss has compared the current CRT controversy with that over sex education which occurred over 50 years ago, stating that what matters in these "culture wars" aren't facts, but fear (Strauss 2021). Common anxieties around teaching CRT in schools include how one student can only get ahead at the expense of another; the fueling of hostility toward white people; and the idea that the U.S. is not, in fact, a land of equal opportunity for all. The reality is that most K-12 teachers don't teach CRT; what they teach "are foundational issues in U.S. history that are very much connected to racial inequity [and] segregation" (Presha et al. 2021). Moreover, most K-12 teachers are committed to teaching racial literacy, which equips "young people to see and

act on our racialized world" (Guo and Vulchi 2021). Critics of CRT in schools argue that, if taught at all, race should be presented as a past problem, since they believe that teachers politicize the K-12 classroom when they tell students that the U.S. is still a systemic racist nation.

All teaching and all classrooms, however, are political. The idea that education is neutral is a myth. As Kishimoto explained, "education has often been exclusionary and functioned to assimilate students by normalizing dominant knowledge and values" (Kishimoto 2018: 541). Although CRT has been adapted by scholars in various disciplines to examine racial disparities in higher education, antiracist pedagogy (ARP) involves the application of CRT in the context of education. ARP is "not about simply incorporating racial content into courses, curriculum, and discipline [but] also…*how* one teaches, even in courses where race is not the subject matter" (Kishimoto 2018: 540). ARP aims not just to diversify the classroom and curriculum, but also involves "consciousness raising, which reflects psychological and social development" (Blakeney 2005: 124; Freire 2020). ARP exposes and challenges the ways in which white privilege has shaped educational environments, critiquing in particular the "culture of positivism," which privileges an objective and universal truth, and ignores the effects of social and political context. As a result, personal narratives, particularly those of people of color, are considered to be less reliable than evidence-based "facts" (usually provided from a white perspective) and are often omitted from conversations surrounding race in antiquity.

Despite what many believe, ARP, like CRT, does not refer to diversity and inclusion initiatives, but "requires a commitment to educat[ing] students in ways that make racialized power relations explicit" (Hassouneh 2006: 256). Requiring students to read about or view films which center the experiences of marginalized communities or feature BIPOC is not enough. Instructors "need to teach all students how to critically interrogate the authenticity of stories of experience and to recognize that all accounts are mediated by power, politics, and ideology" (Brunsma et al. 2012: 728). In other words, we need to be teaching racial literacy in our courses, regardless of the subject matter being taught.

REFLECTIONS, RESOURCES, AND TEACHING STRATEGIES

Because ARP provides archaeologists with an opportunity to acknowledge and reconcile our field's role in creating and maintaining racial hierarchy, ethically-minded instructors can implement antiracist teaching strategies to promote equity within and beyond the classroom. What follows are some general guidelines for teaching an antiracist archaeology of the ancient Mediterranean. We offer these guidelines alongside reflections on our respective experiences and positionality with race and pedagogy, Nadhira as a Black female graduate student and instructor and Maggie as a white female instructor, and provide some practical recommendations and resources for antiracist teaching. These guidelines represent a starting point in the process of developing antiracist teaching strategies for archaeological instruction and can be adapted to a variety of instructional settings.

Guidelines for Teaching an Antiracist Archaeology of the Ancient Mediterranean

1. *Acknowledge racism in archaeological practice (Maggie Beeler)*

My experience with antiracist pedagogy comes from teaching "Race in the Ancient Mediterranean" at Temple University, which is offered by the Greek and Roman Classics department and satisfies the race and diversity requirement for the university's General Education program. I started teaching this course in 2017, right after the deadly Charlottesville Unite the Right rally that drew attention to the rising tide of white nationalism in the U.S. As a white instructor teaching race history to a diverse student body, I knew that to create an inclusive learning environment I needed to be transparent about my positionality in discussions of race and power and center the experiences of students who face

racism on- and off-campus. I wanted to make the course relevant to and conversant with the various social and academic backgrounds of students in the large classes of mostly General Education students. I decided at the outset to structure the course around issues of reception to highlight the impact of ancient ideas of social difference on modern racial ideologies. Although the concept of race is anachronistic for the ancient Mediterranean, ancient identities and ideas are modern reconstructions shaped by the racial ideologies and biases of the modern scholars. A reception-based approach to ancient social difference locates the analysis of race not in the ancient sources but rather in their modern interpretations and appropriations.

Focusing on racialized receptions of antiquity provides the opportunity to introduce ARP into the classroom by tackling race head-on, though not to the exclusion of ethnicity. Both ethnicity and race are productive frameworks for examining ancient social difference but they are complementary rather than interchangeable. While ethnicity draws attention to the fluidity and constructed-ness of collective identities, race provides a critical framework for examining the power dynamics of past personhood as a modern reconstruction. For example, in the race class we examine white supremacist groups such as those at the Unite the Rally in 2017 or the insurrectionists at the U.S. Capitol in 2021 who cosplayed ancient Greekness by wearing reproduction helmets and armor. An excellent resource for this topic is Curtis Dozier's blog *Pharos* (Dozier 2017; 2019), which tracks appropriation by white supremacist groups that seek to attach themselves to the prestige and authority of ancient Greece to legitimize their ethnonationalist ideology. Approaching the topic of race in archaeology through its reception today prompts students to consider who is invested in historical narratives of "classical" antiquity or the "cradle of civilization," who is excluded, and why. Such critical discussions underscore the ethical concerns that attend archaeological interpretation and acknowledge the experiences of students who face an often-unstated form of racism in white academic spaces.

Discussions of race can be integrated into any course on archaeology by introducing the history of the concept of race and archaeology's role in its development (see above, Race and Archaeology). Challenging students to consider how archaeology is implicated in the creation and maintenance of racial hierarchy, especially through legitimation of craniometry and other pseudoscience methods to identify ancient peoples, is one strategy for integrating ARP into everyday archaeological instruction. I start the race class each semester by examining the history of race as a concept from its invention in Enlightenment era classifications, institutionalization through 19th and 20th century scientific racism, and post-World War II reconceptualization as a social construct. Providing students with this historical context establishes that racial categories are constructed, a social intervention rather than an essential truth or biological reality, which is new information to many students since discouraging its discussion upholds white supremacist perspectives. A valuable resource for teaching racial constructivism is the U.S. Census' website, which traces changing racial categories from an initial distinction between "Free" and "Slave" in 1790 to a white/Black dichotomy and beyond (Pew Research Center 2020; U.S. Census Bureau 2020). Relating America's changing racial categories to contemporary historical events, such as new immigrant groups arrivals in the 19th century or the Civil Rights movements, illustrates the concept of social constructivism and introduces an analysis of power. Using reception studies to connect the dots between this modern history and the ancient material allows instructors to integrate ARP into their teaching by acknowledging the permanence of racism, a core tenet of CRT.

2. *Model critical approaches to archaeological evidence and questions in your lectures (Nadhira Hill)*

In October 2020, I was invited to give a guest lecture for Professor Beeler's "Race in the Ancient Mediterranean" course. The topic of my lecture was cultural interaction between Greeks and Scythians, a nomadic group who lived in the Black Sea region in antiquity. I began my lecture by complicating the popular notion that non-Greeks frequently "imitated" Greek culture, proposing that, in reality, at least three types of interaction were possible: imitation (copying something wholesale without alteration), adaptation (copying something but altering it to better fit the specific needs of one's culture or environment), or appropriation (members of one culture adopting element[s] of another culture). Doing this was necessary because it highlighted the ways that the different terminologies we use to describe cultural interaction have been used to perpetuate myths about who had power and agency in the ancient world and who did not. As Kishimoto has shown, confronting and deconstructing such myths reveals "their functions, which are to justify the unequal treatment of people of color and maintain white privilege" (Kishimoto 2018: 545). In particular, advancing the notion that non-Greeks frequently imitated Greek culture reinforces moral and value judgments which place the Greeks at the top of a cultural hierarchy and everyone else (including the Romans) below them. This view of Greek hegemony is dangerous because it has often been mobilized in supremacist narratives, from ranking human skulls from primate to the Apollo Belvedere sculpture (a.k.a. the European "ideal") in the 18th century to contemporary propaganda campaigns by alt-right groups linking the classical tradition to white European heritage.

While broadening our definition of cultural interaction in antiquity is important in deconstructing the dominant view that Greece was the pinnacle of civilization, it still faces the problem of viewing the Greeks as the primary or only agents in their interactions with other Mediterranean populations. This is largely due to the privileging of texts, depictions, and perspectives of non-Greek groups produced by Greeks, which inevitably paint those groups as passive victims. My approach moved away from this portrayal by restoring agency to the Scythians. Their agency was demonstrated by deliberately placing them within their chronological, historical, and geographic context. While Greek texts and images were used in my lecture, incorporating and discussing images produced by Scythians alongside Greek ones was also important in this endeavor, because it demonstrated that their culture was just as complex as that of the Greeks (i.e., not inferior to Greek culture), challenging the Greek/barbarian dichotomy which persists in modern discussions of cultural interaction in the Mediterranean. Moreover, the images produced by the Scythians provided an opportunity to explore how they thought of themselves, since written personal narratives were unavailable. The local depictions were compared with those found in oft-cited Greek texts, inviting students to consider how the types of evidence we privilege serve to oppress and distort the realities and lived experiences of marginalized populations.

Not all students, however, are willing to acknowledge or accept the continuing relevance of race and racism in the contemporary world. Although some have argued for the importance of telling students "the truth" about race and racism, Brunsma et al. warn against positioning oneself as an "authority" on race and racism in the classroom, which may "produce white resistance to being 'told' the 'truth' about racism" (Brunsma et al. 2012: 728). This is particularly the case when attempting to engage with white students who are willfully ignorant about the realities of racism and/or voice racist ideas in class. A common solution has been to omit discussions of racism altogether and designate our classrooms as "safe spaces." But who does this designation serve? Students of color are likely to feel unsafe in our classrooms if white students are allowed to voice racist ideas unchallenged; on the other hand, white students are likely to feel unsafe if we *do* challenge them in these situations, particularly if you are a woman or an instructor of color. A more equitable solution involves encouraging dialogic, inquiry-based pedagogy that gives students a more active role in the construction of knowledge in the classroom. The role of the teacher should be more than just a provider of information; a teacher should also give students the opportunity to reflect on and share their own lived experiences (Carr and Klassen 1996).

3. Diversify instructional methods and materials to center marginalized voices (Nadhira Hill)

When we as instructors present ourselves as objective authorities in the classroom, we tend to privilege dominant perspectives at the expense of those which have been historically excluded and silenced. Centering white historical narratives runs the risk of painting a rosier picture of the past than actually existed, as has been the case when instructors claim that "slavery in the ancient world was not that bad" because many were freed, had "good" relationships with their masters, and slavery wasn't predicated on race (Bostick 2018). Such an uncritical approach also risks homogenizing past populations by obscuring people of color from view. Those that do emerge are marked as exceptional or unusual. When I was an undergraduate student, I took many courses that used images on Greek painted pottery as illustrations of historical and mythological events. While usually straightforward and unproblematic, occasionally there would be examples which included depictions of individuals with clear African features alongside ones with more European (a.k.a. "Greek") ones. One professor noted that the name of one painter (Amasis), which was found inscribed on two pots above figures with African features, was Egyptian in origin without further discussion of the broader cultural implications of these depictions. One scholar suggested we view the attribution as "a humorous shorthand reference to Amasis' origin" (Boegehold 1985: 31), but this argument has not been revisited or developed. Scholars have only recently begun to present alternative approaches to the study of Greek vessels, particularly ones in the form of figural heads (e.g., Derbew 2022; Gates-Foster 2021).

Interpretations of the depictions of non-Greeks in both ancient and modern media have traditionally been reductive. They focus on how these depictions exemplify "barbarity" as opposed to "Greekness." Although the term "barbarian" was originally used to indicate peoples who did not speak Greek nor practice Greek customs, it has come to be closely associated with inferiority, "or at least an inherent value judgement condoning inequality" (Southern 2015: 325). Despite this, the term continues to be used uncritically in university classrooms. It is unsurprising, then, that the Greek/barbarian dichotomy was central to our discussion of the vase painter's self-portrait, and continues to be implicated in the choice by many instructors to assign white-washed film adaptations (*Troy*; *300*; *Cleopatra*) in their courses without interrogating the role of racism in their production and subsequent popularity in the discipline.

Presenting presumably alluring source material, such as texts written by marginalized individuals or images depicting them, and films which feature more diverse casts is not enough on its own. As instructors, we have an ethical responsibility to attend to "the experiences of marginalized populations in ways that guard against the re-inscribing of patterns of domination, ensuring that marginalized peoples are not objectified, appropriated, interpreted, or taken over by those who dominate" (Hassouneh 2006: 256). This means not only acknowledging that people of color existed in antiquity, but also interrogating and being explicit about how that existence was shaped by overlapping systems of power. Moreover, it also means both contextualizing and validating the personal narratives of individuals from marginalized groups, both ancient and modern. As Sterling has observed from her own experiences, "points of view that deviate from the White, male, upper-class, cisgendered standard are seen as coming from a special interest perspective, and the objectivity is suspect" (Sterling 2015: 99). When inviting guest speakers or assigning readings by scholars from historically excluded backgrounds, be clear with your students about why you are highlighting their particular work or perspective. A common rationale is wanting to decenter oneself as a white authority on certain topics and to amplify BIPOC voices which have otherwise been overlooked. Confronting one's own complicity in the systems of oppression that have shaped the field of archaeology is not easy, but it is important to show that no one is exempt from these systems.

Racism affects everyone—either you are harmed by it or you benefit from it. By having honest conversations about issues of representation, privilege, and power dynamics in our field (see Heath-Stout, this volume), in education, and in the world more generally, we can make students—especially students from historically excluded backgrounds—feel more included (Oland 2020).

4. *Create opportunities for collaborative learning to empower students as authorities in the classroom (Maggie Beeler)*

In addition to acknowledging that racism is real in archaeology, modeling critical approaches to archaeological research, and diversifying instructional methods and materials, instructors must acknowledge that racism is real in our student's lives, whether they face racism or benefit from white supremacy. We need to develop teaching strategies that make discussions of race reiterative rather than a special topic of discussion by creating opportunities for collaborative learning to empower students as authorities on race and racism in the classroom. One way we can promote inclusive learning environments is to create opportunities for collaborative learning and peer engagement. Many of us already integrate active learning into our teaching through in-class exercises such as group work and discussions, which promote peer learning by allowing students to explore issues together as a process of discovery. Discussions and other group projects can be adapted for ARP to create opportunities for peer teaching and counter storytelling when students are willing to share their personal experiences with racism. But instructors cannot simply expect students who face racism to be willing to share their experiences with their peers, thereby placing the burden on them to educate their white peers. We need to develop a curriculum that delivers the historical context for race history and fosters a dialogue among students to relate their lived experiences within a structured and collegial framework. In other words, we need to create classroom environments that students are willing to invest in because it invests in them.

I view my role in discussions of race as a facilitator and aim to provide a venue and vocabulary for students to discuss race and racism by centering students' lived experiences as authoritative sources of information in the classroom. In order to facilitate productive discussions, a classroom code of conduct must first be established. I structure this as an in-class activity in which students help edit an existing document and propose new ones, creating consensus on collegial discussions. I have found it helpful at this stage to clarify concepts such as systemic and colorblind racism to protect BIPOC students from potentially racist comments from their peers during group discussions.

Discussions present an ideal opportunity to position students as an authoritative source of information in the classroom. I have found in my teaching that structured and recurring discussions foster more meaningful dialogues through student self-reflection and reiterative peer engagement. I adapted my existing discussion format to facilitate collaborative, inquiry-based learning by: 1) identifying a series of topics that build knowledge and analytical skills, 2) formulating discussion questions to guide students to an understanding of the material, and 3) prompting students to relate the questions under study to their own ideas and experiences. In addition, structuring discussions in three parts (written, small group, all-class) maximizes self-reflection and diversifies peer engagements. Students first submit written responses to discussion questions before class, next share their responses in small discussion groups that rotate throughout the semester, and finally reconvene as a class to discuss their group's questions or insights. This allows students to fully digest and reflect on discussion questions before they tackle them with their peers, making learning a process of group discovery. I find that the combination of a collaborative classroom code of conduct and structured, recurring discussions can facilitate productive conversations that are more likely to expose students to their peers' diverse perspectives. On the first day of class, I describe my teaching methods and detail discussions and other in-class activities so that students can decide if that format works for them. This is necessary for discussions of racism because prompting students to reflect on their experience of racism, even just benefiting from it, puts pressure on BIPOC students to educate their peers. For this reason, it is important for instructors to deliver the historical content and theoretical context in lectures before each discussion.

The most productive conversations that I have facilitated on the subject of race tackled the issue of white supremacy head-on. When I began teaching the "Race in the Ancient Mediterranean" class in 2017, the timing was such that I could cite two current events directly relevant to race and the study of the ancient world. The first is the deadly "Unite the Right" rally in Charlottesville that attracted white nationalist extremist groups like Identity Evropa (now the American Identity Movement), who explicitly invokes "classical" Greece and Rome in their racist agenda to "preserve western culture" by intellectualizing and legitimizing white supremacy (Southern Poverty Law Center 2020). One Identity Evropa campus recruiting poster depicts the famous Greek statue Apollo Belvedere that early race pseudoscientists used in craniometry to justify white supremacy and racial slavery. The image of the statue, visual shorthand for their claim of "classical" heritage, is overlain by the phrase, "Our Future Belongs to Us," an allusion to "displacement theory," the idea that white people will be displaced by BIPOC as the demographic with the most political power (Dozier 2017). In addition, earlier that same summer white supremacists harassed scholars Sarah Bond and Mary Beard for their work highlighting the diversity of the ancient Mediterranean, Bond's article about white marble statues being perceived as white skin (Bond 2017) and Beard's defense of the historical accuracy of a BBC cartoon depicting racial diversity in the Roman word (Zhang 2017).

Invoking these two recent and relevant events introduces key themes in the study of race and antiquity: ancient ideas about social difference and their modern, racialized reception; the history and constructedness of racial categories; and archaeology's role in the continued maintenance of (white) nationalist historical narrative. Resources for teaching these two events include Bond's original article and its coverage (Bond 2017; Zhang 2017; McCoskey 2018), video clips of interviews with Bond (Vice 2017), news stories about Charlottesville, and Curtis Dozier's blog *Pharos: Doing Justice to the Classics*, which tracks misappropriations of the classical tradition by white supremacist groups in real-time (cf. Dozier 2017; 2019). They present ideal conversation starters to create opportunities for collaborative learning and can be integrated into any archaeological curriculum.

Conclusion: Towards a Framework for an Antiracist Archaeology of the Ancient Mediterranean

We have argued in this chapter that antiracist archaeological instruction is an ethical imperative, citing insights gained from critical race theory, antiracist pedagogy, and our personal and professional experiences with race and pedagogy as both a Black female and white female instructor. Summarized here are some general guidelines that provide a starting point for teaching an antiracist archaeology of the ancient Mediterranean, which can be adapted to a variety of instructional settings:

Guidelines for Teaching an Antiracist Archaeology of the Ancient Mediterranean:

1. *Acknowledge racism and white supremacy in archaeological practice.* Make a concerted effort to address archaeology's role in the creation of racial hierarchy. Be explicit about your own positionality in these discussions as an authority on archaeology and your experience with race and racism. Be transparent with your students about your teaching methods by explaining what, why, and how they are learning about race and antiracism.

2. *Model critical approaches to archaeological evidence and questions in your lectures.* Select topics and case studies that allow students to

analyze the power dynamics of ancient representations of the 'other'. Use archaeological evidence to respond to representations of foreigners.

3. *Diversify instructional methods and materials to center marginalized voices.* Include the work of BIPOC scholars on your syllabus and in your lecture. Collaborate with peers to share syllabi and resources, guest lecture, and attend webinars and workshops.

4. *Create opportunities for collaborative learning to empower students as authorities in the classroom.* Create opportunities for collaborative learning through in-class exercises that promote peer engagement, such as writing a classroom code of conduct together and recurring, structured discussions. Solicit student feedback with midterm surveys to adapt lesson content and format to each new class configuration. Integrate current events to engage students in their own language.

These guidelines contribute to a wider disciplinary conversation about antiracist archaeology that was initiated by historical archaeologists. They provide a starting point for teaching an antiracist archaeology of the ancient Mediterranean that should be used in tandem with the resources found in contributions to the Society of Black Archaeologist's "'Archaeology in the Time of Black Lives Matter' Resource List" (SBA et al. 2020), "'The Future of Archaeology Is Antiracist': Archaeology in the Time of Black Lives Matter" forum (Flewellen et al. 2021), April Beisaw's "Archaeology of Racism" reading list (Beisaw 2020), Black-Centered Resources for Ancient Mediterranean Studies (Gao et al. 2020), and the Society for American Archaeology's list of publications related to race, inequality, and colonization (SAA 2020).

We offer guidelines rather than a checklist of actions, which are neither effective nor sustainable for teaching in dynamic classroom settings. A more ethical and sustainable approach to teaching an antiracist archaeology of the ancient

Mediterranean involves focusing on processes for shifting perspectives, behaviors, and culture, such as those outlined in the guidelines above. Through conscious and coordinated efforts to create more inclusive learning environments for our students, archaeologists stand to contribute meaningfully to a more equitable academy by recruiting, retaining, and promoting more diverse students into our faculty ranks.

REFERENCES

Agbe-Davies, A. S.
2002   Black Scholars, Black Pasts. *SAA Archaeological Record* 2.4: 24–28.
2020   Race. Pp. 80–94 in *Handbook of Global Historical Archaeology*, ed. C. E. Orser, Jr., P. Funari, S. Lawrence, J. Symonds, and A. Zarankin. New York: Routledge.

American Society of Overseas Research (ASOR)
2019   *Policy on Professional Conduct* (adopted April 18, 2015, amended November 24, 2019). https://www.asor.org/about-asor/policies/ (accessed 1 September 2020).

Archaeological Institute of America (AIA)
2016   *Code of Professional Standards* (adopted December 29, 1994, amended December 29, 1997, January 5, 2008, and January 8, 2016). https://www.archaeological.org/about/governance/policies/ (accessed 1 September 2020).
2020   AIA Webinars: Critical Conversations on Race, Teaching, and Antiquity. Archaeological Institute of America. https://www.archaeological.org/aia-seminars-critical-conversations-on-race-teaching-and-antiquity/ (accessed 1 September 2020).

Arnold, B.
2002   Justifying Genocide: Archaeology and the Construction of Difference. Pp. 95–116 in *Annihilating Difference: The Anthropology of Genocide*, ed. A. L. Hinton and K. Roth. Berkeley: University of California.

Ash, A. N.; Hill, R.; Risdon, S. N.; and Jun, A.
2020   Anti-Racism in Higher Education: A Model for Change. *Race and Pedagogy Journal* 4.3: 1–35.

Bahrani, Z.
2006   Race and Ethnicity in Mesopotamian Antiquity. *World Archaeology* 38.1: 48–59.

Beisaw, A. M.
2020   Archaeology of Racism Bibliography. https://docs.google.com/document/d/1D6pMXn1xXZ62sRyKF1t39prpaymmopKMq_maZbNOxko/ (accessed 1 September 2020).

Bindman, D.
2002   *Ape to Apollo: Aesthetics and the Idea of Race in the Eighteenth Century*. London: Reaktion.

Blakeney, A. M.
2005   Antiracist Pedagogy: Definition, Theory, and Professional Development. *Journal of Curriculum and Pedagogy* 2.1: 119–32.

Blakey, M. L.
2001   Bioarchaeology of the African Diaspora in the Americas: Its Origins and Scope. *Annual Review of Anthropology* 30: 387–422.
2020   Archaeology under the Blinding Light of Race. *Current Anthropology* 61.S22: 183–97.

Boegehold, A. L.
1985   The Time of the Amasis Painter. Pp. 15–32 in *The Amasis Painter and His World: Vase Painting in Sixth-Century B.C. Athens*, ed. D. von Bothmer. New York: Thames and Hudson.

Bond, S. E.
2017   Why We Need to Start Seeing the Classical World in Color. *Hyperallergic*, June 7, 2017. https://hyperallergic.com/383776/why-we-need-to-start-seeing-the-classical-world-in-color/ (accessed 1 September 2020).

Bostick, D.
2018   Teaching Slavery in the High School Latin Classroom. *In Medias Res*, February 23, 2018. https://medium.com/in-medias-res/teaching-slavery-in-the-high-school-

latin-classroom-ce4146827abe (accessed 16 August 2021).

Bowdery, D.
2015   An Enigma Revisited: Identification of Palm Phytoliths Extracted from the 1983 Rapa Nui, Rano Kao2 Core. *Vegetation History and Archaeobotany* 24.1: 455–66.

Brunsma, D. L.; Brown, E. S.; and Placier, P.
2012   Teaching Race at Historically White Colleges and Universities: Identifying and Dismantling the Walls of Whiteness. *Critical Sociology* 39.5: 717–38.

Bryce, T. R.
2014   Hittites and Anatolian Ethnic Diversity. Pp. 127–41 in *A Companion to Ethnicity in the Ancient Mediterranean,* ed. J. McInerney. Oxford: Wiley Blackwell.

Carr, P., and Klassen, T.
1996   The Role of Racial Minority Teachers in Anti-Racist Education. *Canadian Ethnic Studies* 28.2: 126–38.

Challis, D.
2013   *The Archaeology of Race: The Eugenics Ideas of Francis Galton and Flinders Petrie.* New York: Bloomsbury.

Childe, V. G.
1929   *The Danube in Prehistory.* Oxford: Clarendon.

Crimmins, P.
2021   Penn Museum Apologizes for 'Unethical Possession of Human Remains'. NPR, April 27, 2021. https://www.npr.org/2021/04/27/988972736/penn-museum-apologizes-for-unethical-possession-of-human-remains

von Däniken, E.
1971   *Chariots of the Gods? Unsolved Mysteries of the Past,* transl. M. Heron. London: Transworld.

DeBenedetto, P.
2021   In Texas, 666 Laws Take Effect Wednesday, Including Many Conservative Priorities. *NPR,* September 1, 2021. https://www.npr.org/2021/09/01/1032894148/in-texas-666-laws-take-effect-sept-1-including-many-conservative-priorities (accessed 1 September 2021).

Delgado, R. and Stefancic, J.
2012   *Critical Race Theory: An Introduction. Critical America,* 2nd ed. New York: New York University.
2013   *Critical Race Theory: The Cutting Edge,* 3rd ed. Philadelphia: Temple University.

DeCuir, J. T., and Dixson, A. D.
2004   "So When It Comes Out, They Aren't That Surprised That It Is There": Using Critical Race Theory as a Tool of Analysis of Race and Racism in Education. *Educational Researcher* 33.5: 26–31.

Derbew, S. F.
2022   *Untangling Blackness in Greek Antiquity.* Cambridge: Cambridge University.

DeSanto, J.
2021   Museum Announces the Repatriation of the Morton Cranial Collection. *Penn Museum,* April 12, 2021. https://www.penn.museum/documents/pressroom/MortonCollectionRepatriation-Press%20release.pdf (accessed 1 August 2021).

Dietler, M.
2015   *Archaeologies of Colonialism: Consumption, Entanglement, and Violence in Ancient Mediterranean France.* Berkeley: University of California.

Dozier, C.
2017   This Is Not Sparta. *Pharos,* November 18, 2017. http://pages.vassar.edu/pharos/2017/11/18/this-is-not-sparta/ (accessed 1 September 2020).
2019   Classical Antiquity and the fear of "White Extinction". *Pharos,* March 29, 2019. http://pages.vassar.edu/pharos/2019/03/29/classical-antiquity-and-the-fear-of-white-extinction/ (accessed 1 September 2020).

Duesterberg, S.
2015   *Popular Receptions of Archaeology: Fictional and Factual Texts in 19th and Early 20th Century Britain.* London: Transcript.

Emberling, G.
1997   Ethnicity in Complex Societies: Anthro-
        pological Perspectives. *Journal of Archaeo-
        logical Research* 5: 295–344.
2014   Ethnicity in Empire: Assyrians and Others.
        Pp. 158–74 in *A Companion to Ethnicity in
        the Ancient Mediterranean,* ed. J. McInerney.
        Oxford: Wiley Blackwell.

Evans, J.
2012   *The Lives of Sumerian Sculpture: An
        Archaeology of the Early Dynastic Temple.*
        Cambridge: Cambridge University.

Executive Order 13950 (September 22, 2020)

Evelyn, K.
2021   Historians Rail Against Trump Adminis-
        tration's 1776 Commission. *The Guardian,*
        January 22, 2021. https://www.theguardian.
        com/us-news/2021/jan/22/1776-commis
        sion-report-trump-administration-histori
        ans (accessed 16 August 2021).

Flenley, J. R., and King, A. S. M.
1984   Late Quaternary pollen records from Easter
        Island. *Nature* 307: 47–50.

Flewellen, A.; Dunnavant, J.; Odewale, A;
Jones, A.; Wolde-Michael, T.; Crossland, Z.;
and Franklin, M.
2021   The Future of Archaeology Is Antiracist:
        Archaeology in the Time of Black Lives
        Matter. *American Antiquity* 86.2: 224–43.

Franklin, M.
1997   Why Are There So Few Black American
        Archaeologists? *Antiquity* 71: 799–801.

Franklin, M.; Dunnavant, J. P.; Flewellen, A. O.;
and Odewale, A.
2020   The Future Is Now: Archaeology and the
        Eradication of Anti-Blackness. *Interna-
        tional Journal of Historical Archaeology* 24:
        753–66.

Freire, J.
2020   *Pedagogy of the Oppressed.* 50th anni-
        versary edition. New York: Bloomsbury
        Academic.

Gao, D.; Hill, N.; Ross, S.; and Thomas, Z. E.
2020   Black-Centered Resources for Ancient Medi-
        terranean Studies. https://docs.google.com/
        document/d/1Ktd0wxlAeuMsK99uIH1-
        tY1G8DJ5r8SdxrW2SMmK-2E/ (accessed
        1 September 2020).

Gates-Foster, J.
2021   Out of Egypt: Provenance, Racial Represen-
        tation, and Miniature Images of Nubians in
        the Menil Collection. Pp. 106–25 in *Object
        Biographies: Collaborative Approaches to
        Ancient Mediterranean Art,* ed. J. N. Hop-
        kins, S. K. Costello and P. R. Davis. Hous-
        ton: Menil Collection.

Gosden, C.
2006   Race and Racism in Archaeology: Introduc-
        tion. *World Archaeology* 38.1: 1–7.

Gould, S. J.
2006   *The Mismeasure of Man.* New York: Norton.

Guo, W., and P. Vulchi
2021   American Schools are Failing to Equip Stu-
        dents with Racial Literacy – And We've Seen
        Firsthand How it Happens. *Time,* August
        13, 2021. https://time.com/6089533/critical-
        race-theory-student-perspective/?amp
        =true (accessed 15 August 2021).

Hall, J. M.
1997   *Ethnic Identity in Greek Antiquity.* Cam-
        bridge: Cambridge University.

Hamilakis, Y.
2012   Are We Postcolonial Yet? Tales from the
        Battlefield. *Archaeologies* 8: 67–76.

Hassouneh, D.
2006   Anti-Racist Pedagogy: Challenges Faced by
        Faculty of Color in Predominantly White
        Schools of Nursing. *Journal of Nursing
        Education* 45.7: 255–62.

Herbert, S.
2020   Update From President Sharon Herbert Re-
        garding ASOR'S Name. ASOR, August 20,
        2020. https://www.asor.org/news/2020/08/
        asor-name-change (accessed 1 August
        2021).

Hiraldo, P.
2010   The Role of Critical Race Theory in Higher Education. *The Vermont Connection*: 31.7: 53–59.

Hunt, T. L., and Lipo, C. P.
2012   *The Statues that Walked: Unraveling the Mystery of Easter Island.* New York: Simon and Schuster.

Isaac, B.
2004   *The Invention of Racism in Classical Antiquity.* Princeton, NJ: Princeton University.

Jones, S.
1997   *The Archaeology of Ethnicity: Constructing Identities in the Past and the Present.* London: Routledge.

Killebrew, A. E.
2014   Hybridity, Hapiru, and the Archaeology of Ethnicity in Second Millennium BCE Western Asia. Pp. 142-157 in *A Companion to Ethnicity in the Ancient Mediterranean*, ed. J. McInerney. Oxford: Wiley Blackwell.

Kishimoto, K.
2018   Anti-racist Pedagogy: From Faculty's Self-reflection To Organizing Within And Beyond The Classroom. *Race, Ethnicity and Education* 21.4: 540–54.

Koutonin, M.
2016   Lost cities #9: Racism and Ruins - The Plundering of Great Zimbabwe. *The Guardian*, August 18, 2016. https://www.theguardian.com/cities/2016/aug/18/great-zimbabwe-medieval-lost-city-racism-ruins-plundering (accessed 19 August 2021).

Krebs, C. B.
2009   A Dangerous Book: The Reception of Tacitus' *Germania*. Pp. 280–99 in *The Cambridge Companion to Tacitus*, ed. A. J. Woodman. Cambridge: Cambridge University.

Ladson-Billings, G., and Tate, W.F.
1995   Toward A Critical Race Theory of Education. *Teachers College Record* 97: 47–68.

Leahy, A.
1995   Ethnic Diversity in Ancient Egypt. Pp. 225–34 in *Civilizations of the Ancient Near East*, Vol. 1, ed. J. M. Sasson, J. Baines, G. Beckman, and K. Robinson. New York: Scribner.

Malkin, I. (ed.)
2001   *Ancient Perceptions of Greek Ethnicity.* Center for Hellenic Studies Colloquia 5. Cambridge, MA: Center for Hellenic Studies, Trustees for Harvard University.

Matić, U.
2018   De-colonizing Historiography and Archaeology of Ancient Egypt and Nubia Part 1: Scientific Racism. *Journal of Egyptian History* 11.1–2: 19–44.
2020   *Ethnic Identities in the Land of the Pharaohs: Past and Present Approaches in Egyptology.* Elements in Ancient Egypt in Context. Cambridge: Cambridge University.

McCoskey, D. E.
2018   Beware of Greeks Bearing Gifts: How Neo-Nazis and Ancient Greeks Met in Charlottesville. *Origins* 11.11. http://origins.osu.edu/article/beware-greeks-bearing-gifts-how-neo-nazis-and-ancient-greeks-met-charlottesville (accessed 1 September 2020).

McInerney, J. (ed.)
2014   *A Companion to Ethnicity in the Ancient Mediterranean.* Oxford: Wiley Blackwell.

Monoson, S. S.
2011   Recollecting Aristotle. Pp. 247–78 in *Ancient Slavery and Abolition: From Hobbes to Hollywood*, ed. R. Alston, E. Hall, and J. McConnell. New York: Oxford University.

Moreno García, J. C. M.
2018   Ethnicity in Ancient Egypt: An Introduction to Key Issues. *Journal of Egyptian History* 11.1–2: 1–17.

Oland, M. H.
2020   Teaching Archaeology with Inclusive Pedagogy. *Journal of Archaeology and Pedagogy* 4.1: 1–25.

Orser, C. E.
2004   *Race and Practice in Archaeological In-terpretation.* Philadelphia: University of Pennsylvania.
2014   Race in Archaeology. Pp. 6223–26 in *Encyclopedia of Global Archaeology*, ed. C. Smith. New York: Springer.

Pew Research Center
2020   What Census Calls Us. https://www.pewresearch.org/interactives/what-census-calls-us/ (accessed 1 September 2020).

Phillips, J. A.; Risdon, N.; Lamsma, M;
Hambrick, A.; and Jun, A.
2019   Incorporating Anti-Racist Pedagogy in the College Classroom: Barriers and Strategies by White Faculty Who Incorporate Anti-Racist Pedagogy. *Race and Pedagogy Journal* 3.2: 1–27.

Porter, B. W.
2010   Near Eastern Archaeology: Imperial Pasts, Postcolonial Presents, and the Possibilities of a Decolonized Future. Pp. 51–60 in *Handbook of Postcolonial Archaeology*, ed. J. Lydon and U. Z. Rizvi. Abingdon: Routledge.

Presha, A.; Shakya, T.; Stewart, B.;
and McAfee, M.
2021   Teachers, Students Speak Out Against Texas Laws Targeting Critical Race Theory *ABC News*, August 12, 2021. https://abcnews.go.com/amp/US/teachers-students-speak-texas-laws-targeting-critical-race/story?id=79391492 (accessed 16 August 2021).

Relethford, J. H.
2017   Biological Anthropology, Population Genetics, and Race. Pp. 160–69 in *The Oxford Handbook of Philosophy and Race*, ed. N. Zack. New York: Oxford University.

Serwer, A.
2019   The Fight About the 1619 Project is Not About the Facts. *The Atlantic*, December 23, 2019. https://www.theatlantic.com/ideas/archive/2019/12/historians-clash-1619-project/604093/ (accessed 16 August 2021).

Siapkas, J.
2014   Ancient Ethnicity and Modern Identity. Pp. 66–81 in *A Companion to Ethnicity in the Ancient Mediterranean*, ed. J. McInerney. Oxford: Wiley Blackwell.
2016   Skulls from the Past: Archaeological Negotiations of Scientific Racism. *Bulletin of the History of Archaeology* 26.1, Art. 7.

Smiles, D. A.
2021   Review Essay: Elizabeth Weiss and James W. Springer. *Repatriation and Erasing the Past.* University of Florida Press, 2020. 278 pp. ISBN: 9781683401575. https://journals.kent.ac.uk/index.php/transmotion/article/view/993/1918 (accessed 18 August 2021).

Smith, S. T.
2018   Ethnicity: Constructions of Self and Other in Ancient Egypt. *Journal of Egyptian History* 11: 113–46.
2020   Black Pharaohs? Egyptological Bias, Racism, and Egypt and Nubia as African Civilizations. Virtual lecture at the Hutchins Center for African & African American Research, Harvard University, September 22, 2020. https://www.youtube.com/watch?v=4QK7P0Bdpj0 (accessed 18 August 2021).

Society for American Archaeology (SAA)
2018   *Principles of Archaeological Ethics* (adopted 1996, amended 2018). https://www.saa.org/career-practice/ethics-in-professional-archaeology (accessed 1 September 2020).
2020   A Note from the SAA Publications Committee on a Selection of SAA Publications on Race, Inequality, and Decolonization. https://www.saa.org/publications/saa-contributions-on-race (accessed 1 September 2020).

Society of Black Archaeologists; Theoretical Archaeology Group (North America);
and Columbia Center for Archaeology (eds.)
2020   *Archaeology in the Time of Black Lives Matter.* https://vimeo.com/433155008 (accessed 1 September 2020).

Southern, P.

2015   *The Roman Empire from Severus to Constantine.* Milton Park: Taylor & Francis.

Southern Poverty Law Center

2020   Identity Evropa/American Identity Movement. http://www.splcenter.org/fighting-hate/extremist-files/group/identity-evropa american-identity-movement (accessed 1 September 2020).

Sterling, K.

2015   Black Feminist Theory in Prehistory. *Archaeologies* 11: 93–120.

Strauss, V.

2021   The Culture War Over Critical Race Theory Looks Like the One Waged 50 Years Ago Over Sex Education. *The Washington Post,* July 25, 2021. https://www.washingtonpost.com/education/2021/07/25/critical-race-theory-sex-education-culture-wars/ (accessed 15 August 2021).

Sussman, R. W.

2014   *The Myth of Race: The Troubling Persistence of an Unscientific Idea.* Cambridge, MA: Harvard University.

Trigger, B. G.

2006   *A History of Archaeological Thought,* 2nd ed. Cambridge: Cambridge University.

Tumin, R.

2022   Penn Museum to Bury Skulls of Enslaved People. *The New York Times,* August 9, 2022. https://www.nytimes.com/2022/08/09/us/university-pennsylvania-black-skulls-burial.html (accessed Aug 15 2022).

U.S. Census Bureau

2020   About Race. https://www.census.gov/topics/population/race/about.html (accessed 1 September 2020).

Van Soldt, W.

2005   *Race and Ethnicity in Ancient Mesopotamia.* Proceedings of the 48th Rencontre Assyriologique Internationale at Leiden, 1–4 July 2002. Leiden: Netherlands Institute for the Near East.

Van Tilburg, J. A.

1996   Mechanics, Logistics, and Economics of Transporting Easter Island Statues. *Rapa Nui Journal* 10.4: 110–15.

Vice News

2017   Why Ancient Marble Statues Aren't Meant To Be Seen As "White." July 18, 2017. https://www.youtube.com/watch?v=86PD8o6xe_4 (accessed 1 September 2020).

Zender, M. A.

1997   *The American Archaeologist: A Profile.* Walnut Creek, CA: AltaMira.

Zhang, S.

2017   A Kerfuffle About Diversity in the Roman Empire. *The Atlantic.* August 2, 2017. https://www.theatlantic.com/science/archive/2017/08/dna-romans/535701/ (accessed 1 September 2020).

Chapter 6

Looking beyond 1970

Addressing "Orphan" Objects and Paths Forward

Sarah Kielt Costello

Abstract

Scholars have, in recent years, made strong cases for the importance for academics and museum professionals to adhere to ethical guidelines in the acquisition and publication of archaeological objects. One area that has evaded a consensus view is the problem of "orphan objects," objects which typically cannot be acquired or published due to their insufficient provenance history. These objects reside in private and public collections yet are in essence off-limits to publication by scholars, or acquisition by public collections, according to the ethical guidelines of various scholarly societies, such as the Archaeological Institute of America (AIA), the American Schools of Overseas Research (ASOR), the Society for American Archaeology (SAA), and the American Alliance of Museums (AAM), since their study or purchase could fuel the antiquities market and, by extension, the looting of archaeological sites.

This chapter will review the various ways that stakeholders define the term "orphan," and argue that its usage should be abandoned. The importance of the 1970 date is reviewed, and further steps are suggested. I urge scholars working in museums and in academia to be guided by the intentions of the "1970 rule," rather than by finding its loopholes and weak spots, and to consider those intentions in all aspects of object publication. I argue that professional ethics oblige all archaeologists and historians of ancient art to engage in the problems of provenance and bring these issues to a broader public awareness.

Introduction

Archaeological excavation is destructive by nature; when sites are excavated, contexts are destroyed in the process and artifacts are displaced from their depositional location. Careful record-keeping along with non-invasive archaeological practices (survey, experimental archaeology, ethnography, archival studies, etc.) mitigate data loss. In contrast, the removal of artifacts through looting is fully destructive of archaeological context, obliterating the record not only of the looted object, but everything in the vicinity (Barker 2018: 457). Looted objects often enter the art market, where, transformed into *objets d'art* or relics imbued with a lost past, they are purchased into private or public collections. The two categories of objects—properly excavated and documented, or looted—seem discrete, yet older excavations and practices blur the lines. Furthermore, we rely on documentation to determine an object's history; when documentation is incomplete or suspect, the status of an object can be uncertain.

A thriving market for antiquities can drive the looting of sites and even museums, as well as contributing to the likelihood of forgeries in the market, all to meet the demands of buyers. Museums can impact the market when they add ancient works to their collections, if their interest demonstrates demand for such works. A recent example is the Museum of the Bible in Washington, DC, and its voracious acquisition of objects from ancient western Asia; the impact of that buying spree changed the type of objects appearing in the licensed market in Israel, as detailed by Morag Kersel. Market principles indicate that demand creates supply; Kersel cites evidence for that link (Kersel 2023). Archaeologists and art historians, likewise, may amplify the market value of looted objects if they publish articles, books, or museum entries on them. An infamous example is the "Guennol lioness," an 8.3 cm limestone figurine that sold at auction for 57 million dollars in 2007 (Witmore and Harmanşah 2007). While its charms are many, that a tiny figurine with few parallels fetched such a high price was no doubt helped by the fact that Columbia University scholar Edith Porada dedicated an article to the unprovenienced figure, giving it an impressive scholarly pedigree (Porada 1950). In recognition of these problems, and in an effort to limit future looting, our various professional organizations have developed ethical codes of conduct to ensure that our behaviors as scholars and professionals do not contribute to demand in the antiquities market, and thus to the looting, forgery and theft that feed that market. Recent decades have seen archaeologists, art historians, and museum professionals (these are often overlapping identities) coalesce around certain ethical principles that guide how we engage with objects lacking a full archaeological pedigree; these principles have guided the drafting and revision of our professional ethical codes.

What happens, however, to objects already on the market, or in collections, that do not meet the provenance requirements of those guidelines, and therefore are off-limits to study, publication, or acquisition (depending upon the details of the particular example)? Such works have been called "orphan objects." The term is not consistently defined or applied (see below), nor is there agreement over how such objects should be handled, from an ethical perspective. This chapter aims to further our discussion of the ethics surrounding objects lacking adequate provenance records. In the following sections, I define the terminology employed in this chapter and in related scholarship (including provenance and provenience). I outline the history and the significance of the 1970 date, and how various professional organizations have implemented ethical guidelines based around that date. That history provides the context for how the category of "orphan" objects emerged. I argue that "orphan" is not a descriptor well-suited to archaeological objects, and that it distracts from important questions that remain controversial in the stewardship of antiquities. Finally, I propose several ways to move forward towards more ethical approaches to this challenging category of material.

Scholars have, in recent decades, made powerful arguments for the importance of adhering to ethical guidelines in the acquisition, display, and publication of archaeological objects. Archaeologists have presented the many facets of the negative impacts of the trade in antiquities, outlining in detail the various "material and intellectual consequences of esteem" for archaeological works (Gill and Chippindale 1993). At issue is the practice of treating archaeological objects as art commodities and subjecting them to the same collecting practices, market forces, and display practices as other types of art found in museums, to the detriment of their value as sources of information about both past societies as well as the collecting practices of modern society. Beyond that issue lie a host of related problems: the question of legal ownership versus ethical stewardship of ancient works; the destruction of archaeological sites; heritage management; and the biases and violence driven by colonialism, nationalism, and racism. These issues cannot be disentangled from the practice of museum collection, display, and scholarly treatment of ancient objects. While some remain committed to the notion of art versus artifact (e.g., Timothy Potts at the Getty, as cited in Marlowe 2020: 326; and in his own words: https://blogs.getty.edu/iris/a-new-vision-for-the-collection-at-the-getty-villa/), the current intellectual environment favors the recognition that much is lost when archaeological context is ignored, unknown, or destroyed, and that ethical practice should be aimed at discouraging the trade in antiquities that supports such losses.

The consensus around that point is evident through the widespread adoption of a 1970 date as a line in the sand: objects should have an ownership history showing they were outside their country of origin before 1970 (or legally exported after that point), or the object should not be purchased or published. The importance of 1970, and the various policies and guidelines subsequently adopted by archaeological and museum organizations, are discussed below. First, I present a short discussion of the terminology used within those policies, to clarify both points of overlap and distinction among similar terms.

Terminology

There is some overlap and inconsistency in the terms used by the many scholars engaged in discussions on the topic of cultural heritage. The following terms are used and/or cited in this chapter.

Provenance: The history of ownership of a work. It is the record of sales, gifts, bequests, or other transfers through which an object changed hands over the years, since its creation. In the case of antiquities, however, the provenance is typically the *modern* ownership history of the object. Provenance research seeks to establish the documentation of that history.

Provenience: Provenience, an anglicization of "provenance," is commonly used as a synonym for archaeological findspot. Hence, prove-nience often points towards the ancient origin of the work.

Looting: The unscientific removal of archaeological material.

Findspot: The archaeological context in which an object was discovered. While archaeological findspot is often quite specific, down to the specific archaeological context and even spatial coordinates, "findspot" in provenance research can be far less precise, such as a site name or even a broad locality. Synonymous with "provenience," "findspot" is perhaps to be preferred since the provenience/provenance distinction can be confusing, particular in a context of French and English speakers. "Findspot" also emphasizes the active, physical removal of a work from the ground, while "provenience" leaves the manner of its discovery unquestioned.

Grounded: An object with a known provenience or findspot (as per Marlowe 2016a).

Ungrounded: An object lacking a known provenience or findspot (as per Marlowe 2016a).

Documented: An object with a known provenance extending back to 1970.

Undocumented: An object lacking a known provenance back to 1970.

History: 1970 and Subsequent Policy

The 1970 date is that of the United Nations Educational, Scientific, and Cultural Organization (UNESCO) *Convention on the Means of Prohibiting and Preventing the Illicit Import, Export and Transfer of Ownership of Cultural Property* (Unesco.org), which formally recognized the threat to heritage worldwide posed by the looting of archaeological sites. The convention represents a global effort to stem the widespread looting of archaeological sites to supply the international art market. In response to that convention (recognized by the United States in 1983 through the Convention on Cultural Property Implementation Act), the various professional organizations in our field have adopted guidelines for members, and 1970 is widely viewed as an important marker in policies around the acquisition and treatment of antiquities. Neil Brodie and Colin Renfrew write that the "'1970 Rule' seems an effective and practical response to an ethical problem, and one that is capable of rigorous enforcement" (Brodie and Renfrew 2005: 352). Claire Lyons, of the Getty Museum, calls it a "bright line," a "date after which provenance must be documented" (Lyons 2009: 421). The idea is that once UNESCO formally identified the connection between the art market and the looting of archaeological sites, the world was put on notice, and no further trafficking past that date should be tolerated. If an object's provenance can be traced back before 1970, it can ethically be purchased, studied, and published, even if it lacks archaeological provenience. If its modern provenance cannot be documented to that date, it should be considered unethically acquired. This, in short, is the "1970 rule."

The 1970 UNESCO Convention and the professional responses to it have been extensively discussed (e.g., Reed 2021; Gerstenblith 2013; Brodie and Renfrew 2005); I present here a brief summary of the policies of organizations most relevant to the ASOR membership and the American audience. Neither the Convention itself, nor the various codes of conduct implemented by the organizations discussed below, establish legality of actions; this discussion is directed at the guidance of ethical behavior, which encompasses the protection of cultural heritage.

ASOR's Policy on Professional Conduct, as it pertains to stewardship of the past, supports the UNESCO Convention (ASOR 2019). ASOR's policy directs members not to engage in activities that add to the value of artifacts in illicit markets. Recommendations around publication are detailed and should be read in full, but broadly, ASOR publications cannot serve as first publication of an object lacking a provenance prior to April 1972, the date of entry into force of the 1970 Convention. Publication is allowed, however, if it serves primarily to emphasize the loss of heritage. Publications of objects lacking findspots, even if not first publication, should clearly identify

those objects as such. There is a further exception related to cuneiform texts. Conflicts in Iraq and Syria in recent decades gave rise to considerable looting of sites in the region; this exception was made to allow for the acquisition, study, and then return of cuneiform texts to their region of origin, or "to some other publicly-accessible repository, if return to its country of origin is not feasible" (ASOR 2019).

The AIA's directives to members include a number of separate policies that pertain to these issues: a Code of Ethics (adopted 1990, last amended 2016), a Code of Professional Standards (adopted 1994, last amended 2016), a Resolution on the Importance of Antiquities (adopted 1970), a Resolution on the Acquisition of Antiquities by Museums (adopted 1973), and a Policy on the Presentation and Publication of Undocumented Antiquities, adopted in 2020. The AIA endorsed the UNESCO Convention in December 1970 (www.archaeological.org). Publication guidelines were first established in 1978, when the Institute's journal, the *American Journal of Archaeology* (*AJA*) adopted a first-publication prohibition for pre-1973 works. The 1973 date is when the AIA adopted a similar restriction for presentation at its Annual Meeting (Gerstenblith 2013: 365). The first-publication prohibition was revised in 2004 to allow for exceptions that emphasize the loss of archaeological context (Norman 2005: 135).

The SAA's "Principles of Archaeological Ethics" differ in not referencing the 1970 UNESCO Convention, instead emphasizing the responsibility of archaeologists for prioritizing stewardship and preservation of artifacts, and avoiding scholarship that risks "enhancing the commercial value of archaeological object." In the same clause, objects that are not "curated in public collections" are emphasized, suggesting room for scholarship on those that are (SAA 2016). On the museum side, the Association of Art Museum Directors (AAMD) enacted guidelines in 2004, which have been amended twice since then (AAMD 2013). The initial guidelines, intended to limit purchases of art and artifacts that could incentivize looting, recommended that any object considered for purchase have a ten-year documented history of ownership outside of its country of origin. The "ten-year policy" was criticized for allowing dealers to too easily circumvent the intended restriction, for example by warehousing purchases for ten years (Lyons 2009: 429). A searing critique of museums by Brodie and Renfrew asserts that the AAMD acquisition guidelines of 2004 represent a move backwards by museums in actively working to prevent the looting of archaeological sites, going so far as to call it a "looter's charter" (Brodie and Renfrew 2005: 353).

That policy was amended in 2008, the same year that the American Alliance of Museums (AAM) also drafted and adopted a related policy (AAM 2008; Gerstenblith 2013: 367). The AAM's guidelines use the 1970 date, suggesting that if a museum acquires a work lacking the 1970 pedigree, they should seek documentation that it was exported legally. The policy allows for exceptions, however, within the public's interest and in "alignment with the institution's collections policy and applicable ethical codes," a rather lenient loophole (www.aam-us.org). The AAMD also adopted the 1970 date as a standard in its 2008 revision, allowing, however, broad exceptions to the rule. Objects acquired outside of the standards are meant to be placed on a public-facing registry for transparency (Gerstenblith 2013: 368).[1]

A further change to the AAMD policy in 2013 represents yet looser adherence to the 1970 rule, by allowing museums to purchase objects lacking the 1970 provenance if research allows the museum to "make an informed judgment that the Work was outside its probable country of modern discovery before 1970 or legally exported from its probable country of modern discovery after 1970" (AAMD 2013). The term "informed judgement" leaves ample room for the justification of a desired but suspect work. Victoria Reed stresses that the latitude afforded to museums by the guidelines leaves space for decision making by the museum, but that such decision making should be guided by the acquisition policies of the individual museum, along with full consideration of legal concerns and financial risks (Reed 2021: 223–24). The new guidelines also allow museums

to accept gifts that had been discussed or intended prior to 2008, even if they lack provenance. Such exceptions are meant to be documented on the registry (Gerstenblith 2013: 369).

Adherence to the 1970 rule is a critical starting point both for museums and scholars. These guidelines establish a basis from which to make decisions about acquisition, display, and publication. However, as Gerstenblith recounts, there have been many claims by nations for restitution of objects acquired *before* 1970, as well as the continued acquisition of post-1970 objects by museums, making it plain that the current guidelines, based on the 1970 rule, do not fully solve the problems associated with the purchase of antiquities (Gerstenblith 2013: 370).

Two questions in particular remain contentious:

1. What should become of objects not currently in public collections that lack a 1970 provenance? Can they be purchased by a public or academic institution, so as to be subject to care and study?

2. What should become of objects already in public collections that do not meet the UNESCO standards? How should they be displayed? How should they be treated by scholars?

As to the first question, Lyons notes that "[t]he issue of how to address undocumented antiquities, acquired after 1970, remains a matter for further consideration" (Lyons 2009: 430), referring to such objects as "orphaned" (Lyons 2009: 432). In fact, both of those sets of objects have been referred to as "orphans" because they are left out of the guidelines for ethical stewardship. Not only is there disagreement about the proper fate for these works, there is also disagreement about which ones should be called "orphans." A review of how this term has been applied reveals how the old fault lines between archaeologists and museums, and art versus artifact, remain divisive.

"Orphan" Objects

The policy and practice gaps that remain, once a 1970 date is generally adhered to, become evident very quickly to any scholar working with

1   https://aamd.org/object-registry

material not recently excavated. Whether in a museum or university setting, one encounters objects without findspots, works not previously published, works that entered the market recently as a result of conflict, pieces from private collections now offered for sale or as gifts, and any number of other situations that seem to fall in a "gray area." In some cases, such works have also been referred to as "orphans."

The term "orphan" has been applied in a variety of ways in connection to ancient or other archaeological works. Below I discuss five different usages, all from recent decades. The first three correspond to the list assembled by Richard M. Leventhal and Brian Daniels when they assessed the term in 2013 (Leventhal and Daniels 2013).

1. One narrow and specific use of the term "orphans" is in reference to fragments of Greek vases by known artists, sold in pieces as a deeply-problematic way of moving them into collections with less scrutiny than a full vessel would attract. This practice, "the sale of the orphans," is referenced by Peter Watson and Cecilia Todeschini in their exposé of the antiquities market (2006: 77; more recent discussions of the practice include Gill 2022; Leventhal and Daniels 2013: 340). An interesting possible case of such a "sale of the orphans" is detailed in a 2023 *New York Times* piece highlighting a Greek kylix at the Metropolitan Museum of Art (now returned to Italy). The museum asserts that the vase was assembled from sherds acquired over nearly twenty years thanks to the expertise of researchers. In contrast, some scholars contend that the reassembled work is the result of the intentional scattering of pieces into sales over a period of years to evade notice, later "surprisingly" reassembled. The authors, in reference to the museum's position, cite researchers' ability to match pieces from "a universe of orphaned shards" (Bowley and Mashberg 2023).

2. In contrast to that narrow usage, a very broad use of the term "orphan" refers to any ancient object lacking findspot data (Leventhal and Daniels 2013: 342). Gill and Chippindale cite this use of the term by Getz-Preziosi, who states, "To me, an orphaned Cycladic idol is just as much an orphan whether it surfaced in 1874 or 1974..." (Getz-Preziosi, cited in Gill and Chippindale 1993: 612). Despite their critique of her usage and the modern "burden" it carries, directing the reader to think of the Cycladic sculpture as an individual person (Gill and Chippindale 1993: 657), Chippindale and Gill themselves employ this terminology in their later influential article on unprovenienced Classical antiquities. They refer to works that have no "declared or credible findspots," as orphans, or more poignantly, "orphans without history" (Chippindale and Gill 2000: 463; see also 500). John Henry Merryman follows suit, calling objects lacking documentation "orphans" (2005: 29).

3. The third definition refers to objects in private collections that museums do not acquire because they lack documentation back to 1970. This usage is related to the adoption of the 1970 rule and was the impetus behind the changes to the AAMD guidelines in 2013, both discussed above (Leventhal and Daniels 2013: 347). Works that might have been offered as gifts by collectors to museums could not be accepted, as per the 2008 AAMD guidelines, if they lacked the 1970 documentation. Unacquirable, they were therefore "orphans" (Cultural Policy Research Institute, 2009). The 2013 changes in the AAMD guidelines discussed above made it possible for museums to accept those gifts under certain conditions. In her discussion of these issues, Lyons employs the term in this way, defining "orphaned" objects as "undocumented antiquities in public and private collections, acquired since 1970" (Lyons 2009: 432). The 2013 rule change allowing such gifts could be viewed as a way to provide a proper home to an orphan. Elizabeth Marlowe presents a nuanced discussion of the ethics of such an unprovenienced private collection entering a university's possession in a 2022 article; she employs the term "orphans" throughout in reference to the antiquities in question (Marlowe 2022).

4. There is another usage related to museum collections. Janet Ulph defines orphans as "objects in museum collections where legal title is uncertain" (2017: 3). She goes on to define "orphan

collections" in museums as those objects that museums "cannot confidently say that they own" (Ulph 2017). This usage is paralleled in discussions of copyright, where the term "orphans" is commonly used to refer to works for which the copyright owner cannot be identified or located (Burri 2014; Hansen et al. 2013).

5. Related to the notion of lacking title, the term may be used in reference to a collection of archaeological materials without a clear owner. An archaeological collection is "orphaned" when it is abandoned by its owner or loses curatorial support (Voss 2012: 147). Barbara Voss's discussion of orphaned collections points to the ethical need for archaeology, as a field, to take more responsibility for the stewardship of already-excavated objects, as opposed to putting the lion's share of resources into new excavations. Her advocacy for a more active and engaged relationship between scholars and existing collections, even those that were divorced from study and care at some point in the past, is echoed in Van de Ven's call for a more critical and active engagement with archives (this volume).

That the term is used in at least five different ways makes evident that it lacks clarity and precision. Among these five different usages of the term "orphan," the fourth gains legitimacy from its connection to usage in the copyright realm, though perhaps given the range of ways "orphan" has been used for antiquities, scholars might do well to avoid it. The fifth usage makes good sense and has a bibliography associated with it, particular in the Society for American Archaeology (SAA), as outlined in Voss (Voss 2012: 147–48). It is the first, second, and third definition that are the focus of this chapter.

The first usage is quite narrow and the associated issues have been well-explored by Leventhal and Daniels; nevertheless, the 2023 study of the Makron kylix, cited above, demonstrates how the term is still injected into controversial cases, potentially eliciting an emotional bias. It is in the space of the second and third usage that we find the most trouble, however. Broadly speaking, some archaeologists are using "orphan" to mean

any unprovenienced work, while some museum professionals are using it to mean a select group of works lacking a provenance prior to 1970 and also, in their view, in need of an institutional "home." Below, I refer to these as the "archaeological usage" and the "museum usage," though only as a shorthand for the purpose of this discussion, not to further the division. These two groups have more shared goals than differences. I argue that the term "orphan" should be avoided, both because of the conflicting definitions and the unnecessary burden on discourse of the emotional weight of the word.

The poignancy of the term bears discussion. Gill and Chippindale pointed to the emotional power of the word "orphan" in their influential study of Cycladic figures, noting that our sense of orphans as little lost souls affects how we view objects referred to as such (1993: 657, as cited in Leventhal and Daniels 2013: 5). There is tension in this topic. There are stakes. How we treat orphans is a measure of what kind of society we have and what kind of people we are. Then-director of the Metropolitan Museum of Art, Philippe de Montebello, used that reasoning to question the motives of archaeologists who would deny him the opportunity to acquire undocumented works, asking, "would these… archaeologists abandon a shivering orphan child on a cold rainy day in the street or would they look for an orphanage?" (de Montebello 2006, cited in Leventhal and Daniels 2013: 8). Marlowe cites a similar, more recent example of a colleague angrily saying "archaeologists don't care about orphans!" (Marlowe 2022: 33).

Archaeologists, trying to protect sites, and museum professionals, trying to properly curate objects, are all interested in stewardship. Yet by leveraging the term "orphan," these positions become antagonistic and suggest both blame and callousness. In fact, my own interest in the topic arose when I used the term "orphan" in a discussion on provenance at the annual meetings of the AIA in Toronto in 2017. A museum professional sharply rebuked me because I was following the archaeological usage, referring to broadly unprovenienced works, and she preferred the narrower museum definition, referring to unprovenienced works outside of museum collections. The emotional power of the term, and the desire to control its use, was perhaps at the root of that dispute. Both usages are emotionally manipulative, even if not consciously intended as such. Progress will not be made when discussions are shut down by emotionally charged terminology.

In both of these usages—works lacking provenience no matter their date of acquisition, or works outside of public collections lacking documentation to 1970—objects are personified into orphans, a transference that invokes an emotional response of pathos and outrage. Pathos because orphans are to be pitied, and outrage because orphans should have proper families and not be left uncared for. The term *orphan* brings with it this emotional baggage. In the archaeological usage, the pathos is directed toward the object and the archaeological context hurt by the act of looting and the outrage at the destructive act of looting and subsequent sale. Implicitly blamed is anyone complicit with the sale. In the museum usage, the pathos is again for the object, though not the archaeological context; the implication is that the damage is done, but the poor orphan can still find a home. The outrage, if any, is directed implicitly toward the ethics guidelines that make it challenging for museums to be proper stewards of the objects. Again, I do not accuse individuals of intentional emotional manipulation. I argue that the term itself generates feelings of pathos and outrage. The shift of terminology from unprovenienced, ungrounded, or looted to *orphaned* anthropomorphizes objects. Worse, it anthropomorphizes them as victims of human neglect. It renders emotional a situation that is better treated by an objective, transparent, and thorough description of the state of affairs.

If we abandon the term "orphan," and its concomitant anthropomorphizing and emotional baggage, stakeholders, whether representing archaeological or institutional priorities, could work more effectively towards solutions that prioritize stewardship. In other words, we could focus on the question of how to most ethically and effectively treat unprovenienced archaeological

objects while also discouraging further looting. This is a problem that people on all sides of the issue have a common interest in solving.

ETHICS, AND WAYS FORWARD

In the Museum

"Prioritizing stewardship of the past" is, I argue, the ethical goal in the context of this discussion. And as argued above, it is a goal shared by most stakeholders (though see Hamilakis 2007: 27–28 for alternative perspectives). The desire to properly care for and steward ancient objects may lie behind an institution's desire to circumvent the 1970 rule and acquire a work lacking proper documentation, so it is not lost to a private collection. Is that stewardship of the past, however, if it perpetuates the market for looted objects? I have long argued that the many exceptions in our various professional ethical codes, whether pertaining to cuneiform tablets or museum acquisitions, are loopholes that allow looting to continue (Costello 2012). Alex W. Barker confirms that the scale of looting is only increasing, despite the half-century since the UNESCO accord and the changes in practices that it spurred (Barker 2018: 456). Have too many concessions been made to coin collectors, epigraphers, museum directors, and other devotees of ancient objects (Elkins 2008; Gill 2020)? "Saving" this object or that object, individually, can contribute to much broader archaeological destruction. If our ethical position is that we should be stewards of the past, then in some cases, we must leave works uncurated and unstudied. Reed explores in detail the decision process and due diligence that a museum should undertake before acquiring a work of antiquity, to ensure that the piece is not looted or fake (Reed 2021: 229–34); these are important guidelines. And when in doubt, when there is a chance that the acquisition would defy the purpose of the ethical guidelines (even if a loophole allows it), the work should not be acquired.

I would apply this same no-holes logic to the proposal that works that don't meet the AAM/AAMD guidelines could be acquired, instead, by a university museum for research purposes. Marlowe makes a nuanced argument in favor of such a solution, arguing that it is preferable to the works going to a private auction, or even to a market of last resort such as Ebay if the reputable auction houses refused. A purchase by a university could keep a collection intact, better preserving the objects' provenance. In a university museum, students can engage in provenance research and other forms of object-based learning (Marlowe 2022). While there is much of value in this idea, I maintain that it punctures yet one more hole in the ethical policies that are intended to slow the traffic in antiquities, and therefore is untenable.

While the "bright line" established by the 1970 UNESCO Convention is a critical benchmark in policies regarding acquisitions of new works by museums and scholarly publications, it is not enough. Whether provenance goes back to 1968 or 1975, the problem is essentially the same: if we do not know the details of the findspot, then it is possible that an archaeological context was destroyed in the acquisition of the work, or that the work is a forgery (and would therefore contribute to a false version of history). Even if a work has provenance information prior to 1970, a museum is not necessarily "safe" in acquiring it. As Lyons points out through examples of restitution cases, when there is clear evidence that a work was stolen prior to 1970, restitution can and should proceed; "there is no statute of limitation" (Lyons 2009: 425). Brian Rose makes a similar point when discussing the repatriation agreement in the case of the Trojan Gold at the Penn Museum (Rose 2021: 251–54). For works that are already in museum collections, an emphasis on both provenance and provenience is critical, no matter when the work was acquired. The possibility that a work might be looted or a forgery should be acknowledged if the findspot is unknown, no matter when the work was acquired. Many museums publish or display the presumed place of origin of a work, but do not reveal how that conclusion was drawn—through archaeological records, the report of a dealer, or connoisseurship. Including that information should be standard practice (Van de Ven and Costello 2024). Increasingly, institutions are us-

ing their websites and chat labels in the galleries to provide more information about provenance and provenience. More attention to provenance research can strengthen the museum's ability to share the full stories of the works in their collections with the public (e.g., Reed 2021).

Marlowe's (2016a) article on provenance makes a strong case for more transparency in the study and display of all archaeological material, whether recently acquired or not. She argues for a straightforward labeling of archaeological objects in museums as either having a secure findspot (she uses the term "grounded") or lacking one ("ungrounded"). In her proposal, a work that is "said to be from..." or "probably from..." a place would lose that uncertain affinity and be labeled as "findspot unknown" (2016a: 224). Such definitive clarity makes it less likely that inaccurate conclusions about regional style, chronology, or even authenticity would be drawn from the uncertain or unconfirmed findspot.

Treating all objects with such transparency is one answer to the question of how best to manage works that are currently in museum collections, but which are looted or lack a findspot for some other reason. Transparency about the missing findspot foregrounds the problem: it makes clear that much is lost when works are looted, or changed hands illicitly post-excavation, or any number of complex—and interesting—ways that works moved across borders and into public collections. Such transparency can bring the issue of looting to the attention of the public, raising awareness of the global problem of the destruction of cultural heritage. It also clarifies the process of the production of knowledge: the public becomes more aware of where artifacts come from and how "the museum" knows their histories. Such an approach is critical at a time like this when calls for social justice are reaching into all corners of our lives. The public should not be placed in a subaltern position in a museum, allowed only a small, carefully curated peephole into the world of an object. There are myriad ways to provide a fuller picture.

When repatriation is called for, cultural memoranda of understanding (MOUs) between institutions and source countries present a means of moving beyond strict concepts of ownership and towards stewardship as a goal; such arrangements can allow for mutually beneficial repatriation of works to their source countries, while the partner institution gains something in return, such as other objects for exhibition (Lyons 2014). As Lyons explains, "More than just a quid pro quo exchange of objects to place in vitrines, arrangements that provide a basis for long-term, open-ended partnerships are the most fruitful. These may entail loan exhibitions, conservation treatment and training, publications, inventory, and data exchanges, all of which should aim to enhance understanding, expertise, and public enjoyment" (Lyons 2009: 426). Successful examples abound; Rose details such an arrangement made between the Penn Museum and Turkey (Rose 2021: 251–54). Museums cannot rely on a pre-1970 provenance as security against repatriation and therefore should be prepared to negotiate creatively for solutions that find good results for the works in question and for the global community.

Works lacking the 1970 documentation required for purchase by a museum face an uncertain fate. Ideally, they would be forfeited by law as stolen property and returned to their place of origin. Such legal action is challenging, however, since it typically requires proof of ownership, which may not exist. Brodie and Renfrew discuss "repositories of last resort," as defined in the International Council of Museums (ICOM) Code of Ethics as a potential solution (Brodie and Renfrew 2005: 351; ICOM). Restitution is implied; someone must purchase the work, then return it to the locality of its origin. An example of this type of "safe haven" restitution would be the purchase of the Byzantine Frescos by the Menil Foundation; they were purchased to "rescue" them from the art market, but the purchase was done with the agreement of the Republic of Cyprus. After residing temporarily in Houston, Texas, the frescoes were returned to Cyprus (Kersel 2021: 268–69).

The case of the Cypriot frescoes and the Menil Foundation, unfortunately, stands out for its exceptionality. Many works may not find their way to such a safe haven. It should also be noted that in the case of the frescoes, the market was still rewarded, and so by the logic I have been advocating here, further looting was potentially encouraged. The "safe haven" notion is therefore inherently flawed. Unfortunately, I think we must accept a measure of loss: there will be objects that cannot be purchased or returned and may be lost to a private collection or storage unit indefinitely.

In Scholarship

Just as museums can present a fuller picture of provenance and provenience, scholars can employ a similar approach in their scholarship, highlighting the gaps in our knowledge about an object. I have advocated for the "object biography" approach as one solution to the problem of how to find meaning in looted objects while foregrounding the problems associated with their lost context. Rather than emphasizing a single moment in the history of an object, object biography addresses the long history of a work, from its creation through the various phases of its use, to its deposition, excavation, and modern provenance (e.g., Costello 2021; Costello, Davis and Hopkins 2021; Gill 2012; Marlowe 2020: 324; Joyce 2012; Chippindale and Gill 2000: 467–68). While some of that information may not be available, the approach encourages consideration of the full history and acknowledgement of the gaps in the story. It could be argued that object biography anthropomorphizes ancient works, something I warn against above with the use of the term "orphan." To avoid anthropomorphizing and adding an emotional imperative to the analysis, the object biography model should be applied only in the sense that we allow the object's history to be viewed as a long, complex history, with many moments of meaning and many active engagements with other subjects.

Our recent project attempted just that: a transparent presentation of works in a museum, together with scholarship that foregrounds missing information about objects that were looted at some point in the past (Hopkins, Costello and Davis 2021). The Collections Analysis Collaborative at the Menil Collection in Houston, Texas, gathered scholars, museum professionals, and students to focus new attention on the museum's collection of antiquities from the Mediterranean, most of which lack provenience. In the newly-installed galleries, curator Paul R. Davis has maintained the museum's policy of minimal labeling, while also reporting more faithfully the unknown provenience and modern interventions for certain works, through brief indications on the label. The project's publication provides much more information about the pieces, using object biography to tell a fuller story of the works than one often sees reflected in catalogs. The chapters dedicated to objects from the collection foreground the information missing as a result of looting and the art market, yet still tell fascinating tales about the other chapters in the lives of the objects, from likely ancient contexts, to excavation information, to modern provenance histories (Hopkins, Costello and Davis 2021).

Scholars should adhere to the ethical guidelines of our professional organizations, of course; it is incumbent upon us to be familiar with them and abide by the spirit of the intent as well as the letter of it. These guidelines are not enough, however; as noted above, more discussion of provenance and findspot (or the lack of findspot) is urgently needed in our work, no matter when the work surfaced. Discussion of artifacts should include provenance and provenience information as a matter of course. Marlowe tries to guide scholars more carefully through the "grey area" by constructing several "decision trees" for publication (Marlowe 2016b: 263–65). These raise questions such as the trustworthiness of a reported findspot, previous publication, and any paper trail.

Archaeologists and the Public

Ideally, ancient objects should have their stories presented to the public. Scholars and museum professionals have an ethical responsibility to share their research, to share the stories of ancient works, sites, and histories. Archaeology is destructive, which is why good record-keeping is so critical. But records that go unread might as well not be written. Archaeological reports

should not be written only with other scholars as an intended audience; these results should be shared with a wider public, emcompassing museum-goers, students, enthusiasts, tourists, and collectors. In our classrooms, public lectures, and publications, educators must talk about the problems of looting and the connections to the art market. As Marlowe points out, most students do not encounter a museum studies course (Marlowe 2022: 32), but they are likely to take a course in history, archaeology, art history, anthropology, or classics. These courses present an opportunity to increase awareness of the problems inherent to the antiquities market.

This is not a museum problem. It is an archaeology problem; the sites we work at, our data, and the heritage we are committed to protect is what is at stake. As professionals in our field, we must educate and advocate—in museums, university and K-12 classrooms; in our home and in our fieldwork locales; in our academic publications; through public lectures and writing aimed at a broader public; and etc.—in order to educate a wide public about the damage wrought by looting and its connection to the antiquities market.

Acknowledgements

I wrote the initial draft of this chapter with the support of Faculty Development Leave from the University of Houston-Clear Lake. I am grateful to conversations and communications with Sarah Lepinski, John Hopkins, Paul Davis, Joseph Newland, Annelies Van de Ven, Elizabeth Marlowe, and David Gill, as well as the panel of the "Defining Provenance" session of ASOR 2022, all of whom helped me shape my thoughts. Alexis Castor and two anonymous reviewers offered helpful comments. Writing during the initial phases of the Covid-19 pandemic of 2020 was challenging and I thank Leo, James, and Connor for their support and patience. I also appreciate the librarians at the Neumann Library at UHCL, who continued to provide services such as ILL during those months of shutdown.

REFERENCES

Archaeological Institute of America (AIA)
Policies. https://www.archaeological.org/about/ governance/policies/

American Schools of Oriental Research (ASOR)
ASOR policy on professional conduct. http://www. asor.org/about-asor/policies/policy-on-professional-conduct/

Association of Art Museum Directors
2013   Guidelines on the Acquisition of Archaeological Material and Ancient Art (revised 2013). https://aamd.org/sites/default/files/ document/Guidelines%20on%20the%20 Acquisition%20of%20Archaeological%20 Material%20and%20Ancient%20Art%20 revised%202013_0.pdf

Barker, A. W
2018   Looting, the Antiquities Trade, and Competing Valuations of the Past. *Annual Review of Anthropology* 47: 455–74.

Bell, M.
2016   Notes on Marlowe's "What We Talk about When We Talk about Provenance." *International Journal of Cultural Property* 23: 254–56.

Bowley, G., and Mashberg, T.
2023   The Kylix Marvel: Why Experts Distrust the Story of an Ancient Cup's Rebirth. *New York Times*, 19 April 2023. https:// www.nytimes.com/2023/04/19/arts/kylix-cup-greek-metropolitan-museum.html? smtyp=cur&smid=tw-nytimesarts

Brodie, N., and Renfrew, C.
2005   Looting and The World's Archaeological Heritage: The Inadequate Response. *Annual Review of Anthropology* 34.1: 343–61.

Burri, M.
2014   Global Cultural Law and Policy in the Age of Ubiquitous Internet. *International Journal of Cultural Property* 21: 349–64.

Chippindale, C., and Gill, D. W. J.
2000   Material Consequences of Contemporary Classical Collecting. *American Journal of Archaeology* 104: 463–511.

Coggins, C. C.
1998   United States Cultural Property Legislation: Observations of a Combatant. *International Journal of Cultural Property* 7: 57.

Costello, S. K.
2012   Defining Principles, Determining Value. Paper presented at the Annual Meeting of ASOR, Chicago, IL.
2021   "Who was King? Who was not King?" (Re)Writing the Biography of a Votive Figure. Pp. 29–44 in *Object Biographies: Collaborative Approaches to Ancient Mediterranean Art*, ed. J. N. Hopkins, S. K. Costello and P. R. Davis. New Haven, CT: Yale University.

Costello, S. K.; Davis, P. R.; and Hopkins, J. N.
2021   Introduction: The Long Biographies of Ancient Objects. Pp. 1–28 in *Object Biographies: Collaborative Approaches to Ancient Mediterranean Art*, ed. J. N. Hopkins, S. K. Costello and P. R. Davis. New Haven, CT: Yale University.

Cultural Policy Research Institute
2009   Project on Unprovenanced Ancient Objects in Private US Hands. Research Study #1. November 10, 2009. https://sites. google.com/a/cprinst.org/www/Home/ issues/project-on-unprovenanced-ancient-objects-in-private-us-hands

de Montebello, P.
2006   Public Lecture at the National Press Club: Museums and Cultural Property, 17 April, 2006).

Elkins, N. T.
2008   A Survey of the Material and Intellectual Consequences of Trading in Undocumented Ancient Coins: A Case Study on the North American Trade. *Frankfurter elektronische Rundschau zur Altertumskunde* 7: 1–13.

Gerstenblith, P.
2013   The Meaning of 1970 for the Acquisition of Archaeological Objects, *Journal of Field Archaeology* 38.4: 364–73.

Gill, D. W. J.
2012   The Material and Intellectual Consequences of Acquiring the Sarpedon Krater. Pp. 25–42 in *All the King's Horses: Essays on the Impact of Looting and the Illicit Antiquities Trade on our Knowledge of the Past*, ed. P. K. Lazrus and A. W. Barker. Washington DC: Society for American Archaeology.
2022   Context Matters: Fragmented Athenian Cups. *Journal of Art Crime* 27: 77–84.

Gill, D. W. J. and Chippindale, C.
1993   Material and Intellectual Consequences of Esteem for Cycladic Figures. *American Journal of Archaeology* 97: 601–59.

Hamilakis, Y.
2007   Archaeology and Capitalism: From Ethics to Politics. Pp. 15–40 in *Archaeology and Capitalism: From Ethics to Politics*, ed. Y. Hamilakis and P. Duke. Walnut Creek, CA: Taylor & Francis.

Hansen, D. R.; Hinze, G.; Hashimoto, K.; Samuelson, P.; and Urban, J. M
2013   Solving the Orphan Works Problem for the United States. *Columbia Journal of Law & the Arts* 37: 1.

Hopkins, J. N.; Costello, S. K.; and Davis, P. R. (eds.)
2021   *Object Biographies: Collaborative Approaches to Ancient Mediterranean Art*. New Haven, CT: Yale University.

International Council of Museums (ICOM)
2004   Code of Ethics for Museums. Paris: ICOM.

Joyce, R. A.
2012   From Place to Place: Provenience, Provenance, and Archaeology. Pp. 48–60 in *Provenance: An Alternate History of Art*, ed. G. Feigenbaum and I. Reist. Los Angeles: Getty Research Institute.

Kersel, M.
2021   Telling Stories of Objects. Pp. 261–72 in *Object Biographies: Collaborative Approaches to Ancient Mediterranean Art*, ed. J. N. Hopkins, S. K. Costello and P. R. Davis. New Haven, CT: Yale University.
2023   Innocents Abroad? The Consumption of Antiquities from the Holy Land. *Journal of Ancient Judaism* 14.2: 263–90.

Leventhal, R. M., and Daniels, B. I.
2013   "Orphaned Objects", Ethical Standards, and the Acquisition of Antiquities, *DePaul Journal of Art, Technology & Intellectual Property* 23: 2, 1–34.

Lyons, C.
2009   Museums as Sites of Reconciliation. Pp. 421–32 in *Cultural Heritage Issues: The Legacy of Conquest, Colonization, and Commerce*, ed. J. A. R. Nafziger and A. M. Nicgorski. Leiden: Nijhoff.
2014   Thinking about Antiquities: Museums and Internationalism. *International Journal of Cultural Property* 21.3: 251–65.
2016   On Provenance and the Long Lives of Antiquities. *International Journal of Cultural Property* 23: 245–53.

Marlowe, E.
2016a   What we Talk about when we Talk about Provenance: A Response to Chippindale and Gill. *International Journal of Cultural Property* 23: 217–36.
2016b   Response to responses to "What we Talk about when we Talk about Provenance." *International Journal of Cultural Property* 23: 257–66.
2020   The Reinstallation of the Getty Villa: Plenty of Beauty but Only Partial Truth. *American Journal of Archaeology* 124.2: 321–32.
2022   Orphan Antiquities at Kenyon College: The Lessons of the Harris Bequest. *Peregrinations: Journal of Medieval Art and Architecture* 8.1: 26–40.

Merryman, J. H.
2005   Cultural Property Internationalism. *International Journal of Cultural Property* 12: 11–39.

Norman, N. J.
2005   Editorial Policy on the Publication of Recently Acquired Antiquities. *American Journal of Archaeology* 109: 135–36.

O'Keefe, P. J.
1997   *Trade in Antiquities: Reducing Destruction and Theft.* London: Archetype; Paris: UNESCO.

Porada, E.
1950   A Leonine Figure of the Protoliterate Period of Mesopotamia." *Journal of the American Oriental Society* 70.4: 223.

Reed, V.
2021   Collecting Antiquities since 2008: A Look at Guidelines and Best Practices for American Museums. Pp. 221–41 in *Object Biographies: Collaborative Approaches to Ancient Mediterranean Art*, ed. J. N. Hopkins, S. K. Costello and P. R. Davis. New Haven, CT: Yale University.

Ulph, J.
2017   Frozen in Time: Orphans and Uncollected Objects in Museum Collections. *International Journal of Cultural Property* 24: 3–30.

United Nations Educational, Scientific and Cultural Organization (UNESCO)
1970   Convention on the Means of Prohibiting and Preventing the Illicit Import, Export and Transfer of Ownership of Cultural Property. Geneva: United Nations Education, Scientific and Cultural Organization. http://portal.unesco.org/en/ev.php-URL_ID=13039&URL_DO=DO_TOPIC&URL_SECTION=201.html

Van de Ven, A., and Costello, S. K.
2024   Provenance inconnu and other stories: developing engaging labels for ancient history collections. *Museums and Society* 22.1: 158–73.

Watson, P., and Todeschini, C.
2006   *The Medici Conspiracy: The Illicit Journey of Looted Antiquities from Italy's Tomb Raiders to the World's Greatest Museums.* New York: Public Affairs.

Witmore, C., and Harmanşah, Ö.
2007   The Endangered Future of the Past. *The New York Times*, 21 Dec. 2007. https://www.nytimes.com/2007/12/21/opinion/21iht-edwhitmore.html

Chapter 7

Museumification and Demuseumification of Sacred Sites in Turkey

Practices and Politics of Archaeology, Heritage, and Faith

Tuğba Tanyeri-Erdemir

ABSTRACT

In this chapter, I investigate the museumification of religious heritage sites, looking at the challenges of these processes from the perspectives of site preservation, religious practice, identity politics, and state sectarianism. I compare three case studies from Turkey: Hagia Sophia Museum, Soumela Monastery, and Akhtamar Church.

All three sites are iconic for the various faith communities that lay claims on them, and one or more faith communities have demands to use these four historical heritage sites, administered as museums by the Turkish state, for religious worship. A comparative analysis of these three cases reveals a hidden sectarian logic that shapes the Turkish government's differential treatment of sacred heritage sites and various faith communities that lay claims on them. While site preservation concerns are often a key component of public discourse around museum practices, sectarian underpinnings of policy and practice are rarely articulated or revealed. For archaeologists and museum professionals, balancing conflicting demands of religious freedom, site preservation, and sectarian politics poses unique professional and moral challenges, as they are forced to navigate conflict-ridden encounters between often antagonistic stakeholders.

By presenting a comparative analysis of these three cases of religious heritage sites, I explore complications and shortcomings of the current heritage regime. How do we mediate archaeological heritage, religion and the public, including local, national, and global stakeholders? What kind of challenges do the dual practices of heritage and faith present for fostering inclusivity and equality? Through these questions I explore the ethical responsibility of scholars in the fields of archaeology, heritage management, and museology and call for more policy literacy and religious literacy.

INTRODUCTION

Sites of religious heritage, such as churches, mosques, synagogues, and temples of any historical era are part of what we study as archaeologists. Some of these ancient sites continue to be sacred for existing communities and are revered by multiple groups, sometimes in competition and conflict with each other. Furthermore, religious, ethnic, and class hierarchies in any given country determine who owns and controls these sites, who can access them, and how they are interpreted. In this chapter, I examine how heritage policy is put to use for exclusivist and discriminatory purposes through museumification and demuseumification processes at sacred sites in Turkey. In so doing, I highlight ethical responsibilities for scholars and practitioners as well as caveats on work in contested sacred sites more generally.

Museumification and demuseumification of religious heritage sites pose significant ethical challenges for practitioners in the fields of archaeology, art and architectural history, and museum and heritage studies. Balancing demands of worship and devotion with heritage management requirements at sacred sites is one of the most important challenges. Another challenge is the changing dynamics of power and hierarchies at these sites. All these factors have significant impact on the people who use the sites and/or have an emotional bond with them. They also have an impact on the work of the professionals who take on the responsibility of protecting the sites.

While working on ancient sacred sites, our ethical responsibilities are two-fold. On the one hand, our foremost responsibility is to ensure the protection of these sites for future generations. Designating sacred sites as museums and heritage sites grants them legal protection and enables us to develop effective long term heritage management plans. On the other hand, we have a responsibility for contemporary users, such as local communities, domestic and international tourists, and globally dispersed diasporas that continue to have an emotional attachment to the site. These different groups of users may have different, and

at times clashing, interpretations of what the site is and how it should be used. Of those who regard the site as a sacred space, some may wish to revere the site but may be limited in their access. In most cases our dual responsibilities to the site itself and its users may be in conflict.

Museumification of sacred sites can take place in different formats. For instance, an archaeologically excavated prehistoric sacred site may have long lost its worship function. In such cases, turning the site into a museum/heritage site may take place without conflict. In some cases, the site may either obtain a new contemporary religious interpretation (like Göbeklitepe in southeastern Turkey), or it may continue to carry deep sentimental value for various faith communities (like Stonehenge in the United Kingdom). A functioning historic religious site may turn into a museum, which may abruptly end ritual activities (like Hagia Sophia in Istanbul, Turkey). Turning a functioning worship hall into a museum often entails a change of legal ownership of the site. Unless the religious site is turned into a museum by the faith communities themselves, the ownership of the site is transferred to the state or another party designated by those in power. In most cases, access to sites becomes limited and controlled through museum or heritage authorities and related government agencies.

The process of museumification often means that curators, restorers, conservators, and heritage specialists will take the necessary measures to protect, curate, and manage the site and its components, either limiting or preventing worship practices at sacred sites. As such, the site's sacredness and ritual practices become part of the curatorial narrative. This narrative may exclude or partially conceal the history of the site depending on the specific political context of museumification, and whether the community/communities that have a connection to the site are part of the group in power or whether they are subjugated.

The reverse process of demuseumification, where formerly museumified sites reopen as places of worship, can be equally problematic. Demuseumification often brings about a significant change in heritage management practices.

Once the historic site reopens as a functioning worship hall, the increased visitor traffic and the lack of specialized personnel to monitor and maintain the site have a detrimental effect on the long-term management and protection of the site. Although these are the most critical issues, there are also other aspects to consider, especially for sites with multiple layers and histories of conflict and contestation. In these instances, museumification may offer a balance in which contested identities of the site may be recognized, and thus may contribute to an inclusive interpretation and utilization of the site.

In both museumification and demuseumification of sacred sites, social hierarchies and power structures determine the change in the function of the sites. It is crucial that we are aware of these power structures and how they affect the lives of current and future generations. Ethical challenges are further heightened when the heritage sites in question were built by communities who are marginalized and vulnerable minorities within polities that now control these monuments. Further complications arise in the cases where control of and access to such heritage sites are contested by different stakeholders following forced conversion, destruction, and abandonment (Prodromou 2020; Tanyeri-Erdemir 2016). While we need to be aware of local sensitivities throughout our work, we also need to operate within the framework of our discipline and maintain an awareness that our research and fieldwork may deepen existing societal cleavages and feed into conflict.

Heritage work has always been implicated in power dynamics among states, heritage practitioners, and other stakeholders, including competing constituencies with various claims to heritage sites. International heritage organizations such as UNESCO are also part of these dynamics (Meskell 2018). Within that framework, heritage can be utilized to strengthen government hegemony and legitimize its policies and practices. Laurajane Smith, in her discussion of heritage practices and how they affect subaltern and indigenous groups' rights, highlights the necessity of "a critical and engaged understanding of the power and authority of competing heritage discourses, and

the relative power and authority that underpins them" (Smith 2006: 38). As such, I contend that it is an ethical responsibility and necessity of practitioners of archaeology, museums, and heritage to be aware of competing heritage discourses, the political context, and how they affect living populations.

Based on a survey of the power dynamics shaping the Turkish government's heritage practices at Hagia Sophia (Istanbul), the Surp Khach Cathedral (Van), and the Soumela Monastery (Trabzon), I argue that museumification and demuseumification processes reinforce religious hierarchies between dominant Muslim majority and minority Christian communities in Turkey while also tokenizing Christian heritage as part of the Turkish government's efforts to deflect criticism through spectacles and performances of tolerance (Erdemir 2019; 2021). In so doing, I demonstrate the caveats of working on museumified and demuseumified sacred sites. Through this analysis, I highlight the importance of our awareness of political contexts in which we operate as heritage professionals, and I exemplify cautionary elements of working ethically with sacred sites and their faith communities.

Hagia Sophia: Demuseumified and Reconquered

The Hagia Sophia of Istanbul/Constantinople is arguably one of the most impressive and politically-charged buildings in history. It also has a complicated and contested history. Justinian I built it as an imperial church to epitomize his power in the sixth century CE. In 1453, Ottoman Sultan Mehmet II converted it into a mosque after his conquest of Constantinople as a potent symbol of his rule and the domination of Islam over Christianity, and of Turks over Byzantines. Mustafa Kemal Atatürk, the founder of the Republic of Turkey, transformed Hagia Sophia into a museum in 1934, in part out of a commitment to build a secular polity of equal citizens and to promote peaceful relations with the West. In so doing, he assured the preservation of Hagia Sophia with its multi-layered Christian and

Muslim pasts, while also contributing to defusing interfaith tensions by protecting this monument in the form of a museum as humanity's common heritage (Katipoğlu and Caner-Yüksel 2010; Nelson 2004). UNESCO inscribed Hagia Sophia on its World Heritage List in 1984 due to its outstanding universal value.[1]

On July 10, 2020, Turkey's Council of State annulled the 1934 decree of the Cabinet of Ministers transforming Hagia Sophia into a museum (Gall 2020). A few hours after the announcement of the verdict, Turkish President Recep Tayyip Erdoğan appeared on television announcing the conversion of the Hagia Sophia Museum into Ayasofya Mosque.[2] Two weeks later, Erdoğan attended the first Friday prayer, officially consecrating and redefining the monument as a functioning mosque.

Although this was a shock to the international community, various developments taking place in the decades leading to Hagia Sophia's demuseumification had already displayed the exclusivist and discriminatory logic of Turkey's heritage framework, which prioritized the Ottoman past of Hagia Sophia as a mosque over the monument's Christian and secular histories that preceded and followed it, respectively. On the following pages, I will present a review of Hagia Sophia's transition(s) from mosque to museum, and from museum to mosque.

The Hagia Sophia Museum

In 1934, after serving as an Ottoman imperial mosque for almost 500 years, and a Byzantine imperial church for a millennium before that, Hagia Sophia became a museum. This transition marked the cessation of its religious use, and it became an internationally renowned museum. Although the museumification process secularized the space, Hagia Sophia continued to be revered both by Muslims and Christians.

1　https://whc.unesco.org/en/list/356/ (accessed 10 December 2020).

2　https://www.tccb.gov.tr/haberler/410/120583/-insanligin-ortak-mirasi-olan-ayasofya-yeni-statusuyle-herkesi-kucaklamaya-cok-daha-samimi-cok-daha-ozgun-sekilde-devam-edecektir- (accessed 4 December 2020).

The museumification of Hagia Sophia entailed physical and operational changes at the site. As a mosque, it was open to the public for 24 hours, and especially for the five Islamic daily prayer times. Colorful carpets covered the marble floor, and the figural mosaics of the church were covered with plaster. Thomas Whittemore, an American scholar and the founder of the Byzantine Institute of America, was appointed by the Turkish Government for the task of restoring the edifice. His team meticulously uncovered the brilliant Byzantine mosaics. Carpets were removed to display the marble floors of the Byzantine church. Once Hagia Sophia became a museum it was only accessible during designated hours each day and visitors were now required to purchase a ticket.

Hagia Sophia's museumification in 1934 was part of a secularizing and modernizing set of reforms that followed the fall of the Ottoman Empire (Katipoğlu and Caner-Yüksel 2010). It was a potent political move marking the ascendancy of the new Turkish Republic. Museumification of Hagia Sophia underlined the monument's universal value and ensured its protection. It was also a way of acknowledging both the Christian-Byzantine and Islamic-Ottoman histories and architectural characteristics of the contested site. Although the Hagia Sophia Museum's curatorial practices never fully embraced the entirety of its multi-layered and contested pasts, the juxtaposition of Byzantine and Ottoman art and architecture presented a sense of coexistence for the complex heritage of the converted building.

The Hagia Sophia Grand Mosque

For Turkish Islamists of the mid-20th century, Hagia Sophia's museumification was a major source of resentment and symbolized a monumental loss. In their view, Hagia Sophia was a conquered edifice of the Muslim sultans and, in its museumified state, it was denied to them (Eldem 2015). These feelings of discontent amongst the ultranationalist and Islamist circles culminated in the demands to reopen Hagia Sophia as a mosque (Azak 2014; Özekmekçi

2012). Although these demands were continuous throughout the 20th century, at the outset they were mostly fringe ideas. They became increasingly mainstream and pronounced in the years following the rise to power of the Islamist-rooted Justice and Development Party (AKP) in 2002 and the ascendancy of its leader Recep Tayyip Erdoğan as the prime minister the following year (Tanyeri-Erdemir 2018). The conversion of Hagia Sophia more than 17 years after his party's rise to power was a defining moment for Erdoğan's rule and, similar to Atatürk's museumification policy, symbolized a turning point for Turkey's identity and its political orientation.

Erdoğan's policies draw from Turkey's Islamist political tradition, Milli Görüş (National Vision). Although his former colleagues, including his former mentor and party leader Necmettin Erbakan, had a very clear position demanding the conversion of Hagia Sophia, Erdoğan's own stance vis-à-vis Hagia Sophia was ambiguous between 2002 and 2019, during which time he never publicly voiced plans to transform the monument's status. In the first decade of his term in office, Erdoğan portrayed himself as a moderate, a Muslim democrat leader similar to European Christian Democrats, who respected rule of law and the rights of religious minorities. Erdoğan's stance changed in 2014, after he became president and consolidated power to an unprecedented level since the establishment of the Turkish Republic in 1923. His new position as president brought him not only greater authority to push his personal agenda but also growing challenges to the legitimacy of his rule.

On the 597th anniversary of the conquest of Constantinople on May 29, 2020, Erdoğan appeared on a giant screen set up in the Hagia Sophia Museum, next to an imam reciting the Conquest Verse from the Quran. Meanwhile, a massive screen in the shape of the land walls of Istanbul was set up outside Hagia Sophia, where crowds watched Erdoğan's spirited speech projected on the canvas walls. This was followed by a visual narration of the conquest of Constantinople, complete with the Ottoman army breaching the fortifications and Mehmet II entering the city and riding his white horse into Hagia Sophia. The recitation of the Conquest Verse, Erdoğan's carefully crafted speech, and the vivid references to the conquest of Constantinople in the visual narrative were clear signs indicating that the conversion of Hagia Sophia was now a possibility (Tanyeri-Erdemir 2020). From the outset, the likelihood of such a conversion was framed around the rhetoric of conquest.

On July 10, six weeks following Erdoğan's conquest spectacle, Turkey's Council of State overturned the 1934 Council of Ministers decree that museumified Hagia Sophia and Erdoğan immediately announced his decision to convert Hagia Sophia into a mosque. In his speech, the Turkish president highlighted how Hagia Sophia's conversion would gratify "the spirit of conquest" of Mehmet II. On July 24, Ali Erbaş, the head of Turkey's Directorate of Religious Affairs, gave the first Friday sermon at Hagia Sophia with a sword at hand, symbolizing an Ottoman tradition of conquest. Such rhetoric and posturing risked branding Turkey's non-Muslim citizens as reconquered subjects, and thereby as second-class citizens (Erdemir and Tanyeri-Erdemir 2020). The conquest rhetoric was particularly distressing for the Greek Orthodox inhabitants of Istanbul, the descendants of the city's Byzantine population, and such a supremacist discourse risks making them targets of hate speech and hate crimes (Romain Örs and Tanyeri-Erdemir 2020).

There are also concerns about how this conversion affects the short- and long-term preservation efforts and site management at Hagia Sophia. The edifice was transformed into a mosque in fourteen days between the July 10 decision of the Council of State and the first prayers at the site on July 24, 2020. This hasty and non-transparent transition did not allow an in-depth analysis by heritage experts to deliberate and discuss minimally intrusive and sustainable solutions.

While international heritage organizations cannot dictate the use of any heritage monument by states, because Hagia Sophia is inscribed on UNESCO's World Heritage List, there are certain preservation and maintenance criteria that the Turkish government is required to comply with

(Ahunbay 2017; 2015). One of these is to consult with UNESCO experts prior to any physical changes to the fabric of the site. The Turkish authorities failed to inform UNESCO of Hagia Sophia's conversion and the physical transformations at the site to accommodate Islamic prayers, despite numerous attempts by UNESCO leadership to open a dialogue.[3] This prompted UNESCO to issue a statement in which its Director-General expressed "deep regrets" concerning the Turkish government's move "made without prior discussion." UNESCO also reminded Turkey that "effective, inclusive and equitable participation of communities and other stakeholders concerned by the property is necessary to preserve this heritage and highlight its uniqueness and significance."[4] UNESCO's interference was of little consequence. As Lynn Meskell's work illustrates, the current structure of UNESCO with representative nation-states, which may be complicit in endangering heritage or oppressing minorities through their actions, is not equipped to effectively engage in actions taken by government authorities (Meskell 2018).

The physical transformation of Hagia Sophia into a functioning mosque also significantly altered the visitor experience of the building. With the Byzantine marble floor covered with wall-to-wall carpets and the figural mosaics concealed behind canvas curtains, the Islamic elements are highlighted at the expense of the Byzantine features. The gradual transformation of the site over the last few decades from a multi-layered monument to one selectively favoring its Islamic past was finalized with the conversion of Hagia Sophia from a secular museum to the Hagia Sophia Grand Mosque.

Since Hagia Sophia started serving as an active worship hall in 2020, there have been numerous reports in the press of damage to the site, such as people breaking off pieces from the ceremonial doors, visitors collecting pieces of frescoes, or damaging a historical Ottoman water basin to use it as a shoe storage. The most concerning ongoing hazard factor is the uncontrolled and increased traffic, contributing significantly to the fast deterioration of this world-renowned sacred heritage site.

Prelude to Hagia Sophia's Conversion: Patterns of Demuseumification

Hagia Sophia's conversion in July 2020 was a major development that attracted global attention. However, this was not the first instance of a museumified monument's conversion into a functioning mosque in Turkey. Three namesakes of the famed Hagia Sophia of Istanbul (Constantinople), namely the Hagia Sophias of İznik (Nicaea), Trabzon (Trebizond), and Vize (Bizye) were also turned into functioning mosques over the last decade (Aykaç 2019). The Hagia Sophias of İznik and Trabzon share very similar histories to the Hagia Sophia of Istanbul. Both were major Byzantine churches, earlier converted into mosques during the Ottoman period, and were later transformed into museums in the 1970s.

The Hagia Sophias of İznik and Trabzon were converted into functioning mosques in 2011 and 2013, respectively. In the case of İznik, the General Directorate of Pious Foundations (GDPF) took the site under its jurisdiction after the site reopened in 2011 following a restoration project that started in 2008 (Aykaç 2019; Ermis 2012). In Trabzon, the GDPF started a legal procedure and brought the case to court, claiming that the Ministry of Culture and Tourism was illegally occupying the edifice. In 2013, the court decided in favor of the GDPF and gave the control of the site to the directorate. In both cases, the former churches—converted into mosques—serving as museums were opened as worship halls for Islamic prayers.

In November 2019, there was yet another alarming development that signaled the future awaiting Hagia Sophia. This was the decision of the Council of State annulling the 1945 Cabinet of Ministers decree that transformed the Kariye Mosque/Chora Church into a museum (Yackley 2019). Like Hagia Sophia, the Byzantine Chora

---

3   https://en.unesco.org/news/unesco-statement-hagia-sophia-istanbul (accessed 4 December 2020).

4   https://en.unesco.org/news/unesco-statement-hagia-sophia-istanbul (accessed 4 December 2020).

Church was converted into the Kariye Mosque after the conquest of Istanbul, and became a museum in the 1940s. The Chora/Kariye Museum is famous for its spectacular late Byzantine mosaics and frescos depicting Biblical scenes. Erdoğan signed the presidential decree to turn Chora/Kariye Museum into a functioning mosque a few months after the conversion of Hagia Sophia, in September 2020.

In all these cases, namely the Hagia Sophias of Istanbul, İznik, Trabzon, and the Chora/Kariye, the conversion from a museum into a mosque was not only a change in function, but also a transfer of jurisdiction between government agencies. As museums, these monuments were listed under the Ministry of Culture and Tourism. As mosques, they are currently under the jurisdiction of the General Directorate of Pious Foundations (GDPF).

The preservation, maintenance, and management of cultural heritage in Turkey has a complicated system governing it, composed of various institutions and bodies, each with a different set of responsibilities and obligations, which may have overlapping areas of control and responsibility (Bonini Baraldi et al. 2013). Historical developments related to the management and control of religious diversity in the early decades following the founding of the Turkish Republic have brought about a particular division of authority and responsibility between the Ministry of Culture and Tourism and the GDPF, two major bodies within the government for listing cultural property and organizing funds for conservation of heritage (Tanyeri-Erdemir 2015).

When a monument is under the jurisdiction of either the Ministry of Culture and Tourism or the GDPF, the overseeing institution is responsible for issuing permissions for conservation and restoration projects. Each institution has its own internal logic and distinctive criteria for classifying monuments. These criteria are best understood when considered alongside the trajectory of the historical developments that brought about the related institutions and how they are formulated to function (Tanyeri-Erdemir 2015). Most ancient and archaeological sites, museums, and the organization of cultural events and func-

tions fall under the domain of the Ministry of Culture and Tourism. The GDPF has a specific area of jurisdiction that encompasses the historic monuments that were parts of the pious endowments during the Ottoman Empire. As such, many sites of religious cultural heritage fall under the control of the GDPF.

The institutional structure of the GDPF represents a significant continuation of the Ottoman system of administration and is therefore based on Sunni-Muslim religio-ideological underpinnings. This has ramifications in terms of how priorities are designated in relation to the preservation of historic religious heritage. For the GDPF, preserving the function of any monument in accordance with its Islamic endowment is a priority. As such, from the perspective and legal reasoning of the GDPF, Byzantine churches that were converted into mosques are to be restored as functioning mosques, regardless of their previous functions.

The particular prioritization and focus of GDPF poses critical challenges from the perspective of preserving multi-layered and converted religious sites because the process of re-conversion of such multi-layered sites results in selective preservation focusing on Islamic features and functions of sites and the neglect and occasional damage to the non-Islamic elements.

Museumification of Christian Heritage

Turkey has a rich Christian heritage. The Greek-Orthodox, Armenian, and Syriac Christian communities lived and built churches, chapels, and monasteries across Turkey. The demographics across Turkey changed following two traumatic event horizons of the early 20th century: the Armenian Genocide of 1915 and the compulsory population exchange between Turkey and Greece in 1923. After the mass killing and deportation of Armenians by the Ottomans in 1915, the Armenian population significantly decreased. A great proportion of Armenian religious structures and complexes across Anatolia were left to decay and became forgotten relics of a once-vibrant Armenian community living under Ottoman rule. Over the century following the Armenian genocide, many of these churches and monastic complexes were destroyed (Mildanoğlu 2012).[5] The compulsory population exchange between Turkey and Greece in 1923 limited the Greek-Orthodox community's presence to Istanbul (Clark 2006; Hirschon 2003). By the end of the first quarter of the 20th century, thousands of Greek Orthodox and Armenian churches, monasteries, and cemeteries in Turkey were left without their faith communities. In the decades to follow, many of these monuments were destroyed by natural elements and through vandalism. Only a handful were designated as heritage sites including the Surp Khach Cathedral in Van and the Soumela Monastery in Trabzon, which were restored by the Turkish Ministry of Culture and opened as museums.

Surp Khach Cathedral on Akhtamar Island, Lake Van

The 10th-century Surp Khach Cathedral (The Cathedral of the Holy Cross) stands on the island of Akhtamar in Lake Van in eastern Turkey. It was built as part of a Medieval Armenian monastic complex (Pogossian and Vardanyan 2019). In 2015, Turkey submitted Akhtamar to be considered for UNESCO's tentative list of World Heritage Monuments.[6]

In the 1990s, Hrant Dink, a Turkish journalist of Armenian descent, envisaged an inclusive and collaborative restoration process that would bring Armenians and Turks together. In his 1997 article, "Ahtamar Amele Taburu" (Ahtamar Labor Battalion), he expressed his belief that the restoration of Akhtamar would bring an opportunity for healing and amends-making if Turkish, Armenian, and Armenian diaspora youth were to work together in this pursuit. In 2007, shortly before he was murdered by a Turkish nationalist, he reiter-

ated his vision and expressed his disappointment in how the Turkish state decided to pursue the museumification of Akhtamar (Dink 2007).

In 2005, the Turkish Ministry of Culture and Tourism started the restoration of Surp Khach Cathedral on Akhtamar, but the project did not proceed as Hrant Dink envisioned. Although the Armenian Patriarchate had been demanding the restoration of Surp Khach for years, the project started without any consultation with the Patriarchate or engagement with the Armenian community living in Turkey. Zakarya Mildanoğlu, a Turkish-Armenian architect, was included as an advisor to the team after the Patriarchate demanded representation of the Armenian community in the project. Hrant Dink thought that the process would bring the countries of Armenia and Turkey together, as equal partners. Although several Armenian experts worked in different parts of the project, it did not turn into a bridge-building exercise.

In 2007, after a lengthy restoration project, the monastic complex was opened as a museum listed under the Ministry of Culture and Tourism. Between 2010 and 2015, the Armenian Patriarchate based in Istanbul was invited by the Turkish government to perform an annual liturgy, which became a major tourist attraction for the region and remains a significant event for globally dispersed Armenians (Över 2016). The liturgies were conducted under the authority, protection, and with the invitation and permission of the Turkish state.

For globally dispersed Armenian descendants of the 1915 genocide, this liturgy was an emotional event. Despite the controversial restoration process and problems with site presentation, this annual ceremony at the Surp Khach Cathedral became an event that fostered intercommunal interactions between Turks and Armenians (Demoyan 2010; Egresi et al. 2012; Kaya et al. 2013). However, as Demoyan and Över point out, the site presentation and the choreography of the annual liturgy perpetuates the idea of Turkey as a "tolerant country," even as Turkish authorities continue to deny the Armenian Genocide (Demoyan 2010; Över 2016). While Akhtamar and

---

5   Zakarya Mildanoğlu identified remnants of 90 surviving religious structures in larger Van region in 2010. Before 1915, there were 218 recorded monasteries and probably more than 500 churches in the area.

6   https://whc.unesco.org/en/tentativelists/6035/ (accessed 19 November 2020).

the annual liturgy at the site bring in significant tourism revenue to the region, the descendants of the Armenian community who built the edifice and have a strong emotional connection to it are no longer part of the local population, and therefore do not benefit from that revenue.

Presentation of information to the visitors at Akhtamar is yet another problematic issue from the perspective of site curation. The site presentation narrative is selective of the historical account and omits critical facts. There are four plaques placed outside each wall of the cathedral illustrating and explaining the visual narrative of the relief sculptures. Upon entry to the Akhtamar Island, there is a panel presenting a short description of the site, its history, and its features. Until 2014, as Turkey's Armenian weekly *Agos* reported, this presentation panel omitted the word "Armenian" and described the site as part of the Medieval Vaspurakan principality (October 31, 2014). In 2014, the panel title was changed to "Akdamar Armenian Church of the Holy Cross." Although this panel offers brief historical details about the date of the site and its utilization, it portrays the site as a Medieval relic and fails to mention that it continued to function under the Ottoman Empire as an Armenian monastery well into the early 20th century, and that it was abandoned after the mass deportation and killing of the region's Armenians in 1915. The lack of a narrative explaining the site as part of the vibrant Armenian population of Van before the genocide is a major grievance for the Armenians.

The museumification of Akthamar and its listing under the Ministry of Culture and Tourism enables the site to be regularly maintained and preserved. Yet the critical issue is the fact that the Armenian community, living in Turkey or in the diaspora, is not part of the decision-making mechanisms defining the function, curatorship, and presentation of the site.

Soumela Monastery, Trabzon

The Holy Monastery of Panagia Soumela, built into a mountain cliff in Trabzon, was a major center of monastic life in the northeastern Black Sea region of Turkey (Bryer and Winfield 1985: 254). In 2000, Turkey submitted Soumela Monastery for the UNESCO World Heritage Sites, and it currently remains under consideration—twenty-two years later.[7] The monastery was one of the wealthiest Christian institutions of the Pontic region until the mass atrocities conducted against the local Greeks in the early 20th century and the compulsory population exchange between Turkey and Greece in 1923 (Bryer and Winfield 1985). Thereafter, Soumela Monastery became one of the thousands of structures left without its community in the aftermath of the population exchange.

In 1972, Soumela Monastery was placed under the protection of the Trabzon Museum and was designated as a heritage site and a museum under the Ministry of Culture and Tourism, and it became one of the most popular tourist attractions of Trabzon. At the time of its designation as a museum, Soumela Monastery/Sümela Museum had been abandoned for decades. Left to decay after 1923, the monastery suffered damage from the elements and vandalism throughout the 20th century. Although the designation of the site as a museum granted it protection, acts of vandalism and decay continued for decades following 1972. Frescoes of Soumela's many chapels were defaced, and uncontrolled visitor access destabilized the site's architecture.

The descendants of displaced Pontic Greeks have a strong emotional connection to Soumela. In 2009, *Haber61*, a local newspaper, reported that a group including the governor of Thessaloniki, who is of Pontic-Greek exchangee background, and a member of the Russian parliament requested permission to hold a liturgy at the site, and was turned down by the authorities (August 15, 2009).

In 2010, Turkish authorities invited the Ecumenical Patriarchate to organize a divine liturgy for the Feast of the Dormition, commemorating the death of Virgin Mary. This was the first time such a liturgy was conducted at the site since 1922. In addition to the flock of the Patriarchate in Istanbul, globally dispersed Orthodox Greeks,

7   https://whc.unesco.org/en/tentativelists/1397/ (accessed 4 December 2020).

many of whom have Pontic origins, also participated in the liturgy. The annual liturgy has become a regular event for the commemoration of the Feast of the Dormition at Soumela Monastery. In a similar fashion to Akthamar, the site functions as a worship hall for one day per year and for the rest of the year it serves as a museum. While the worship at the site acknowledges its sacred importance, it happens under the control and with the permission of the Turkish government.

In 2016, Sümela Museum was closed for restoration, which brought the annual liturgies to a halt. The restoration focused on improving the visitor experience by paving visitor paths, conserving the remaining frescoes, and stabilizing the architecture. While some parts of the monastery opened for visitation in 2019, the Patriarchate did not receive an invitation to hold the annual divine liturgy. The invitation came the next year, on July 28, 2020. Turkish president Erdoğan announced the re-opening of the Soumela Museum on live TV only four days after the conversion of Hagia Sophia.[8] He invited the Patriarchate to hold their annual liturgy at the Soumela Monastery on August 15. This invitation at the height of the COVID-19 pandemic was not only patronizing but also reckless. The Ecumenical Patriarch thanked Erdoğan for his invitation and stated that he would not be able to lead the ceremonies because of the public health risks posed by the pandemic, and the divine liturgy took place at the absence of the Ecumenical Patriarch (Antonopaulos 2020). The site was closed again for restorations in the following month, which strongly suggests that it was briefly opened to host the liturgy as a public relations campaign, possibly to deflect the global criticism Turkey and Erdoğan received for the conversion of Hagia Sophia.

In terms of curatorship, the museum in its current form offers little historical information to its visitors. In addition to one panel explaining the history of the site and its main architectural features, there are only a few sporadic labels at the entrances of various parts of the complex. There is minimal information on the former use and history of the site, and scarcely any indication that the monastery was once part of a prosperous Pontic-Greek culture of the region and served as a major pilgrimage center up until 1922. There is no mention of the traumatic past of the Pontic-Greek population.

The Sümela Museum/Soumela Monastery is revered by the descendants of the Pontic Greek-Orthodox population. The faith community that built and used this significant religious historical heritage is globally displaced after the forced population exchange of 1923. As such, their interaction with the space is defined by the rules and regulations set by the Turkish authorities. While the annual liturgy hosted at the site is a significant event, it clearly defines the Turkish authorities as the hosts and the Orthodox Christian religious officials and worshippers as the guests. The Greek Orthodox community of Turkey and the Ecumenical Patriarchate have no control over the site and are excluded from heritage management decisions.

Tokenizing Christian Heritage as a Performance of Tolerance

The restoration of the religious heritage of Turkey's Armenian and Greek Orthodox communities is a positive step towards acknowledging their historic presence in the country. The annual liturgies at Akhtamar and Soumela also underscore their religious importance. However, both the exclusion of faith communities in the restoration projects and site management plans, as well as the once-a-year invitation extended by the Turkish government to these communities to perform rites at the museumified religious sites, are formulated as spectacles of tolerance showcasing Turkey's benevolent treatment of its minorities.

Both Akthamar and Soumela hosted liturgies in 2010, when Turkey's European Union membership was still a priority and the Turkish government intended to project an image of tolerance and inclusion. These events were so critical that

---

8   https://www.tccb.gov.tr/en/news/542/120736/-sumela-monastery-is-the-epitome-of-how-turkey-protects-all-kinds-of-civilization-heritages-on-its-lands- (accessed 4 December 2020).

then-Deputy Prime Minister Bülent Arınç listed the restoration of Akhtamar Church and Soumela Monastery and the annual liturgies hosted at each site after 2010 amongst the significant accomplishments in the domain of human rights in a 2013 report (Arınç 2013).

This being the case, however, then-Prime Minister Erdoğan's comment on April 14, 2011, in Strasbourg, at the Parliamentary Assembly of the Council of Europe, hints at the sectarian logic of these heritage practices. As part of his reply to a question regarding the freedom of religion or belief in Turkey, Erdoğan stated: "In Van, the Armenian Orthodox Church was about to fall apart. We restored that church, paid for its restoration with our own funds, and opened it to worship" (*Hürriyet*, April 14, 2011). Erdoğan's framing of Akthamar's restoration process indicates that he perceives spending "our own funds" on Christian heritage as a favor, thereby excluding Turkey's Christian citizens from a nation that only includes Muslims as one of "us." Erdoğan's tone in talking about the restoration of Akthamar as benevolence furthermore underlines the discriminatory framework of the state when it comes to the protection of minority heritage.

The spectacles of tolerance and inclusion orchestrated by the Turkish government at Soumela and Akhtamar not only to fail to convey the complex history of these monuments, but also put further political pressure on the communities as they have no control over the heritage management strategies of these sites other than participating in the ritual ceremonies if and when invited by the Turkish government.

ETHICAL CONSIDERATIONS FOR ARCHAEOLOGISTS

The demuseumification and conversion of Hagia Sophia into a functioning mosque in July 2020 was a spectacle of dominance performed by the ruling Islamist-cum-ultranationalist political elite over the country's secular and ethno-religious minorities. The museumification of the Armenian Apostolic Akhtamar Cathedral in Van and the Greek Orthodox Soumela Monastery in Trabzon were also choreographed spectacles, but they aimed at deflecting international criticism by showcasing the tolerant and inclusive attitude of the Turkish state towards its minorities. A comparative study of these cases of museumification and demuseumification illustrates the exclusivist and discriminatory underpinnings of Turkish heritage policy and practices.

While site preservation concerns are often a key component of public discourse around museum practices, exclusivist underpinnings of policy and practice are rarely visible and articulated. For archaeologists, art and architectural historians, and museum professionals, balancing conflicting demands of freedom of religion or belief, site preservation, and politics poses unique professional and moral challenges, as we are forced to navigate conflict-ridden encounters among often-antagonistic stakeholders.

As practitioners in the field, we need to be keenly aware that "[t]he issue of control over heritage is political because it is a struggle over power not only because different interests will have different and usually unequal access to resources of power, but also heritage is a political resource" (Smith 2006: 281). This being the case, as practitioners in the fields of archaeology, art and architectural history, and museum and heritage studies, we have ethical responsibilities.

The first among these responsibilities is for scholars to educate themselves to understand the political context in which they operate. All too often, as archaeologists, for example, we focus only on our temporally and geographically defined narrow area of specialization, often separated by centuries if not millennia from the period in which we operate. However, understanding the present context is crucial, as it determines how the past is told and negotiated by different agents today.

This awareness becomes particularly critical when we are working on sites of minority religious heritage. In some cases, like those of Akhtamar and Soumela, we may be dealing with ancient sites that are sacred to communities who are no longer part of the local context and the accompanying heritage practices. In such cases, we need to have a firm grasp of the exclusivist and discriminatory practices of the political authorities, and existing nationalist and/or sectarian narratives and policies of heritage.

Our research, therefore, may have significant consequences not only for vulnerable minorities but also for dominant and/or majority communities. It is our responsibility to be aware of the current impact of our work, which in some cases may further victimize at-risk groups. Consequently, our work also has the potential to empower them.

As Alexandra Vukovich suggests, a "participative and informed management" of ancient and historical remains with a stress for "equitable access and use is key for forming a democratic consciousness" (Vukovich 2022: 16). As archaeologists, our efforts in framing the narrative of the past should contribute to an inclusive future. Ensuring the transparency and accessibility of our research is critical, especially in cases in which our data challenge the exclusivist narratives and discourses deployed to reinforce hierarchies. An awareness of the challenges outlined above leads to inclusive heritage practices, which in turn can be a resource to promote reconciliation, amends-making, and peacebuilding.

REFERENCES

Ahunbay, Z.
2017   Bir Dünya Mirasının Korunmasi: Ayasofya. Pp. 1–20 in *Tarihi Yapıların Korunması ve Güçlendirilmesi Sempozyumu: Trabzon, 2nd – 4th Kasım, 2017*. Uluslararası Katılımlı 6. Trabzon and Istanbul: İnşaat Mühendisleri Odası Trabzon Şubesi; İnşaat Mühendisleri Odası İstanbul Şubesi.
2015   Dünya mirası olarak Ayasofya ve Korumaya İlişkin Sorunlar. *Toplumsal Tarih* 254: 86–91.

Antonopoulos, P.
2020   Assumption of Mary celebrated in Pontian monastery among icons destroyed by Turkish Vandals. *Greek City Times*, August 15, 2020.

Arınç, B.
2013   *Human Rights and the Transformation Process in Turkey*. Center for Strategic Research (SAM).

Aykaç, P.
2019   Contesting the Byzantine Past: Four Hagia Sophias as Ideological Battlegrounds of Architectural Conservation in Turkey. *Heritage & Society* 11.2: 151–78.

Azak, U.
2014   Muhafazakar Milliyetçiliğin Bitmeyen Davası: "Mahzun Mabed" Ayasofya. *Toplum ve Bilim* 131: 236–64.

Bonini Baraldi, S.; Shoup, D.; and Zan, L.
2013   Understanding Cultural Heritage in Turkey: Institutional Context and Organisational Issues. *International Journal of Heritage Studies*, 19.7: 728–48.

Bryer, A., and Winfield, D.
1985   *The Byzantine Monuments and Topography of the Pontos*. Washington, DC: Dumbarton Oaks Research Library and Collection.

Clark, B.
2006   *Twice a Stranger*. London: Granata.

Demoyan, H.
2010   Akhtamar and Turkish State Identity. *LRAGIR*, August 17, 2010.

Dink, H.
2007   Tarihin Cilvesi. *BirGün*, January 19, 2007.

Egresi, I.; Bayram, B.; Kara, F.: and Ozan, A. F.
2012   Unlocking the Potential of Religious Tourism in Turkey. *GeoJournal of Tourism and Geosites* 1.9: 63–80.

Eldem, E.
2015   Ayasofya: Kilise, Cami, Abide, Müze, Simge. *Toplumsal Tarih* 254: 76–85.

Erdemir, A.
2019   Scapegoats of Wrath, Subjects of Benevolence: Turkey's Minorities Under Erdoğan, *Current Trends in Islamist Ideology* 24: 5–23.
2021   Spectacles of Tolerance: The Precarity of Turkey's Religious Minorities in the Era of

Neo-Ottoman Delusions. *Harvard Journal of Middle Eastern Politics and Polity*: 44–51.

Erdemir, A., and Tanyeri-Erdemir, T.
2020   Turkish Government's Hagia Sophia Rhetoric Adds Insult to Injury. *Providence*, July 24, 2020.

Ermis, M. U.
2012   İznik Ayasofyası'nın Son Restorasyon Çalışmasında Açığa Çıkarılan Freskoları. Pp. 1–27 in *Proceedings of the XVth International Symposium of Medieval and Turkish Era Excavations and Art History Researches,* ed. Z. Demirel Gökalp and N. Çöl. Eskişehir: Eskişehir Anadolu Universitesi.

Gall, C.
2020   Erdogan Signs Decree Allowing Hagia Sophia to be Used as a Mosque Again. *The New York Times*, July 10, 2020.

Harmanşah, R.; Tanyeri-Erdemir, T.;
and Hayden, R.
2015   Secularizing the Unsecularizable: A Comparative Study of the Haci Bektash Veli and the Mevlana Museums in Turkey. Pp. 336–68 in *Choreography of Sacred Spaces,* ed. Elazar Barkan and Karen Barkey. New York: Columbia University.

Hirschon, R.
2003   *Crossing the Aegean: An Appraisal of the 1923 Compulsory Population Exchange Between Greece and Turkey.* New York: Berghahn.

Katipoğlu, C., and Caner-Yüksel, Ç.
2010   Hagia Sophia "Museum": A Humanist Project of the Turkish Republic. Pp. 205–25 in *Constructing Cultural Identity, Representing Social Power,* ed. C. Bilsel, K. Esmark, N. Kızılyürek, Ó. Rastrick. Pisa: Plus-Pisa University.

Kaya, F.; Cankül, D.; and Demirci, B.
2013   Türkiye'nin Önemli İnanç Turizmi Merkezlerinden Biri: Akdamar Kilisesi. *KMÜ Sosyal ve Ekonomik Araştırmalar Dergisi* 15.24: 13–24.

Meskell, L.
2018   *A Future in Ruins: UNESCO, World Heritage, and the Dream of Peace.* Oxford: Oxford University.

Mildanoğlu, Z.
2012   Van Manastirlarina ne oldu? *Agos*, September 22, 2012.

Nelson, R. S.
2004   *Hagia Sophia, 1850–1950: Holy Wisdom Modern Monument.* Chicago: University of Chicago.

Över, D.
2016   Cultural Tourism and Complex Histories: The Armenian Akhtamar Church, the Turkish State and National Identity. *Qualitative Sociology* 39.2: 173–94.

Özekmekçi, İ. M.
2012   Türk Sağında Ayasofya İmgesi. Pp 283–306 in *Türk Sağı,* ed. İ. Özkan Kerestecioğlu and G. G. Öztan. Istanbul: İletişim.

Pogossian, Z., and Vardanyan, E. (eds.)
2019   *The Church of Holy Cross at Aghtamar.* Leiden: Brill.

Prodromou, E. H.
2020   Turkey's Cultural Heritage Cudgel. *Cornerstone Forum* 275: 1–7.

Romain Örs, İ., and Tanyeri-Erdemir, T.
2020   Former Byzantine churches are being converted to mosques — this threathens Istanbul's cosmopolitan identity. *The Conversation*, September15, 2020.

Smith, L.
2006   *Uses of Heritage.* New York: Routledge.

Tanyeri-Erdemir, T.
2015   Historical Trajectories, Institutional Particularities: The Funding Regime for Religious Heritage in Turkey. Pp. 213–26 in *Funding Religious Heritage,* ed. A. Fornerond. New York: Routledge.
2016   The Fate of Tanzimat-era Churches in Anatolia after the Loss of their Congregations. Pp. 219–35 in *Christian Art Under Muslim*

Rule, ed. M. Hartmuth. Leiden: Nederlands Instituut voor het Nabije Oosten.

2018   Remains of the Day: Converted Anatolian Churches. Pp.71–96 in *Spolia Reincarnated: Afterlives of Objects, Materials, and Spaces in Anatolia from Antiquity to the Ottoman Era*, ed. I. Jevtić and S. Yalman. Istanbul: Koç University, Research Center for Anatolian Civilizations (ANAMED).

2019   Erdogan's Ploy to Convert Hagia Sophia into Votes. *The Globalist*, March 29, 2019.

2020   Erdogan and the Hagia Sophia: Will He – Or Won't He? *The Globalist*, June 26, 2020.

United Nationals Educational, Scientific and Cultural Organization (UNESCO) and International Council on Monuments and Sites (ICOMOS)

2009   *Report on the joint UNESCO World Heritage Centre/ICOMOS reactive monitoring mission To the World Heritage site of Historic Areas of Istanbul.* https://whc.unesco.org/en/documents/102199

Vukovich, A.

2022   From Imperial to Postcolonial and National Heritage Management: An Ottoman Ruin in Post-Ottoman Belgrade. Pp. 3–23 in *Thinking Through Ruins: Genealogies, Functions, and Interpretations*, ed. E. Khansa, K. Klein and B. Winckler. Berlin: Kulturverlag.

Yackley, A. J.

2019   Court ruling converting Turkish museum to mosque could set precedent for Hagia Sophia. *The Art Newspaper*, December 3, 2019.

Zaman, A.

2020   Istanbul's Hagia Sophia holds first Friday prayers since reconversion to mosque. *Al-Monitor*, July 24, 2020.

Zaman, M.

2010   Türkiye'nin Önemli İnanç Turizmi Merkezlerinden Biri: Sumela (Meryemana) Manastırı. *Atatürk Üniversitesi Sosyal Bilimler Enstitüsü Dergisi* 6.2: 1–24.

Chapter 8

Ethics in Archaeological Grantmaking and Grantseeking

Sarah Lepinski and Christopher Thornton

ABSTRACT

This chapter addresses grantmaking and grantseeking within the larger landscape of archaeological practices and discusses the principles and standards that underpin funding for archaeological activities including research, publication, fieldwork, and collections management with a specific emphasis on the regions that comprise the work of ASOR members. Our goal is to provide perspectives and insights into the broad terrain of archaeological funding for those seeking grant support and hope that this chapter may serve as a resource for the ASOR community (and beyond). We briefly touch on existing scholarship surrounding ethics and funding and highlight the best practices involved in grant review processes, decision making, and the responsibilities and modes of conduct after receiving grant support.

INTRODUCTION

This chapter discusses the principles and structures that underpin grantmaking for archaeological projects with the goal of providing insights for professionals navigating the archaeological funding landscape. It is not a comprehensive discussion of ethical grantmaking, which is a topic addressed in other publications, but one that we hope will serve to highlight the responsibilities of grantmakers and grantseekers, independently and collectively, in employing best practices in seeking funding to support work in archaeology.

As authors, we approach the topic with multiple professional perspectives, as grantmakers (one current, one former), and as an archaeologist and anthropologist, respectively, with years of experience excavating at sites across the Mediterranean and West Asia. We have each held various roles across a number of institutional structures—in higher education, museums, nonprofit organizations, and in a U.S. federal agency dedicated to humanities grantmaking. In our experience, financial support for work in archaeology is rarely considered alongside other fundamental activities in the field, such as fieldwork, research, publication, collections management, and site preservation, despite its obvious importance to the success of the project. We maintain that understanding the principles and processes that support grantmaking can lead to more successful grant applications and, by extension, more successful projects, while also touching on some of the ethical dilemmas. To this end, we provide a brief introduction to existing scholarship surrounding ethical behaviors and funding as a background and to offer details regarding the best practices involved in grant review processes, decision making, and the ethics of receiving grant support. This chapter is in no way all-inclusive, but is meant to engage archaeologists and archaeological funders with some of the key issues that confront both communities. We understand from our own professional experiences that there is an opacity surrounding grantmaking in general and how attempts to secure funding in many ways informs and affects early planning for projects. In this regard, the activities that are integral to grantseeking directly impact project development and overall success. With this in mind, we offer some practical information on the ins and outs of archaeological grantmaking and seek to align with the broader discussion of ethical behaviors within the field of archaeology.

LITERATURE REVIEW

While there is a plethora of useful books for grantmakers and grantseekers (e.g., Kibbe et al. 1999; Orosz 2000; Bauer 2011; Grant 2012; Gow Petty 2013; Folsom 2019), few deal explicitly with the ethical aspects of the grantmaking process. To our knowledge there are no other publications that specifically address ethical grantmaking in the fields of archaeology and anthropology. A handful of publications offer slightly different approaches to the topic and generally reinforce the importance of shared responsibility on the part of funders and grant recipients in supporting and applying best practices, and the reciprocal relationship between grantmakers and grantseekers, which are paramount in the development of healthy funding ecosystems.

For the interested reader, there is an excellent chapter in Joel Orosz's *The Insider's Guide to Grantmaking* called "The Ethics of Grantmaking" (2000: 252–61), which lays out what he calls the "Seven Deadly Sins of Philanthropy." To Orosz, these sins are: 1) ignoring negative consequences; 2) imperiousness towards applicants; 3) lack of honesty; 4) conflicts of interest; 5) apathy for the cause; 6) risk-averse grantmaking; and 7) formulaic grantmaking. In essence, these "sins" or missteps derive from three essential aspects of the grantmaker's job: helping applicants, designing fair decision-making processes, and always keeping the goal of the grant program in mind. Similarly, grantseekers have a responsibility not to lead or pressure grantmakers into committing these sins and to be open to an honest and fair process that seeks to achieve a goal larger than a single project.

The most comprehensive source on this topic is Michael Josephson's 1992 book, *Ethics in Grantmaking & Grantseeking: Making Philanthropy Better*, published by the Joseph & Edna Josephson Institute of Ethics. The core argument of the book is that grantmaking should advance four principles:

1) the Preservation of Public Trust by "avoiding even the appearance of impropriety;"
2) Public Purpose by assuring that "foundation and nonprofit resources are used to advance significant public purposes rather than the private interests of individual or corporate benefactors;"
3) Institutional Accountability and Stewardship, in which grantmakers should "[accept] responsibility for the foreseeable consequences of institutional actions;" and
4) Institutional Integrity by "assuring that the process and substance of grantmaking decisions are consistent with ethical principles" (Josephson 1992: 22–23).

He also covers some of the most common pitfalls in grantmaking, such as the "Compartmentalization Trap" (Josephson 1992: 21), whereby grantmakers "compartmentalize ethics into private and occupational domains allowing them to justify doing things in the course of their work that they know to be wrong in other contexts;" the "Compliance Trap" (Josephson 1992: 23–24), which argues that "if it's legal, it's ethical;" and the "White Lie Fallacy" (46), which argues that "certain lies and deceptions are inherently justified if the intent is to be helpful, kind or to advance a noble cause." By understanding these pitfalls, and the core tenets of a funder's responsibilities, grantseekers can make sure to keep their requests and their own behavior in line with best ethical practices.

Some of the other books for grantmakers and grantseekers also provide a few overarching points that are helpful, particularly with a view towards "field-wide" and/or "discipline-wide" perspectives and contexts. For example, in *The Business of Giving. The Theory and Practice of Philanthropy, Grantmaking and Social Investment*, Grant (2012) emphasizes the general lack of formal training for both grantmakers and grant recipients. He points to specific pressure points in current philanthropy to highlight important areas of shared responsibility, including community involvement, heritage management, and teambuilding. In archaeology, the ability to work collaboratively with colleagues and communities, and to integrate expertise and knowledge from beyond the traditional academic disciplinary boundaries (e.g., from heritage management sectors), are proficiencies typically acquired and developed over time and with practice (Grant 2012: 8). The same can be said for grantmakers.

Shared responsibilities and strong reciprocal relationships are also underscored in Andrew Watt's forward to *Nonprofit Fundraising Strategy: A Guide to Ethical Decision Making and Regulation for Nonprofit Organizations* (Gow Petty 2013), in which he stresses the importance of maintaining strong bonds between grantmakers and the fields they serve, emphasizing that this bond relies on three critical areas: trust, confidence, and accountability. Each of these, he maintains, rests on a single platform—ethics. As Watt details, "working within an ethical framework commits us, publicly, to certain values; it builds trust in our integrity; it builds confidence in our ability to support the work our organizations are committed to do;

and it demonstrates that we are committed to communicating our impact—and what it took to deliver it" (Gow Petty 2013: xviii). Furthermore, ethics help us to understand the concerns of the world around us, the impact of impropriety, the impact of our approach, how perceptions are formed and trust built—and above all, the context for the decisions we make (Gow Petty 2013: xviii).

Ethics of Grantmaking

Grantmaking is an art and a science—i.e., it requires the precision and rigor of a scientist but also the creativity and sensitivity of an artist. Professional grantmaking processes are similarly a mixture of objective facts and highly subjective interpretations (cf. Lamont 2009). Grantmakers must constantly seek the balance between these two extremes. For example, if a grants program is too reliant on metric evaluation, whether of the applications or of the short-term results, it will quickly amass a fairly homogenous group of grantees and grant projects that are likely to result in general mediocrity. On the other hand, if a grant program is too arbitrary in its decision making, or fails to assess the results of the people and projects funded, the result will likely be a scattershot of ideas and outcomes whose meaning and impact can be imagined in the Rorschach inkblot of grant products. There is no perfect balance between these two endpoints. Instead, grantmakers must be flexible to changing organizational goals, changing times, trends and other dynamic factors, and changing applicant pools. We must expect to adjust our programs and processes to match these changes.

Another way to think about this is to acknowledge that *grantmaking is a means to an end*—a method (one of many potentials) for achieving a goal—and awarding grants should never be considered an end in itself. As an example, when one of the authors (CT) left the nonprofit world to join the Federal workforce, he inherited a number of grant programs that had been in existence since the 1960s and 70s. When he asked the staff what the goals of each program were, they often responded in simple, teleological statements (e.g., "We give research grants in order to support research.") because the original purpose of those grant programs had been lost in time. After a bit of archival research and staff reflection, we realized that certain programs had been designed to help junior faculty or researchers in the earlier stages of their project, while other programs were created to support institutional structures rather than individual scholars. We then reached out to relevant institutions and scholarly organizations to ask if the needs of these communities had changed or were the same as in the 1960s and 70s. Such feedback was essential to reconfiguring certain grant programs to better serve the communities. For example, the old Archaeology program at NEH had become too rigid and old-fashioned, limiting the pool of applicants to very traditional "big dig" projects and restricting more multidisciplinary and postcolonial approaches. In consultation with various archaeological organizations (including ASOR), the Archaeology program was sunsetted and a new Archaeological and Ethnographic Field Research Program was launched. Grantmakers must be responsive and flexible to the changing needs of the communities they are meant to serve and have an ethical imperative to measure and evaluate how well they are meeting those needs.

The continuing evolution of grantmaking goals and processes can be hard to understand from the applicant's perspective, which often leads to confusion and frustration on both sides. For this reason, one of the most important ethical responsibilities of a grantmaker is *transparency*. Applicants must be able to understand what the organization—and its reviewers—are looking for and how those decisions will be made, in order to craft a proposal that explains their projects appropriately. It is the responsibility of the grantmaker to make all review criteria and the decision-making process readily apparent to any interested applicant. At the same time, the grantmaker must then adhere to these processes and criteria. Any deviation from the stated criteria and processes as given to the applicants—even if the grantmaker realizes too late that the criteria or processes are faulty—is a gross violation of trust

and can discredit the entire funding opportunity and the organization. Any organization whose criteria or processes are not made transparent to applicants should be approached with caution, as their decisions are likely made with great prejudice or completely at random.

The need for transparency also extends to the sources of funding being used to award grants (see Josephson's [1992: 61, 157–62] discussion of "Grantseekers' Special Obligation to Avoid Tainted Money"). One of the first things an applicant should do upon discovering a potential source of funding is to look up where the money comes from. While some archaeologists may not care where their funding comes from, many of their peers do, and it can seriously hurt a scholar's career if it becomes known that they accepted a grant from a donor or an organization whose money derives from unethical or illegal activities. Similarly, many private funders have a background in art and artifact collecting (whether legal or illegal), and this too can lead to heated discussions about ethics in archaeological grantmaking. It is the responsibility of every grantmaking organization to make explicit the sources of funding used to award grants, and it is the responsibility of the applicant to understand the pros and cons of accepting funds from a particular source.

While transparency is the gold-standard for granting organizations, the grantmaker also has the ethical responsibility of keeping people's information and their intellectual property a secret. In other words, applicants have the right to *privacy*. When an archaeologist has a brilliant idea or makes a big discovery, one that could make her famous and successful, it is often the grantmaker who first hears about it. Indeed, the seasoned scholar knows that a grantmaker is often the best person to tell, because it is our job to help you find sources of funding (if possible) and to keep your information strictly confidential. In addition, grantmakers hear about people's brilliant ideas and big discoveries every day, so we can often give the applicant a sense of how revolutionary their news is relative to others we've heard.

The need for privacy also extends to the peer-reviewers and decision-makers involved in the grantmaking process. While the applicant has the right to know what sorts of people will be deciding on their application (and using which criteria), it is essential for the fair and honest evaluation of applications that the names and comments of reviewers or decision-makers be kept private. While many organizations will provide the names of individuals who sit on decision-making committees, and may even list the names of peer reviewers used in the process, an applicant should never be able to tie a particular score or comment about their proposal back to a single individual. This level of privacy in the review process is crucial; without it, reviewers are unlikely to give their honest opinion, and decision-makers may fear personal or professional reprisal from applicants.

Just as grantmakers expect fair and honest evaluations from their reviewers and decision-makers, we must also strive to provide *honest and straightforward feedback* to applicants whenever possible. There is no bigger waste of time in the grantmaking world than for an applicant to apply for a project that the grantmaker knows will never be funded. Actually, there is a bigger waste of time: if the applicant is unaware of their chances and therefore re-applies with the same flawed application at every opportunity! This latter scenario, which all grantmakers dread, is truly the biggest waste of everyone's time and resources. The obvious solution is for the grantmaker to have an honest conversation with the applicant—either in the guise of reading a draft, or providing reviewer comments, or simply scheduling a phone call to discuss the application and/or project—and encourage them to seek other sources of funding or to change the scope and pitch of the application. If a grantmaker gives honest and straightforward feedback to an applicant, it is then the responsibility of the applicant to listen to their suggestions and make the appropriate changes. If an applicant doesn't quite understand what the grantmaker is telling him, he should ask for clarification or seek a colleague to help interpret the feedback. Any funding organization that will not provide insight before the application is submitted, nor feedback after an application is rejected, should seriously reevaluate whether their use of staff resources is entirely cost-effective. Similarly, applicants may wish to deprioritize such funding organizations, because the likelihood of wasting one's time by applying is much, much higher.

The most complicated ethical issue in grantmaking, and the one that grantmakers spend the most time discussing internally, is that of "conflict of interest" (or "COI"). Each funding organization will have different rules about what constitutes a COI, ranging from the rather obvious (e.g., "the applicant cannot be your spouse or direct family member") to the incredibly strict (e.g., "you cannot have received a degree from the same institution as the applicant"). Ultimately, it is up to the organization's leadership and legal counsel to determine what constitutes a COI for its staff and its reviewers. The decision usually comes down to what level of reputational risk they are willing to hazard in the pursuit of giving grants. Indeed, for a grantmaker to be accused of having a conflict of interest with a particular application that she did not first recuse herself from reviewing is a serious charge—tantamount to plagiarism in scholarly circles—as it calls into question all previous decisions by the person and their organization. For this reason, smaller private organizations tend to have less strict COI rules, while larger public organizations (who have more to lose) are generally much stricter. As a general rule, grantmakers should recuse themselves from handling or reviewing an application if there is any doubt as to their objectivity or perceived objectivity in assessing an applicant or their proposal.

Ethics of Grantseeking

In the last section, we focused on the ethical responsibilities of grantmakers, which in many respects may all be helpful for applicants. For example, applicants should always determine where a funder's money comes from and whether that source will be considered ethical by their colleagues. These are higher-level ethical questions that applicants should always be asking about the myriad of funding organizations available to them. However, just as grantseekers are looking for ethical funders, grantmakers are looking for ethical grantees to use their funds. In this section, we will give a few suggestions on how to craft an application that convinces reviewers and grantmakers that you are going to use their funds in an appropriate manner with minimal reputational risk to the funder, that you will adhere to the conditions of the award in terms of schedule, budget, and reporting responsibilities, and that you will achieve the stated goals of the proposed work (i.e., the project will be successfully completed).

The most obvious advice in application writing generally, and ethical grant writing specifically, is to plan ahead and *pay attention to details*; as the old adage notes, "A scientist is only as good as her lab is clean." If your application is riddled with typos, or missing key pieces of information requested by the grantmaker, or otherwise outside the guidelines for a successful application, then you have already called yourself into question and diminished your prospects as a successful candidate. Sloppy applications often portend sloppy work, and sloppy work leads to reputational risks for the funding organization. Always have someone else read your application before submitting it to clean up typos and help you clarify what you're trying to convey. For complex grant applications, we suggest that you print out the list of essential documents and attachments and check them off one by-one before you submit the application package. If you have questions regarding the requirements, ask the granting body and seek advice from others who may have received grants from this source. Some grantmakers, especially those supported with public funds such as State and Federal entities, field questions regarding their programs and some also provide one on-one consultation and review project proposals. In these cases, *take advantage of all opportunities to ask questions and receive feedback*. And, while it may seem evident, be open and accepting of the advice, as it is offered by those with first-hand knowledge and understanding of the evaluation process and insights into the overarching goals of the grant program. If the required parts of a proposal are listed in the grant application materials, and the review criteria are given, ask a friend

or colleague to read your application and check off each one when they find it. If they cannot find one, or if it is not obvious, then consider rewriting your application to make all required parts and criteria explicit.

Related to the statement about following requirements and explicitly addressing review criteria is the issue of bibliographic citations in application materials. Unlike publications, grantmakers often restrict the size of bibliographies in their applications, thereby limiting the number of sources to which an applicant can refer. But at the same time, grantmakers and reviewers are looking carefully for any sign of plagiarism, intellectual thievery, or even just missing canonical works that suggest the applicant is not familiar with the existing literature. Providing sufficient citations and sources is one of the trickiest aspects of an application, but it is rarely discussed. As a rule of thumb, it is better to cite too much rather than too little, but the constraints of a bibliography can often make this impossible. One way to demonstrate knowledge of other scholars' work without listing them is to employ rhetorical methods. For example: "Many scholars have discussed the roles of women in Neolithic societies, notably Jane Smith and Robert Jones," rather than "Many scholars have discussed the roles of women in Neolithic societies (see Smith 2008, 2011; Jones 2004, 2007, etc.)" It is also important to give credit for other people's ideas (e.g., "As Henry Martin noted over thirty years ago..."), even if you don't formally cite them in the application as you would in a professional publication. The goal of an application is not to demonstrate that you have read the Chicago Style Guide cover to cover; it is to argue convincingly that you are in control of the existing literature on the subject and are aware of how your project will ultimately add to that body of knowledge.

There is currently an active and lively debate in academia about support letters and letters of reference that engages with a number of key questions: Does the requirement of letters encourage the dominance of elite private schools? Are letters likely to overburden women and people of color? How much weight should reviewers give letters when reading applications? These are all important questions beyond the scope of this paper, but both grantmakers and grantseekers need to be aware of the discourse and adjust accordingly. Many grantmaking organizations require applicants to provide reference letters from scholars who can assess the applicant and their project. These referees are usually separate from the peer review conducted by the organization, so applicants are often free to use former advisors or close colleagues who can help argue their case. The onus is on the applicant to inform the referee that they are requesting the letter and to give them copies of the grant program criteria and the application itself so that they can write the strongest letter possible. Encourage these letter writers to speak to your character as much as to your previous scholarship—a word of confidence about your ability to complete a project in a timely and ethical manner can often sway peer reviewers and decision-makers to take a chance on a risky proposal. More importantly, an ethical application should include a letter of support from any communities or stakeholders involved in the project. It is important for grantmakers to know that you have the support of the local communities in which your research takes place, as the successful completion of your project often depends on that support. There is great reputational risk to the organization if they are perceived to be funding people who are working against the wishes of a local community. Of course, there are often multiple stakeholders with different viewpoints in any community, and the applicant should do their best to seek letters of support from as many stakeholders as possible.

Another area in which applicants often raise doubts about their project is in describing the distribution of work conducted with grant support. Reviewers and grantmakers need to know who is doing what on a multi-person or multi-institutional grant, and this division of responsibilities should be reflected in budgets and budget narratives, as well; any confusion about how funds and workload are being distributed can effectively doom a proposal. Worse, if reviewers come to believe that the application says Person X will be doing certain work, but in actuality Person Y will be carrying out the work, then they will likely be far more suspect of the proposal. Ultimately it does not matter who submits the application (i.e., who the "applicant" is)—it matters who the application says will conduct certain parts of the work plan. It is far better to be honest about the distribution of work, and to express it clearly, than plump the application with names of prestigious scholars who are unlikely to have the time to carry out the described tasks.

BEING AN ETHICAL GRANT RECIPIENT

Once you have received a grant, your ethical responsibilities to the grantmaker and to your fellow grantseekers do not end there. Indeed, you have now entered a legal and professional relationship with that funding organization that, like any relationship, requires communication and trust. Fostering this relationship may reap benefits for years or even decades to come. Beyond the more obvious ethical responsibility to use the funds as detailed in the awarded application, you also have the ethical responsibility to "give back" to the community that has directly or indirectly made your grant possible. In this section we provide a brief list of ways to make the most of your experience as a grantee.

1) *Ask for feedback from reviewers and grantmakers.* Many scholars assume that feedback is only helpful for revising and resubmitting an unsuccessful application, and while that is certainly true, it's only half of the story. Feedback can also inform a funded project. In fact, very rarely are awarded applications considered flawless—retired grantmakers can usually recall a handful of such unicorns throughout their entire career! It is far more common that grants are awarded *despite* the flaws in the application and/or the project design. Peer reviewers and grantmakers have spent hours evaluating your proposal; it behooves you and the project to know and understand what they have to say and to consider amending your project. These adjustments will likely lead to a

better outcome for the project and will ensure that precious grant funds will be spent in the most effective way possible.

2) *Provide feedback to the grantmaking organizations to which you applied.* Scholars whose applications were rejected are understandably reticent to provide helpful feedback to grantmakers about "what worked and what didn't" in the grantseeking process, but successful applicants should have no such concerns. Grantmakers rely on feedback to refine their programs and processes for the sake of future applicants and sadly sometimes lose touch with the applicant's perspective. Perhaps the information provided on the website was unclear, or the review criteria were not made explicit, or the application's formatting was off. Or worse, perhaps there are deeply ingrained biases in the program that are favoring one type of applicant over another. While no applicant should ever fear reprisal for providing honest criticism or commentary, awarded grantees have an ethical obligation to do so on behalf of those less fortunate.

3) *Communicate regularly with your grantor.* The relationship between the grantmaker and the grantee, as we noted above, is built on trust. The grantmaker in particular is trusting the grantee with their limited and fixed funds and with their organization's imprimatur, hoping to see positive change in some chosen area. Trust is built through communication, including short email updates and longer formal reports, phone call "catch-ups" and in-person meetings. If something goes awry and the project has to change, the grantmaker can help determine what is allowable and will work with the grantee to find a solution. In this way, grantmakers can make sure the grantee is not straying too far from the stated goals of the successful application or the requirements of the granting organization, and the grantee can reassure the grantor that their funds and name will continue to be used appropriately. Similarly, once the grant period is over, grantees have an obligation to inform their grantors

of any published results or other outcomes of their grants. The most successful grantseekers are those who cultivate professional relationships with grantmakers, but not (as one might suppose) because of favoritism. Instead, these grantseekers have learned what aspects of their project are important to the organization and have earned the trust of the grantmakers by demonstrating the positive outcomes of their previous grants.

4) *Offer to help your professional community.* Most funding organizations have incredibly low success rates—5 to 15% success is quite normal—so holding a grant is a privilege. Like all privileged positions, the grantee has an ethical obligation to support the wider community of practitioners and those less fortunate. Easy ways to "pay it forward" include offering to serve as a reviewer for grantmaking organizations and offering to provide advice to other grantseekers. Many grantees are happy to share their successful applications as a template, or to provide advice on a draft application, if asked. Giving back to one's professional community is not only ethical, it's often the best way to improve one's own grantseeking skills for the future.

In addition to "giving back" to a funding organization, peer review provides an unparalleled opportunity to see how a review process works from the inside and to gain a "thirty-foot" view of current research directions, methods, and projected results. In short, in addition to providing a service to grantmakers and support the field, peer review affords the opportunity to nurture new relationships and professional networks, and to acquire significant insights that may inform your professional work, broadly and beyond grantseeking.

FINAL THOUGHTS

In this chapter, we aimed to draw attention to important issues facing archaeologists and archaeological funders and to address best practices in ethical grantmaking and grantseeking. We have underscored that grantmaking is both an art and a science, and that flexibility and the ability to adjust processes and programs is necessary for maintaining an equilibrium. We have also stressed that a reciprocal relationship between grantmakers and grantseekers is essential for creating and sustaining a healthy funding ecosystem, and have emphasized key responsibilities for both parties. Grantmakers must be transparent regarding their funding opportunities and decision-making processes, they are obligated to uphold the privacy of their applicants and reviewers, and they must provide honest and straight-forward feedback to grantseekers. Grantseekers and, once supported, grant recipients are committed to adhering to the regulations and requirements of the grantmaking organization and for maintaining communication and trust. In sum, we expect this chapter to be a resource and a point of departure for additional discourse and also for further definition of ethical practices surrounding funding within the archaeological community.

References

Bauer, D. G.
2011   *The "How To" Grants Manual: Successful Grantseeking Techniques for Obtaining Public and Private Grants.* The ACE Series on Higher Education. Lanham, MD: Rowman & Littlefield.

Folsom, R. B.

2019   *How to Get Grant Money in the Humanities and Social Sciences.* New Haven, CT: Yale University.

Gow Petty, J.
2013   *Nonprofit Fundraising Strategy: A Guide to Ethical Decision Making and Regulation for Nonprofit Organizations.* Hoboken, NJ: Wiley & Sons.

Grant, P.
2012   *The Business of Giving. The Theory and Practice of Philanthropy, Grantmaking and Social Investment.* Basingstoke: Palgrave Macmillan.

Josephson, M.
1992   *Ethics in Grantmaking & Grantseeking: Making Philanthropy Better.* Marina del Rey, CA: Joseph and Edna Josephson Institute of Ethics.

Kibbe, B. D.; Setterburg, F.; and Wilbur, C. S.
1999   *Grantmaking Basics, A Field Guide for Funders.* Washington, DC: Council on Foundations.

Lamont, M.
2009   *How Professors Think: Inside the Curious World of Academic Judgment.* Cambridge, MA: Harvard University.

Orosz, J. J.
2000   *The Insider's Guide to Grantmaking.* A Publication of the W. K. Kellogg Foundation. San Francisco: Jossey-Bass.

III. Legacies and Futures

Chapter 9

Never Read Your Heroes

Questioning the Legacies of our Archaeological Forebears through their Archives

Annelies Van de Ven

Abstract

The recent shift to "archive-as-subject" within archaeology has brought with it a questioning of how knowledge is formed within our discipline. Though this reflexive turn has made huge inroads into acknowledging the biases of our interpretive practice, there is still a hesitancy to contend with the ways in which archaeological research has been canonized.

Nowhere is this more the case than in our approaches to major figures within archaeology, the directors of key sites, authors of groundbreaking publications, and donors of large collections or funds. An in-depth critical look at their archives has the potential to destabilize the pedestals upon which many of these figures stand, revealing unethical collecting, political interference, and active discrimination, each carrying its own impact within the further development of the discipline. However, the bias of preservation has meant that their documents are often the most extensive sources we have for researching past events. This begs the question of how we use archives to study the history of our discipline and communicate it in an ethical way, without embodying, reproducing, or legitimating the problematic ideologies of our forebears. This chapter aims to contribute to this discussion by presenting a critical and reflexive deconstruction of one such archive, that of French coptologist Jean Doresse.

Introduction

Institutional and personal archives[1] give us important insights into the archaeological process,

the histories of archaeological sites and artifacts, but they also pose many challenges. The shift to "archive-as-subject" within anthropology and history has brought with it an inquiry into how knowledge is formed within the academic sphere (Stoler 2002: 87; 2009: 44).[2] Archives are not neutral, their construction mirrors the intent of their creators and custodians. Though their sto-

---

1   In this chapter, I use the definition of archive laid out by archivist Dorothy Berry (2021): "An archive, is defined as the materials/permanent records created or collected by an individual or organization because of the enduring value contained in the information they contain, especially if those materials were kept according to provenance, original order, collective control."

2   See also Baird and McFayden 2014; Brusius and Singh 2018; Riggs 2019; Brusius 2020; da Canha 2020.

ries are often collected as a sign of tribute to key actors within the discipline—from the directors of key sites, to the authors of ground-breaking publications, or the donors of large collections and funds—it is not uncommon for these same archives to reveal episodes of questionable collecting, political interference, and active discrimination. Yet, truly critical analyses of their construction remain challenging.

Whether it be the racist comments of James H. Breasted (Ambridge 2013) or the anti-suffragette campaigning of Gertrude Bell (Bush 2002), we have all encountered the disappointment of discovering the unscrupulous practices of our discipline's pioneers. Some would suggest that we should chalk this up to a difference in cultural experience or historical context and stick to assessing the merits of their archaeological contributions alone. However, this context-free approach still falters when we consider that the recorded actions and words of these figures continue to have a deep impact on archaeology to this day. The archive's continued ability to affect our practices implies that we must take a diachronic approach to its analysis, addressing its contents within its historical context as well as through its more problematic legacies (Thompson 2002).[3] Confronting these narratives often proves difficult, and they are all too easily swept under the rug for fear of threats to resources, funding, and public support (Brusius 2017b). In addition to this, there are counter-forces within academia itself, preferring to ignore the existing prejudices baked into the discipline's history, as inquiries into ethical questions and structures of inequality are met with accusations of emotionality and bias.

The exigencies of archaeology as a scientific and objective endeavor positions archives as passive, and thus authentic, witnesses of their time. This neglects both the subjectivity of the archives'

authors, as well as the agency of the archives themselves, as they structure our institutions, methods, and assumptions, not to mention the heritage communities that they engage. These issues beg the question of how we can work ethically, highlighting the value of our discipline and its contributors, through time without embodying, reproducing, or legitimating the problematic practices embedded within it. A key realization in addressing this issue is that we cannot do this alone. Efforts to close off our discipline and our sources to external critique until we have come to grasp with the situation, though often well-meaning, are counterproductive (Colwell 2015). What is needed instead are frameworks that embrace interdisciplinarity, collaboration with museum and archival professionals, and co-creation with heritage communities.

In this chapter, I focus on the ethical mediation of personal and institutional archives within the discipline of archaeology. Ethics, here, is considered not as a purely intellectual endeavor nor as a merely procedural entity,[4] but as the broader foundation for increasing accountability and openness in our everyday practices. I will begin with a personal encounter of an archaeological archive, exploring how heroic images are constructed, using as an example my own research into the collections and archives of Egyptologist Jean Doresse held at the Université Catholique de Louvain (UCLouvain). I will first focus on deconstructing the biases of the archaeological archive, and this will be followed by an examination of the ways in which these challenges can be rendered visible in our practices. Finally, I move to the wider implications of archival (in-)accessibility and the need for collaboration and sensitivity in our practices surrounding these important resources. By placing a case study from my own research within the wider movement of reading archives "against the grain" (Carruthers and Van Damme 2017: 271; Stoler 2009), I highlight the need for reflexivity in our approach to archaeological research.

3 An example of this legacy is the ongoing orientalism, classism, sexism, and ableism of the labor division on archaeological sites as well as the promotion strategies within archaeological departments. The latter are often still based on a need for international excavation experience and leadership, which continues to disadvantage those with disabilities, financial need, or caring obligations.

4 Procedural ethics are written into application procedures and include things like data storage strategies (see Guillemin and Gillam 2004).

Deconstructing our own Pedestals

Reflexivity can be defined as the ability to (re-) examine one's own relationship to the research subject. It is a methodological consideration, as it focuses not on what is being studied but on why and how. This implies an interrogation of "our own ethos and motives" but also "the directions and training which we work" (McKee and Porter 2012: 64–65). As a methodology, reflexivity cannot be achieved through a singular action; it is continuous, requiring both self-discipline and self-awareness throughout the research process. The consideration of one's own positionality and biases makes us more alert to ethical tensions that arise within the research process, as it ensures we are more aware of power relationships across the material and consider our own ability to impact how the archives we work with are engaged with in the future. It does not prescribe a response to any particular ethical dilemma, but rather ensures that we treat each one with openness and sensitivity (Guillemin and Gillam 2004: 277). Acts of reflexivity should also be communicated with the same sense of scientific commitment as other aspects of a project's methodology. Thus, to set the tone, I begin my own chapter with a consideration of how my own engagement with the archive was shaped by my own education and positionality.

As students in archaeology, one of the first things that we are introduced to in our courses is the canon of scholars and patrons that defined our field. From Gertrude Bell to Lewis Binford, these figures occupy pride of place on Archaeology 101 reading lists and are featured in countless undergraduate essays. Luckily, bucking the cannon has become more commonplace in these courses, as staff members acknowledge the importance of exploring diverse approaches to archaeological practice to teach students to look critically and creatively at the development of archaeological practice. However, the presence of these larger-than-life figures continue to impact our collective work and our research environment. Sponsors and founders not only give their names to buildings but also to professorships

and scholarships that we strive to attain. Such constant reminders reinforce the significance of these figures and legitimize their actions as part of mainstream archaeological practice. The sites that these pioneers excavated become the focus of public and academic pilgrimages, as they are placed at the center of a modern hero cult. Their publications are established as foundational texts and our syllabi that reference them form a kind of epic tradition within which we construct our own identities as scholars and professionals. With these archaeological heroes looming so large over our discipline, being able to access their archives comes to feel like a rare privilege and a confirmation of your status as part of the academe (Schwartz and Cook 2002: 1). The sense of attainment that one feels in working with archives is a sign of the success of the archival project. Archival inventories are presented as academic and objective, all the while marking out the narratives that underwrite the canon of our field and normalizing the exclusion of others. The archive has thus been internalized as a symbol of knowledge and power, with archival research being presented as the fieldwork of historical disciplines, "essential to the identity of the historian as a historian" (Decker and McKinlay 2020: 18). This makes it all the more challenging to come to terms with their problematic legacies when confronted with the written record. By researching the archives of heroic figures contained within academic institutions, scholars inevitably contribute to the validation of this canon. It is not just the contents of the archive and the reputation of its creator that is at stake here but their context and their continuing impact on the processes of research.

At UCLouvain, the university museum, Musée L, and the university archives hold collections donated by one such figure, the French coptologist Jean Doresse.[5] Described as one of the greatest "orientalists"[6] of the century by one of his

---

5   These collections were donated to the Institut Orientaliste de Louvain, now also known as the Centre d'études orientales.

6   A problematization of this word within the French-speaking community in Belgium was presented in a 2018

protégés (Rassart-Debergh and Fuchs 2016: 7), Jean Doresse is internationally best known for his work on the Nag Hammadi Codices, which he published not only in the academic milieu but also for a wider public. However, Coptic Studies communities tend to be much better acquainted with his full curriculum vitae, which included translating and analyzing numerous Coptic texts, undertaking a survey of Coptic monuments in Egypt, excavating a ruined Coptic monastery, and being part of the French team that developed their own archaeological service in Ethiopia. In order to carry out this work, he regularly traveled back and forth from his home in France to Egypt and Ethiopia, building up an extensive archive and collection in the process.[7] These collections would ultimately become the key to guaranteeing his legacy, as he donated them to various institutions in order to make them widely accessible to researchers in the hope that they would be able to continue his unfinished work (A_JD_Document_Administration_53).[8] Though he left most of his collection connected to Ethiopia, as well as his manuscript collection, to other institutions, his primary research into Coptic archaeology came to UCLouvain, being acquired as the *Fonds Doresse*.[9]

As a non-coptologist, it was Doresse's collections that first brought me into contact with his legacy. Examining the archaeological collections at Musée L, his are hard to miss. Most of Musée L's collections are a combination of donations coming from collectors and teaching collections inherited from early to mid-20th-century professors. This means that only few came with any clear archaeological provenience[10] attributed to them. In contrast, the material that Jean Doresse donated in the early 1990s all had a known find location, having been collected during his 1948–49 survey and sondage at Deir el-Gizaz (Doresse 1989) and later analyzed and published by Anna Di Bitonto-Kasser (1988; 1989; 1990; 1992; 1994; 1996).[11] The finds are made up primarily of everyday artifacts that would have been used and disposed of during the monastery's lifetime. The collection consists of textile fragments, various bones (mostly related to food preparation), ostraca, fragmented glass, and stone and ceramic objects. They have been used to attribute to Doresse an appreciation of scientific data in spite of his training, which was dominated by a love of philology.

Only four artifacts from the *Fonds Doresse* are on permanent display: a decorated pottery sherd,

---

report by Guillermo Kozlowski. This kind of problematic terminology is slowly being adjusted within the academic environment. This is not happening at the same pace everywhere, and efforts to change the name of chairs and institutions have not been taken up with the same vigor in all communities and in Belgium it continues to be used in academic institutions.

7 Many of the artifacts within his collection came to him as diplomatic gifts and local purchases, though a significant number can also be traced back to purchases from well-known antiquities dealers.

8 These references refer to the archives at Musée L. They are given the initial of the donator, in this case JD, and then organized according to box, folder, and then individual document. The Doresse archive held in the university's archival service is identified as FE 113; however, the individual documents have not yet been given definitive numbers and are therefore referenced by their box number, document type, and, where relevant, their date.

9 Already in 1961 he donated his manuscript collection to the Vatican Library. Between 1972 and 1976, he presented successive batches of archival materials to Claremont College for their publications of the Nag Hammadi Archives. His archives concerning the emperor of Ethiopia he donated

to the University of Addis Ababa in 1991, and he gave his collections of Ethiopian artifacts and material connected to Marianne's work at Antinoe to the Musee d'Histoire Naturelle et d'Ethnographie Colmar in 1999 (see Rassart-Debergh 2004; Rassart-Debergh and Fuchs 2016).

10 Provenience in this chapter refers to the archaeological context in which an artifact was found, while provenance in short indicates the artifact's history in relation to those who use, keep, and study it.

11 It remains unclear exactly how Jean Doresse brought these objects to France. It would have been possible with an explicit permit from the Egyptian authorities, which is not unlikely, given the type of artifacts entailed, but he retained no documentation to confirm this. Though those exporting material during this time highlight that there were no laws impeding export, it is clear that several measures were in fact in place to stop people, particularly archaeological teams, from removing finds (see Kersel 2010). Certain objects from this excavation have also appeared elsewhere, with an alphabetic ostracon from the same hand as the one in Musée L (inv. D103) being found in the library at Leiden (Hoogendijk and van Minnen 1991: 30–31, no. 11).

two ostraca, and a carved wooden seal. Their fragmentary nature, while perhaps less attractive to groups of casual visitors, does a great deal to evoke the reality of archaeological fieldwork, increasing their appeal as sources of archaeological knowledge.[12] Truly challenging to display are the two meters of personal research archives that Jean Doresse deposited in the university alongside his collection.[13] The sheer fact that his archive remains preserved immediately gives Doresse status as an important figure within the field. A shallow read of the correspondence within the archives only confirms this, presenting Doresse as leading the mid-century charge to turn international attention to the under-researched field of Coptic archaeology despite resistance from more established academy figures. The files also contain extensive bibliographic notes, as well as drafts of articles and publications, cut up and rearranged with comments in every margin. The documents that he provided date back to Doresse's own doctoral research, including failed requests for funding and letters to his supervisor seeking support for his efforts. His struggle to manage publication deadlines and wordcounts are recognizable and it is easy to commiserate with his descriptions of familiarly challenging workloads and bureaucratic bottlenecks. In reading his work, I found myself empathizing more and more with his experiences, taking his side in discussions with colleagues and lifting him up as an example of someone who overcame the challenges of an academic career to become a significant donor and well-regarded scholar.

My sense of rapport with Doresse through his archives highlights their role as "affective economies" (Ahmed 2004: 7) with an ability to evoke emotions and influence practice beyond their original context. Though these feelings of familiarity and empathy may make the research process more recognizable, reassuring the researcher and making them feel at home, they also work to obscure inequalities or oppressive practices. Critical approaches require us to question and deconstruct those things we take for granted, allowing us to identify issues and create space for more ethical practices that promote equality, transparency, and care. This does not mean ignoring our own biases. Instead, by adopting an "intimate distance" towards past archaeologists, we are able to claim both "closeness with and distance from" their practices, eschewing the neutrality of the researcher in the process (Bigenho 2012: 123; Harrison 2015: 39). Acknowledging our own positions as "objective partisans" during presentations and articles is part and parcel of this process of self-reflection and should be more mainstream (Hodder 2003; Kamash 2018). This recognition of personal intimacy with the unequal knowledge structures created by archaeological processes refocuses critical arguments against individuals operating in the past towards the wider systems within which they operated. In this way, we acknowledge the urgency of approaching archives in a critical way, ensuring that we read them "against the grain," considering their contexts of creation, the assumptions that they embody, and the structures that they support (Stoler 2009).

Understanding Context

In order to ethically deconstruct Doresse's archive, it is necessary understand its context. The bulk of the material was created after the Second World War,[14] in a period when France held strong to its cultural hegemony in Egypt. It fits within a wider corpus of material left behind by the "heroic" figures who are presented as worthy of

12 The full range of material was recently put on display as part of the exhibition "Parcours d'Archéologues: Entre archives et objets," curated by the author in collaboration with the Musée L collections team between February 18, 2020 and August 16, 2020 (see https://archiveobjets.wordpress.com/).

13 It is important to note here that though a number of fieldwork records in the traditional sense are included in the archive, this is not the bulk of the collection, which is more focused on Doresse's personal research notes and correspondence.

14 The two exceptions being the glass plate photographs from the early 1900s (A_JD_Plaque_Egypte_1-43; A_JD_Plaque_Monastere_1-115) and the inventory of Ptolemaic and late antique terracottas in Parisian museums, which was the work of Jean Doresse and Marianne Guentch-Oglouëff, when they were working at the Louvre and the Musée Guimet, respectively (drafts in FE 113_2).

remembrance thanks to their efforts protecting Egyptian antiquities and history from oblivion. Critical studies of the archives belonging to several of Egyptology's other heroes show imperialist and discriminatory practices upon which they founded the discipline (Carruther 2015), many of which are still ongoing to this day (Abd el Gawad 2019).[15] Auguste Mariette's supposed success in stemming the flow of illicit antiquities out of Egypt is belied by his own clandestine excavations and the exclusion of local scholars (Reid 1985: 234; 2002: 99–103). Gaston Maspero is heralded as a great Egyptologist who contributed to the preservation of Egyptian sites even while he promoted a system of partage and international antiquities collecting that bypassed local rights to heritage (Stevenson 2019; Piacentini 2013; Gady 2011). Sir Flinders Petrie is seen as the father of scientific archaeology, but his methods were grounded in a system derived from the work of eugenicists (Challis 2013; Perry and Challis 2013). Howard Carter, still heralded as the ultimate Egyptologist, went to great lengths to placate international funders with positions on his dig crew, exclusive reporting rights and antiquities that he removed from the country (Riggs 2019).

Doresse actively compared himself against these figures, referencing his own discoveries in comparison to theirs (Doresse 1949; Nice Matin 1949).[16] To this day, Egyptological finds are presented in relation to Tutankhamun, and archaeologists are measured against an idealized picture of the intrepid explorer with boots on the ground. Though we are quick to point out the fallacy of Tomb Raider and Indiana Jones stereotypes in our classes, those credited with founding archaeology through their intrepid travels continue to set the standards of practice that we are expected to follow.[17] The visual records held within Doresse's archives materially support his place as a member of this Egyptological elite. The presence of several sketches and over 2000 photos of monastic architecture give physical weight to the long time he spent traversing Egypt in order to capture the vestiges of Coptic life throughout the country. The images are further supported by letters in the archive, in which Doresse notes his own independence and international intrepidness in stark contrast with the careers of his supervisors, the scholars who followed his work from Europe, but also to the Egyptian Egyptologists who are presented as existing only in a local sphere.[18] His work on the Nag Hammadi Codices was particularly evocative in these reports. His reports of his own unprecedented discovery with the potential to radically alter our perception of religious history were so embedded into popular consciousness that it spawned fictional retellings (e.g., Malarkey 2006).

Key within these retellings is the concept of "discovery" within archaeology. To this day, with-

---

15 This is equally true for other fields of Middle Eastern archaeology (see Brusius 2017a; 2017b; Porter 2010; Larsen 1989).

16 Doresse also shared with these figures his active participation in the antiquities market. He defended his position by stating that he ensured artifacts remained in Egypt through their sale to local museums, institutions, and collectors (Doresse 1958: 138–41). Thus, the reports, publications, and media reports surrounding his research that are included within the archives that he left to UCLouvain present him as a protector of Coptic history in northeast Africa. However, a cross-referencing of his own writings with reports on the antiquities market at the time and local responses show that his connection to dealers was far less altruistic (Gady 2011; JD _VI.4-6; FE 113; two letters from Tano to Doresse on June 29, 1949 and July 1, 1949; letter from Robinson to Doresse November 3, 1972) In addition to this, his sensationalization of the artifacts of his research had an adverse impact on their safety by

increasing their value and appeal to international collectors (Robinson 2014: xxvi).

17 To this day attending fieldschools abroad is seen as a kind of "rite of passage" for students across archaeology. Following this, many tenured archaeological positions continue to be reserved for people who are able to lead a fieldschool or other larger scale academic field project. The requirements of adhering to this intrepid archaeological lifestyle in order to be "successful" in the discipline has an exclusionary effect that has engendered several publications in recent years. Some prominent publications on the problematic ableism that this entails are Smith et al. 2015; Phillips and Gilchrist 2012; Moser 2007..

18 This is particularly evident in his letters to Puech (e.g., FE 113_2; letter from Doresse to Puech, June 29, 1950). There is a continuing issue of exclusion in Egyptology which is discussed in several chapters of William Carruthers' *Histories of Egyptology* (see Doyon 2015; Omar 2015; Elshakry 2015), as well as a forthcoming publication by Usama Gad.

in academia in general and archaeology in particular, a great value is attributed to being the first to report on something. Publication, funding, and awards structures are all built around our ability to prove the novelty of our research. Rewarding scholars for claiming the role of "discoverer" or lead researcher inadvertently increases sensationalism, competition, and guardedness around new finds and their publication. This is true today, and it was true in the case of many of Doresse's projects. We can see the importance of "discovery" emerge in two different ways in Doresse's archive. There is discovery as the identification of archaeological sites or artifacts, and there is discovery as the uncovering of a site or artifact through excavation. Doresse regularly crosses the two, making it difficult at times to ascertain his role in different projects. In the case of Deir el-Gizaz, he did not discover the site; it was a known location among the local population, his "discovery" was in reconnecting the site with the monastery of Apa Samuel. Similarly, in the example of the Nag Hammadi archives, in his publications and his letters to his funders and patrons Doresse named himself the discoverer of these manuscripts (Doresse 1958: 133–59; FE 113_2, letters from Doresse to Schaeffer, De Plin, and Faure on July 24, 1956). However, he did not excavate them, and when challenged on his role, he explains himself by stating that he was "alone in being able to claim the honor of their discovery from a scientific point of view" (FE 113_2; letter from Doresse to Schaeffer on August 21, 1956).

In claiming the sole honor of discovery, Doresse regularly—consciously or not—erases the voices of his collaborators, and not just his international counterparts with whom he felt he was competing but also his local partners—his mentors, guides, and colleagues. The few names that are preserved in the archive largely disappear when it comes to Doresse's formal reporting. This is particularly the case of his excavations at Deir el-Gizaz where several photos include the local workforce but only a single name, that of Coptic Museum conservator Raouf Habib,[19] is retained

in the archive.[20] During his short expedition to locate the find spot of the Nag Hammadi, he noted the names of his guides: Cheikh Abd el Gourmi, Fadullah Mohammed Endauri of Hamra Dam, Mahmoud Abd el Naim of Es Sayyad, Ahmad Mohammed Nur al-Din of Es Sayyad, and the two Coptic priests Dawit (or David) and Ioachim Isaac (FE 113_5; notes regarding Doresse's visit to Nag Hammadi on January 26–27, 1950) allowing us a peek into the collaborative effort that such a "discovery" requires. However, in his final publication, it is only one name that is preserved, that of Coptic priest Dawit, as he remarks that the tales told by the other locals, who he refers to consistently as "peasants" (*paysans*), were just fabrications (Doresse 1950: 437; 1958: 145–56). In creating this value division among local oral histories, he disregards their knowledge and experiences, further cementing the imagined superiority of the foreign archaeologist in determining reliability and legitimizing narratives of the past (Abd el Gawad 2019; Mickel 2019; Doyon 2015; Pollock 2010). This fits within a wider framework of systemic discrimination that marked many of the interactions of French coptologists and wider biblical scholars with Egyptian history, as Egyptian Muslim scholars were distrusted and contemporary local traditions were seen as tainting the "true Christianity" of their forebears (FE 113_5; notes regarding Doresse's visit to Nag Hammadi on January 26–27, 1950; letter from Doresse to Puech 20n April 29, 1950; Doresse 1988: xii; Robinson 2014: xv, 77–92).

This trend of disparaging local knowledge and expertise is not uncommon in the archaeological record.[21] The perpetuation of these stereotypes by those researching these events only serves to further existing inequalities and hierarchies. For the archival researcher deconstructing such statements is not only important for providing proper context, but it is also ethically impera-

---

19 He is also mentioned within Doresse's publication in a disparaging statement about the state of conservation of

Coptic manuscripts in the museum (Doresse 1989: 159).

20 These photos are labeled for the structures behind those excavating, negating their existence completely (e.g., Doresse 1989: 164). See Riggs 2019: ch. 5; Doyon 2015; Quirke 2010.

21 Mickel 2019; Reid 2002.

tive. While the authors of the archives enjoy the power to present themselves and preserve their views, those named in their documents have little agency over how they are represented. While the researcher does not always have the opportunity to discuss consent or collaboration with those implicated second-hand in the archive, they are accountable for how they frame their inclusion in the archive for future users (McKee and Porter 2012: 60). By adopting a critical approach to these kinds of statements we can help to counterbalance practices that were "lacking in ethical care" (Morra 2020: 10), indicating episodes of discrimination and erasure.

TRACING INEQUALITIES

With historiographical research moving towards feminist and postcolonial studies of the archaeological discipline, archives are seen as a space in which we can find traces of underrepresented figures, like Doresse's local collaborators. However, the very archival project is one that emerged from an effort to preserve a limited perception of social significance, one that is often situated in gendered and racialized narratives (Carruthers and Van Damme 2017: 266–67). Archives are by nature temporally, geographically, or thematically circumscribed. These limits are made explicit in archival histories and mission statements. However, there are also more implicit biases, lacunas that reflect the history of archives themselves, the racism, classism, and sexism that excludes people from systems of power. It is thus necessary to research the context of an archive's creation in order to critically assess its contents. In the case of the UCLouvain Archival Services for example, the history of the university provides some insights into the gaps within the archives. The university's Roman Catholic roots mean that many of its staff were members of the clergy, often well-to-do, well-read, and well-traveled individuals whose religious affiliations impacted their views on science, social structures, and global events. Their predominance limits the viewpoints represented in the archive. Women, for example, are vastly underrepresented, ow-

ing to the late acceptance of female students (1920s) and professors (1960s) into the institution (Malfliet et al. 2016). The inequality is also a measure of donation practices within the cultural sector, as documents and artifacts belonging to minorities are often subsumed into the collections of the dominant group. Thus, the Doresse collection and archives include large portions that were written by Marianne Guentch-Ogloueff, his wife, and Togo Mina, the curator of the Coptic Museum in Cairo, yet their contributions are still included within the framework of their connection to Doresse.[22] The echoes of the inequalities that they faced are preserved in the archive, as his work forms the lens through which we are able to see their accomplishments.

This inequality gives an additional layer to the idea of the archive as a "contact zone" (Pratt 1991; 1992). It is a space within which we encounter the context of past archaeologists, but also one in which the unequal relationship between archaeologists and their families, their colleagues, and local populations becomes apparent. On occasion these relationships are defined in the archives through discriminatory language or descriptions of oppressive behaviors, but unequal relations can also be referenced in more subtle ways. Even those archives that don't show overt classism, sexism, or racism can still show indications of implicit biases embedded within a science that was defined with a Eurocentric male reference point. These biases can be most clearly identified by mapping the networks of knowledge and power through scholarly communications and citations.[23] Tracing Doresse's correspondence with powerful diplomats, renowned scholars, and prolific collectors, alongside institutional archives

---

22 This is in contrast to the relatively common practice of women making donations named after their husbands. Women thus more commonly fall into a role of being the maintainer of a man's legacy in both museum and archival spaces, but in this act their own activities and accomplishments are not as often recognized. See Hill 2016: ch. 2.

23 This continues to happen today, as the structures of publication and funding peripherize particular regions and center others along similar lines as the previous colonial efforts (Langer 2017; xiii–xiv; Hountondji 2006).

FIG. 9.1 *Marianne Guentch-Ogloueff in the desert south of Luxor in the winter of 1949/1950, photo taken by Jean Doresse (A_JD_Negatif_Louxor_129, MuséeL, Louvain la Neuve).*

and publications, we see the centers of influence in Egyptology moving across Europe and later America through the creation of scientific committees and the dissemination of publications by a handful of scholars. This is evident in his communication with the various iterations of the Nag Hammadi committee, as the leadership in these efforts shifted from his own French-oriented initiative to one with Swiss, Dutch, German, and finally American leadership. Egyptian members are rarely given the initiative in these initiatives, more often being contacted to obtain approvals than for scientific contributions. The main exception to this is Pahor Labib, who is the source of a number of communications from the mid-1950s to the mid-1960s. However, it is also in this time that we see a decentering of the publication effort, as Doresse and Puech pushed to get their personal interpretations out before Pahor Labib could disseminate an official edition of the codices (e.g., Doresse 1958; 1959; Puech et al. 1955).

Besides mapping power relations through research leadership and publications, the archives of archaeologists also allow us to trace them in a more material way, through the scattering of artifacts (Stevenson 2019; Joyce and Gillespie 2015). In the case of the Doresse donation, the connection between institutions of research, archives, and artifact extraction is particularly

clear, given the presence of the Deir el-Gizaz material alongside Doresse's documentation.[24] However, what the archives are able to do here that would not be possible in another institution is to connect these collections of provenienced artifacts with wider networks of the antiquities trade. Doresse's correspondence shows that, even while he was working to record artifacts in the field, he was also engaged in the trade of artifacts on the antiquities market and collecting on an institutional level through his work at the Louvre and the Coptic Museum.[25] The content of his letters demonstrates the extractive practices made possible by his privileged position. We see the asymmetrical circuits of these artifacts, from local inhabitants, to international middlemen, and finally to wealthy and influential collectors, while their itineraries highlight the geography of the trade and its primary interlocutors (fig. 9.2). It is only through combining artifacts and archives that we see how intertwined the histories of archaeology and collecting are, with 20th-century

24 However, even in such cases of direct deposition, there is a messiness at play, which is evidenced by the presence of Deir el-Gizaz material in Leiden through a secondary channel of deposition (Hoogendijk and van Minnen 1991: 30–31, no. 11).

25 For examples see FE113_2, letters from Gilles Quispel to Doresse on March 20, 1948, July 9, 1948, and August 25, 1949; Robinson 2014, 389–90.

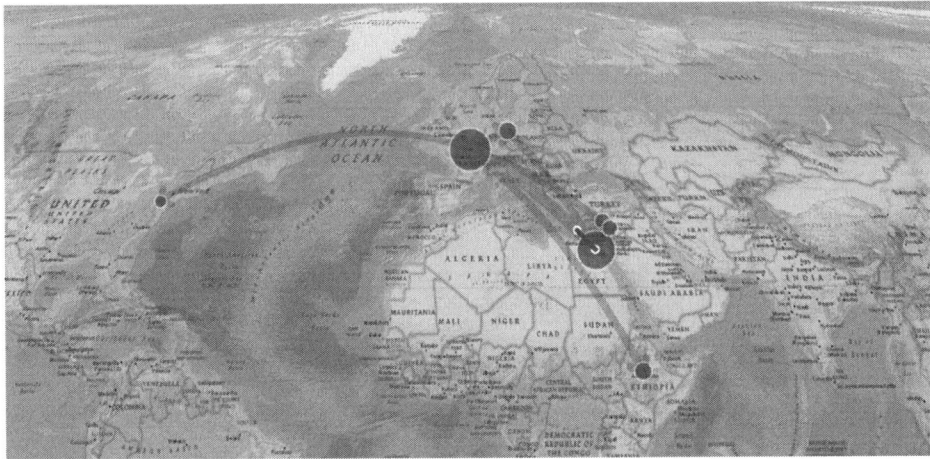

FIG. 9.2 *Visualization of one lot of letters related to Doresse's correspondence with Drioton; created by the author using the Voyant application Dreamscape.*

archaeologists like Doresse moving readily between dig site and antiquities market (Kersel 2019; Brusius forthcoming).

The integration of archaeologists within these networks of power allows us to use their archives as a resource for examining relationships across multiple fields, particularly the inequalities of those connections. However, the dispersal and lack of direct access to both archives and artifacts spread across institutions mean that understandings of such relationships are necessarily fragmentary, as secondary reports become primary research sources. Doresse's own material is spread across at least seven locations,[26] including two at UCLouvain, none of which currently using a linked database through which material can be cross-referenced across institutions. This fragmentation is partially down to colonial politics, like the Deir el-Gizaz material being divided between an Egyptian depot in Gournah and Doresse's own collection through the system of partage imposed by the French-run antiquities service of the 19th and early 20th century to ensure the "compensation" of international teams for their funding of excavations.[27] However, the division of archives is not always this consciously planned, and even within the same institution archives can become fragmented through displacement, as was the case with the Doresse archives at

UCLouvain. When the Oriental Institute became subsumed in the Institute of Civilizations, Arts, and Letters, the documents were inadvertently separated, with half being kept in an office and half getting tucked away in a library drawer. From here the material traveled to the museum and the archival services with neither being aware of the other's holdings until a recent inventorying effort brought the overlap to light.

This is why access across these different institutions is paramount, not only in the research phase of a project, but also in publications and displays engaging with archival materials. By applying the interdisciplinary and multi-method tradition of archaeology to its archive and disseminating the results, these examinations can be made more concrete. This does not mean that we should abandon a contextually informed reading of an archive's contents—an archive should always be considered in relation to its historical context—but rather that we should work to create a more in-depth understanding through methods beyond traditional historical analysis. Network analyses are particularly useful in this effort, as they allow for the mapping and quantification of power connections. Fleshing out the nodes and edges of this network of power allows us to explore the influence that meanings created on a personal and relational level had on archaeological practice. In harnessing these different approaches in our analysis of archives, we can work to "expose

---

26 See footnote 10.

27 Abd el Gawad and Stevenson 2020: 123.

the ways in which the history of archaeology was written to justify some colonialist practices" rather than functioning as a means of bolstering them (Moro-Abadía 2006: 14).

Acknowledging Archival Messiness

The preeminence of archival research has long derived from the perception of their authenticity. Archives are viewed as primary sources, providing an unmediated connection to the past as opposed to the edited nature of published works (Dirks 2015: 28; Schwartz 2006: 69). In this scenario, it is imagined that the researcher is able to re-animate the archives through the act of reading (Stoler 2009: 18–19). However, while archives do give us unique insights into the experiences of past scholars, they also hold in themselves many layers of manipulation and interpretation (Stoler 2009: 22; Derrida 1995). They serve as a means to record events but also to communicate, to persuade, and to validate, creating a relationship between reader and writer that is entangled in a wider network of knowledge and influence. Archivists Joan M. Schwartz and Terry Cook highlight this mediatory role in their definition archives as "active sites where social power is negotiated, contested, confirmed" (2002: 1). This iterative process of archival (re-)construction in order to create meaning is exacted by their creators, maintainers, and users (Spieker 2008: 7). The archives of archaeologists, like the archaeological sites that they contextualize, can therefore be described as having a "taphonomy" (Baird and McFadyen 2014: 20), one that we can deconstruct and analyze.

To examine these processes in the case of the Doresse archive, it is therefore necessary to take his archive out of the realm of the static fact into a space where they can be seen as material and manipulatable (Dever 2019). A material dissection of the archive is necessary to create "intimate distance," allowing the researcher to see its contents framed through their form. If the archival page can be seen as a trace of physical research processes (Fuchsberger et al. 2014), then any page within it can be analyzed as an object with

its own biography (Baird and McFadyen 2014: 16). Each document can be seen as a series of choices, from the material of the support to the medium of communication used, while series of documents show how these choices accumulate as edits are introduced and sections are scrapped. In this way, it becomes easier to distinguish episodes of inexactitude and contradiction but also willful storytelling. This identifies the archive as something constructed, holding the biases of its authors, both individual and institutional. In order to ensure a more equal and thus ethical representation of contributions to the discipline, it is necessary to understand which people and events have been built up in the archive and which have been left out. A taphonomical analysis allows us to do this on a granular level, making it easier to identify not only what choices were made, but also on occasion who made them and to what end.

The bulk of the archival material that Doresse donated to the Oriental Institute of UCLouvain, which later came to the university's museum and archival services, is made up of notes and photographs made by himself, his wife, and his associates,[28] as well as some finished inventories, publications, and course material. These archives are intimately linked to Doresse's fieldwork in Egypt; however, they are surprisingly sparse in their expression of the in-depth archaeological analysis that we would expect from a mid-20th-century scholar. All that remains of his direct archaeological recordings are limited descriptions of pottery and glass fragments, a single site plan, a few images of the site during excavation, and a selection of artifact photographs. There are no detailed descriptions of contexts, no survey coordinates, and no administrative documents to give an indication of the workforce. The central focus of the archive is instead placed on collating ancient sources, translating Coptic texts, and describing the architecture of Coptic monasteries. This omission of archaeological records may suggest a disparity in his own valuation of, or indeed ability in, this area in comparison with

28 The material supplied by others is rarely expressly noted, making it difficult to identify particular hands throughout the archive.

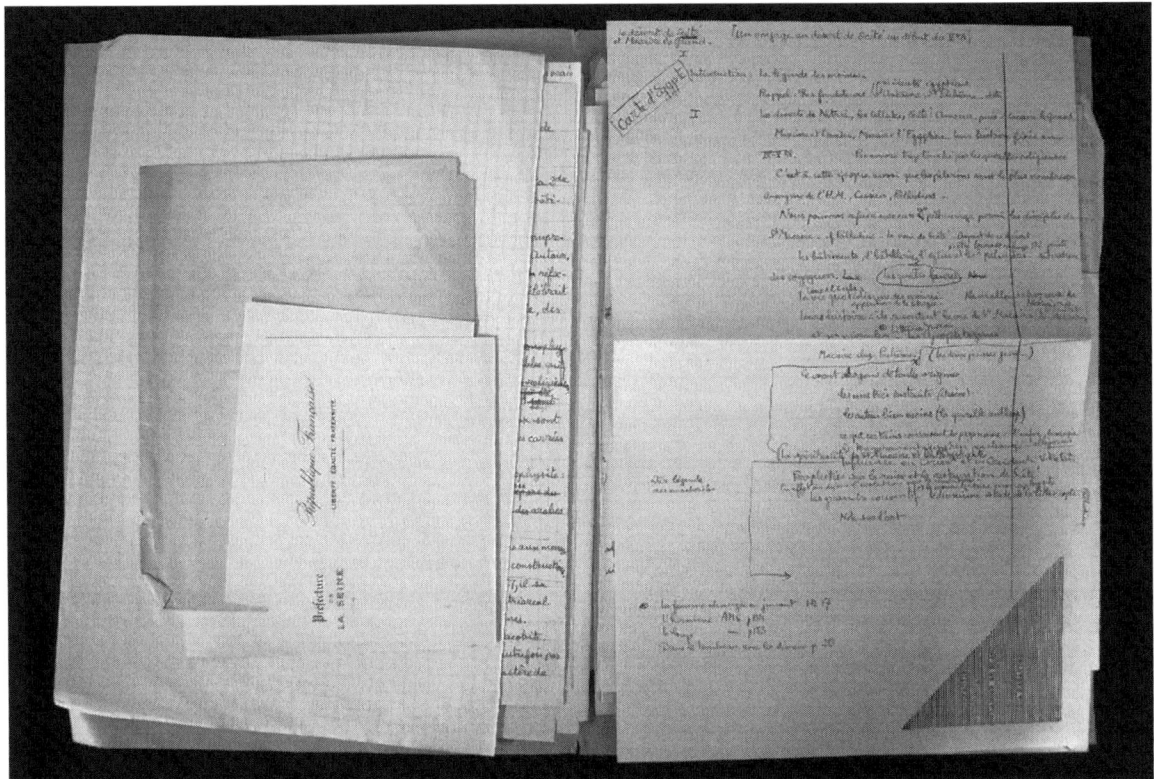

FIG. 9.3 *One of Doresse's research folders showing two notes written on re-used stationery belonging to French institutions (A_JD_Document_Recherche_6, MuséeL, Louvain la Neuve).*

his philological and art historical work, or alternatively an assumption of disinterest on the part of the collecting institution. Whatever Doresse's motivation, the loss of this information problematizes the archaeological categorization of the artifacts that accompany the archive, given the lack of clear data.

The architecturally and philologically-oriented documentation that we do have pertaining to his archaeological survey of Egypt for Coptic sites is divided into different folders. Some contain clear subdivisions, including historiography and bibliography, suggesting the structure of a planned publication. Though there are only a few dated items, primarily letters from Doresse's doctoral advisor, it is possible to organize the folders into different themes that can then be linked to specific times or locations in Doresse's research itinerary. The distinctiveness of each episode is further materially reinforced, as the items reflect technological advances that impacted the development of scholarly research throughout

his lifetime, from early 20th-century glass plate negatives to fax machines in the 1990s. Episodes can equally be distinguished through Doresse's use of different sizes, colors, and types of notepaper, as well as his regular re-use of stationery from certain museums, research institutions, and government departments to take his notes (fig. 9.3), which further aids in reconstructing the precise chronology and geography of his research, as well as his institutional affiliations.

Though outwardly these folders appear organized, a more detailed reading shows a level of messiness within the long period of research undertaken by Doresse. Images and notes are rarely labeled, making it difficult on occasion to find the connection between successive pages. Even in the case of distinct chapter drafts, these are regularly out of order and spread across the folder. Consulting the acquisition records for the archive, there are several references in Doresse's own letters to the Oriental Institute about the process he went through to bring his notes together for donation to UCLouvain. In his first letter dating to 1993 (A_JD_Document_Administration_50), he is still in the process of finalizing his thesis draft for publication,[29] regularly consulting his binders of bibliographic notes and figures. At the time of the first deposit, a number of files containing research notes, as well as the artifacts that made up the *Fonds Doresse*, were still on loan to Anna Di Bitonto-Kasser who was finishing the analysis of material from Deir el-Gizaz (1988; 1989; 1990; 1992; 1994; 1996), a site that had yet to be properly published over 40 years after its excavation (Doresse 1989).[30] In another letter, he references having to squeeze the documents into boxes for transportation, leading them to become disorganized in the process (A_JD_Document_Administration_37). Each of these incidents could attest to the general disarray of those documents, and together they highlight the danger of reading an archive entirely as a singular neat episode of deposition, as the process of acquisition often occurs in a complex and piecemeal fashion.

The situation changes completely when we consider Doresse's correspondence pertaining to his work on the Nag Hammadi archive, a set of manuscripts containing primarily gnostic texts bound together in 13 codices.[31] In contrast to the material diversity of most of his research documents, this collection seems to have been photocopied and brought together in a single concerted effort. The copied letters, though not always equally legible, are not kept in folders but rather incorporated as a stack, neatly subdivided into different thematic sections together, with pertinent notes often highlighting injustices that Doresse felt that certain letters presented against him. In this instance, Doresse organized copies of letters that he received from colleagues with his own responses, which he intentionally copied to en-

sure their preservation. On occasion, he preserves multiple iterations of the same correspondence as he re-drafted letters to shorten them, make them sound more professional, and give himself a greater role in the story being told. Even his wife, Egyptologist Marianne Guentch-Ogloueff, is regularly edited out of their collaborative efforts, as Doresse instead crafts statements about his own discoveries (FE 113_5, notes regarding Doresse's visit to Nag Hammadi, January 26–27, 1950; Robinson 2014: 78–92). In considering the contents of the letters, it becomes clear that Doresse made distinct choices on what to include in his folders. The correspondence was actively collected and subsequently stored and maintained to tell a particular story (Dever 2019: 58–59), in this case both a chronological and a moralistic one in which Doresse is putting himself forward as the one who discovered the manuscripts and worked hardest to see them properly published.

A look into the inventories included in the acquisition documents provides further details through which we can interpret his choices. In a list dated to 1995, the correspondence related to the Nag Hammadi archive is referenced to as the "photocopies Robinson" (A_JD_Document_Administration_32). The Robinson here refers to James M. Robinson, an American coptologist working at Claremont College who wrote to Doresse seeking to obtain documentation to write a series of books on the discovery of the Nag Hammadi Codices (FE 113_3 Dossier 5). A comparison between the original letters held in the Claremont collection and the archive photocopies shows that they are in fact the same texts, allowing us to use Doresse's correspondence about his Claremont deposition to better understand his archive at UCLouvain. Put in order, the correspondence in these files shows Doresse gradually being phased out of research into the Nag Hammadi Codices by colleagues. Doresse's desire to order and send his records to Robinson two decades after the events were an attempt by him to "set the record straight" (Robinson 2014: xix). He states in his own publication that the "discovery" for which he was best known had turned out to be "the worst memory of my [his]

---

29 His thesis would ultimately only be published in 2000.

30 A_JD_Document_Administration_1;25;39. The Deir el-Gizaz material was finally deposited in April of 1999 (A_JD_Document_Administration_18). See the publications of Di Bitonto-Kasser 1988; 1989; 1990; 1992; 1994; 1996; Doresse 1989.

31 For an overview of the codices and their histories see Robinson 2014.

career" (Doresse 1988: vii). Yet his preservation not merely of his contextual notes and translations, but also of his full correspondences relating to the event show a continuing preoccupation with his own place in the Nag Hammadi story. He did not merely collect them, but actively (re-) produced them, an act that can simultaneously be seen as an expression of Doresse's anxiety about being forgotten and his own desire for history to prove him right. Doresse's actions ultimately throw into stark relief the tension between remembering and forgetting that is inherent in the archival project. As Derrida highlights in his description of the archive, they are as much an expression of a desire to create a legacy for our memories as one of "forgetfulness, amnesia, the annihilation of memory" expressed through the selective creation of the archive (Derrida 1995: 11).

ACCESS GRANTED

Doresse was not only crafting a narrative through the individual stories present in each document, but also in the way that he actively displaced, (re-) produced, and fragmented documents, grouped them, and ultimately presented them as a single whole. However, Doresse is not the only author in the biography of the archive. The physical and conceptual heterotopia that constitutes the archive is also dependent on the actions, choices, and assumptions of the institutions that keep and manage it (Mbembe 2002: 20; Foucault 1998: 182). Far from representing a single event, the archive is the result of interwoven and sometimes competing agencies. This is why it is so important to preserve the names and actions not only of the donor, but equally of those who constituted and inventoried the archive, those who helped to provide the documents and records with their present-day framework and value as archives.[32]

Archives constitute sites where multiple fragmentary pasts, presents, and futures are braided together through processes of "interpretation,

production and alteration" (Thakur 2020: 71). This means that an archive can never provide a singular comprehensive overview of the past, but rather enacts particular aggregations of it, defined by those collating, maintaining, and using it—the archivists and scholars who gave it its present form and location (Ernst 2016: 12). As historian David Lowenthal highlights, our ideal images of archives are of democratic spaces that are objective and open, but they equally "conjure up confusion, conspiracy, exclusivity" (Lowenthal 2006: 193). From the taxonomies used to the access systems instated, archives remain in many ways spaces of control and classification that "shelter certain kinds of knowledge" (Colwell 2015: s263). Even without explicit statements of exclusion, the archive-implicit bias and Eurocentric reference point of these structures point to a need for more critical approaches to archiving practices. This does not mean that archivists are willfully or intentionally engaging in systems of oppression, but rather that the system that they operate within is inherently biased. This exclusivity is materially manifested in the Archive as an institution just as it is in the archives within it (Stoler 2009: 45; Mbembe 2002: 19). The separation between the panopticon of the reading room (Ketelaar 2002: 236–37) and archival storage is only porous to a select number of people. However, this does not mean that researchers don't have a role to play. In working with the archives of our archaeological forebears, we enter into this chain of archival custody, the process of legitimation that makes archives appear as neutral sources. In order to address these issues, it is essential for researchers to collaborate with archivists in deconstructing the power relations inherent in the archives.

This starts with how we communicate with members of the archival services themselves. As the example of the Doresse archives showed, interrelated materials are rarely kept together. This disruption happens on multiple levels. The very nature of correspondence implies a dispersal of material, as do recording requirements for excavations determined by funding bodies, local governments, and research institutions. Displacements through extraction and donation show willful

32 Many parallels can be drawn to museums in their common "practices of selecting, storing, and manipulating information" (Riggs 2016: 127; see also Brusius and Singh 2018: 7).

movements but also inheritance through familial or academic lineages. Finally, archiving institutions themselves add to movements through sales, exchanges, and rationalizations after deposition. These archival itineraries make historiographical research interesting but also contribute to barriers and exclusivity. As researchers, we are often granted with a level of mobility and independence that allows us to access disparate archives and collections, drawing ties between institutions, sites, figures, and individual records. By documenting these ties, as well as their implications in past and ongoing relationships of power, not just in academic publications but also in our reporting to the archives that we work with and in our communications with community collaborators, we help to ensure a more equal knowledge distribution. Where possible, and ethical,[33] these links can be incorporated into finding aids and databases to be made accessible on-site and online to account for the ongoing inequalities in mobility faced by certain communities due to historical knowledge and resource extraction.

However, an accessible archival database is not the final answer, it is also necessary to rethink the ways in which our information is structured. In my search for documents relating to the work of Jean Doresse, I am browsing for references not just to his name but also those of his best-known associates, the institutions that he worked for, the sites that he worked on, and the academic fields that he worked in. These are often integrated into the database structure, as they have been built to accommodate research like mine, but if we are to create a truly open and de-colonizing space for archival engagement we must open them up to being more than just finding aids for particular documents. A key foundation for this change lays in the language that we use. The words we use are not neutral, as they indicate the audience that we are communicating with and the intention of that communication. As Wayne Modest highlights "the language we use affects whether groups feel a sense of belonging" (2018: 14). They show the per-

spective of their user, the position that they fulfil, and they define in their enactment the supposed position of the receiver. Thus, something as simple as a site name could be an indicator of what kinds of uses an archive is open to. Jean Doresse's archives describe the early work surrounding the Nag Hammadi Codices, thus named in the majority of sources because Nag Hammadi was the closest large town to the find spot. In the current inventories, there is a note linking all references to Nag Hammadi with those to Chenoboskion. This is done because Doresse himself on occasion labeled his research regarding these codices as being related to the Chenoboskion Manuscripts, a term he preferred due to the Greek roots of the name (Robinson 2014: 7–12). Jabal al-Tarif would be a more accurate description of the location of the find, while the names of villages like al-Qasr, Hamrah Dum, or Ad Dabbah would speak more to the individuals who actually found the manuscripts. While these singular instances of archival taxonomy may seem insignificant, taken together they constitute a skewing of the record towards a specific, and quite Eurocentric, viewpoint. By bringing this level of context back into the mix, we acknowledge that archives are more than sources for historical research—they embody lived realities of communities.

The codification of the archive as an inventory that deploys neutralizing language obscures the realities of archival labor, and this not only negates the important contributions of archivists, but it also conceals bias and process in an impersonal structure (Hedstrom 2002; Elia 2017). This can make it easy to avoid challenging existing taxonomies through regurgitating the neutrality of the archive as a holder of material and the researcher as its objective analyzer. However, this ignores the dynamic nature of language and the powerful ways in which it can be deployed. As Stijn Schoonderwoerd states, "words and norms around language are constantly in transition," so although our collections and archives may be "timeless...the ways we speak about them are not" (Schoonderwoerd 2018: 8). Guides on using inclusive archival voice as well as identifying, contextualizing, and potentially replacing sensi-

---

33 Sharing documents should of course occur within the limits of confidentiality agreements and source community consultation as highlighted in Brusius 2020.

tive words exist in order to address these changes and can be applied as much to archival sources as to research engaging with them (Modest and Lelijveld 2018; Antracoli et al. 2019). We should aim to gain familiarity with the language of colonial and oppressive archives without absorbing it into our own practice. In our dissemination practices, this means an acknowledgement of the harmful term alongside the suggestion of a more sensitive one. In research databases, this could take the form of term-referral, in which discriminatory terms are re-directed in a transparent way (Kunst 2018: 31). This avoids invisible censorship while still ensuring that communities feel welcomed to explore the archive rather than actively inhibited. In this way, we come closer to the "radical transparency" described by Janet Marstine, a critical engagement in which we go beyond description to a deep ethical analysis of our institutional practices (2011: 14).

Besides reconsidering who we are communicating with through research and archival channels, a restructuring of archival connections also implies a change in whose voice is heard, not just behind the scenes but also in public display. This is important in order to redress the historicizing tendencies of archaeological practice, the ways in which the discipline obscures present-day realities through the reading of archaeological landscapes as firmly located in the past. This historizing is present in the Doresse archive as we follow the archaeologist as he goes to map the vestiges of Coptic life in a region where Coptic culture is still very much alive and changing (see Robinson 2014: 127). His photographs, maps, and drawings actively reconstruct a first-millennium ce chronology, effacing modern developments and with them modern people (ex. A_JD_HorsFormat_1–8). Without sweeping the narrative with which Doresse imbued his work under the rug, it is possible to mediate how we read its contents through an act of remixing. As Bruno Latour expresses in his description of how knowledge is inscribed into society, archives can be "superimposed, reshuffled, recombined, and summarized," allowing "totally new phenomena [to] emerge" (1986: 30). This remixing can occur through the use of

existing parallel material within the collection.[34] Thus, the erasure of Doresse's drawings can be highlighted through the superimposition of active Coptic figures in the present day, through images, writings, video, and audio recordings, as was the case in Musée L's 2020 *Parcours d'Archéologues* exhibition (fig. 9.4).[35]

Further remixing can involve the creation of new archival documents altogether. Projects like *Egypt's Dispersed Heritage*, in which Heba Abd el Gawad and Mohammed Nasser respond to Egyptological archives through Arabic comics, explore how colonial knowledge regimes can be effectively disrupted through the use of their own records (Abd el Gawad and Stevenson 2020). This project brings to the fore Achille Mbembe's assertion that every archive "contains within itself the resources of its own refutation" (Mbembe 2015) and can provide a model for other disciplines and research initiatives to follow. Archaeological survey and excavation often involve collaboration across borders and communities, which infinitely improves our ability to interpret and communicate material culture—the same can be done for historiographical projects. The ability for the archives to be remixed provides an opportunity to inscribe them with new voices by giving control to underrepresented communities. Opening archives up to annotation in this way expands the range of archives, making them more usable and relevant in the process. Partner communities will not only highlight episodes of inequality but also contribute new taxonomies and questions mediated by their own experiences and expertise. By bringing these collaborations back to the institutions where our records are held, we not only decentralize the archival ecosystem, but also our discipline as a whole.

---

34 See for example the Early Caribbean Digital Archive https://ecda.northeastern.edu/home/about/decolonizing -the-archive/

35 Credit here must go to Emmanuelle Druart, the collections manager at Musée L, who established the connection between the monasteries photographed by Doresse and the Coptic liturgy recordings in the museum's library collection.

FIG. 9.4 *Photo of the Doresse display in the exhibition "Parcours d'Archéologues: Entre archives et objets," taken by the author on March 16, 2020.*

CONCLUSIONS

As we have seen through the example of the *Fonds Doresse*, archives are not the unmediated sources that some might imagine them to be. Instead, they are the subject of active creation, embodying and transmitting the value structures of their authors and stewards. As affective economies, their ability to stand for authenticity, truth, and objectivity is revealed to be dependent on our own acts of reinterpretation, inscribing them with these values.

In order to avoid reproducing these stereotypes, it is necessary to approach archives with an "intimate distance." This implies acknowledging our own relationship to them as sources of archaeological knowledge and practice, but also as potential reference points for disciplinary transformation, giving equality a more central space in how archaeology is carried out. In enacting multiple iterations of distancing and rapprochement, oscillating from contextual analysis to a close consideration of an individual document, the constructed nature of the archive is laid bare. It becomes clear which groups have controlled representations of the past through the archive and how their investments have negated other possible meanings and voices that merit being heard.

Drawing on notions of reflexivity and critical analysis, this chapter exemplifies one pathway for deconstructing archaeological archives. It is not proposed as an exhaustive model but rather as a case study that presents the possibilities of incorporating ethics more directly into the study of archival material in order to promote transparency and equality within the discipline of archaeology.[36]

ACKNOWLEDGMENTS

Thanks must go to the teams at Musée L for introducing me to the *Fonds Doresse* and for being my collaborators in this research. I also am deeply grateful to the Service des Archives d'UCLouvain for their support in accessing the parallel documentation within their own collection, for digitizing Doresse's glass plate collection, and for sharing their expertise on the archival process.

36 See also Van de Ven 2022.

REFERENCES

Abd el Gawad, H.
2019   "We are the children of Tut-Ankh-Amon!":
       Public discourse as counter-archive of heri-
       tage practices in Egypt. Paper presented at
       From Ruins to Preservation, London.

Abd el Gawad, H., and Stevenson, A.
2020   Egypt's dispersed heritage: A source com-
       munity creative model for confronting co-
       lonial legacies in museums. Paper presented
       at the *Association for Critical Heritage Stud-
       ies Conference*, London.

Ahmed, S.
2004   Affective Economies. *Social Text* 79.22/2:
       117–39.

Ambridge, L. J.
2013   Imperialism and Racial Geography in James
       Henry Breasted's "Ancient Times, a History
       of the Early World." Pp. 12–33 in *Egyptology
       from the First World War to the Third Reich*,
       ed. T. Schneider and P. Raulwing. Leiden:
       Brill.

Antracoli, A. A.; Berdini, A.; Bolding, K.;
Charlton, F.; and Ferrara, A.
2019   Archives for Black Lives in Philadelphia
       Anti-racist Description Resources. Phila-
       delphia: Archives for Black Lives in Phila-
       delphia's Anti-Racist Description Working
       Group.

Baird, J. A., and McFadyen, L.
2014   Towards an Archaeology of Archaeologi-
       cal Archives. *Archaeological Review from
       Cambridge* 29.2: 14–32.

Berry, D.
2021   The House Archives Built. Up//Root June 22,
       2021 https://www.uproot.space/features/
       thehouse-archives-built

Bigenho, M.
2012   *Intimate Distance: Andean Music in Japan.*
       Durham, NC: Duke University.

Brusius, M.
2017a What is Preservation? Diversifying En-
       gagement with the Middle East's Material
       Past, Roundtable. *Review of Middle East
       Studies* 51.2: 177–82.
2017b Hitting Two Birds with One Stone: An
       Afterword on Archeology and the History
       of Science. *History of Science* 55.3: 383–91.
2020   Outside the Archive: Researching and writ-
       ing critical histories of collecting. Paper
       presented at the *Association for Critical
       Heritage Studies Conference*, London.
forthcoming   *The Canon under Threat: Objects
       without Status between Middle Eastern Exca-
       vation Sites and Europe's Museums.* Oxford:
       Oxford University.

Brusius, M., and Singh, K. (eds.)
2018   *Museum Storage and Meaning: Tales from
       the Crypt.* London: Routledge.

Bush, J.
2002   British Women's Anti-suffragism and the
       Forward Policy, 1908–14. *Women's History
       Review* 11.3: 431–54.

Carruthers, W.
2015   *Histories of Egyptology: Interdisciplinary
       Measures.* New York: Routledge.

Carruthers, W., and Van Damme, S.
2017   Disassembling Archeology, Reassembling
       the Modern World. *History of Science* 55.3:
       255–72.

Challis, D.
2013   *The Archaeology of Race: The Eugenic Ideas
       of Francis Galton and Flinders Petrie.* Lon-
       don: Bloomsbury Academic.

Colwell, C.
2015   Curating Secrets: Repatriation, Knowledge
       Flows, and Museum Power Structures. *Cur-
       rent Anthropology* 56.12: s263–75.

Da Canha, O. M. G.
2020   *The Things of Others: Ethnographies, Histo-
       ries, and Other Artefacts.* Leiden: Brill.

Decker, S., and McKinlay, A.

2020   Archival Ethnography. Pp 17–33 in *Routledge Companion to Anthropology and Business*, ed. R. Mir and A. Fayard. New York: Routledge.

Derrida, J.

1995   *Archive Fever: A Freudian Impression.* Chicago: University of Chicago.

Dever, M.

2019   *Paper, Materiality and the Archived Page.* London: Palgrave MacMillan.

Di Bitonto-Kasser, A.

1988   Ostraca Scolastici Copti a Deir El Gizaz. *Aegyptus* 68.1/2: 167–75.

1989   Deir Samuele: Localizzazione e Storia Di Un Monastero Della Regione Tebana. *Aegyptus* 69.1/2: 165–77.

1990   Ostraca Greci e Copti a Deir El Gizāz. *Aegyptus* 70.1/2: 57–72.

1992   Ostraca Copti a Deir El Gizāz. Frammenti Di Lettere. *Aegyptus* 72.1/2: 143–60.

1994   Ostraca Copti a Deir El Gizāz. *Aegyptus* 74.1/2: 75–122.

1996   Iscrizioni, Graffiti e Altri Reperti Archeologici a Deir El Gizāz. *Aegyptus* 76.1/2: 101–55.

Dirks, N. B.

2015   *Autobiography of an Archive: A Scholar's Passage to India.* New York: Columbia University.

Doresse, J.

1949   Les Découvertes Archéologiques: Le gouvernement égyptien acquiert des papyrus d'une importance considérable. *La Bourse Égyptienne*, June 10, 1949.

1958   *Les Livres secrets des gnostiques d'Égypte.* Paris: Librairie Plon.

1959   *L'Évangile selon Thomas: Les paroles secrètes de Jésus.* Paris: Librairie Plon.

1988   *L'Évangile selon Thomas: Les Paroles Secrètes de Jésus, 2nd édition.* Monaco: Le Rocher.

1989   Deir el-Gizaz, ou couvent de Samuel: Un monastère thébain oublié…et même disparu. *Aegyptus* 69: 153–63.

2000   *Les anciens monastères coptes de Moyenne Égypte (du Gebel-el-Teir à kôm-Ishgaou) d'après l'archéologie et l'hagiographie*, Yverdon: Institut d'archéologie yverdonnoise.

Doyon, W.

2015   On Archaeological Labor in Modern Egypt. Pp. 141–56 in *Histories of Egyptology: Interdisciplinary Measures*, ed. W. E. Carruthers. New York: Routledge.

Elia, M.

2017   Documenting the Process: The processing note as access point. Paper presented at *From Dust to Dawn: Archival Studies After the Archival Turn*, Uppsala.

Elshakry, M.

2015   Histories of Egyptology in Egypt: Some Thoughts. Pp. 185–97 in *Histories of Egyptology: Interdisciplinary Measures*, ed. W. E. Carruthers. New York: Routledge.

Ernst, W.

2016   Radically De-historicising the Archive: Decolonising archival memory from the supremacy of historical discourse. Pp. 9–16 in *Decolonising Archives*, ed. N. Petrešin-Bachelez. L'Internationale Online. https://e-artexte.ca/id/eprint/30628/1/03-decolonisingarchives_pdf-final.pdf

Foucault, M.

1998   Different Spaces (trans. R. Hurle). Pp. 175–85 in *Essential Works of Foucault 1954–1984, Vol. 2*, ed. M. Foucault. London: Penguin.

Fuchsberger, V.; Murer, M.; Wurhofer, D.: Meneweger, T.; Neureiter, K.: Meschtscherjakov, A.; and Tscheligi, M.

2014   The Multiple Layers of Materiality. Pp. 73–76 in *DIS Companion '14 Proceedings*, ed. R. Wakkary and S. Harrison. New York: ACM.

Gad, U.

forthcoming   Receptions of Classical Antiquity in Egypt and the Arabic-Speaking World: Parallel narratives, invisible corpora and a troubled archive. In *Modern Arabic Scholarship on the Ancient and Medieval Periods*, ed. A. Baadji. Leiden: Brill.

Gady, É.
2011   L'archéologie de l'Égypte antique pendant
       la période coloniale de l'occupation bri-
       tannique à la découverte du tombeau de
       Toutankhamon. *Archéologie(s) en situation
       coloniale* 126: 47–50.

Guillemin, M., and Gillam, L.
2004   Ethics, Reflexivity, and "Ethically Important
       Moments". *Research: Qualitative Inquiry* 10:
       261–80.

Harrison, R.
2015   Beyond "Natural" and "Cultural" Heritage:
       Toward an Ontological Politics of Heritage
       in the Age of Anthropocene, *Heritage &
       Society* 8.1: 24–42.

Hedstrom, M.
2002   Archives, Memory, and Interfaces with the
       Past. *Archival Science* 2: 21–43.

Hill, K.
2016   *Women and Museums 1850–1914: Modernity
       and the Gendering of Knowledge.* Manches-
       ter: Manchester University.

Hodder, I.
2003   Archaeological Reflexivity and the "Local"
       Voice. *Anthropological Quarterly* 76.1: 55–69.

Hoogendijk, F. A. J., and van Minnen, P.
1991   *Papyri, Ostraca, Parchments and Waxed
       Tablets in the Leiden Papyrological Institute.*
       Leiden: Brill.

Hountondji, P. J.
2006   Global Knowledge: Imbalances and Cur-
       rent Tasks. Pp. 41–60 in *Knowledge, Power
       and Dissent: Critical Perspectives on Higher
       Education and Research in Knowledge Soci-
       ety*, ed. G. Neave. Paris: Unesco.

Joyce, R. A.; and Gillespie, S. D.
2015   *Things in Motion: Object Itineraries in An-
       thropological Practice.* Santa Fe: School for
       Advanced Research.

Kamash, Z.
2018   Embracing Customization in Post-conflict
       Reconstruction. Paper presented at the
       UCL DigiClass, London.

Kersel, M.
2010   The Changing Legal Landscape for Middle
       Eastern Archaeology in the Colonial Era,
       1800–1930. Pp. 85–90 in *Pioneers to the
       Past: American Archaeologists in the Middle
       East 1919–1920*, ed. G. Emberling. Chicago:
       Museum of The Oriental Institute.
2019   Itinerant Objects: The Legal Lives of Le-
       vantine Artifacts. Pp. 594–612 in *The Social
       Archaeology of the Levant*, ed. A. Yasur-Lan-
       dau, E. H. Cline, and Y. Rowan. Cambridge:
       Cambridge University.

Ketelaar, E.
2002   Archival Temples, Archival Prisons: Modes
       of Power and Protection. *Archival Science*
       2: 236–37.

Kozlowski, G.
2018   Le Savoir des Racistes. *Collectif Forma-
       tion Société.* http://ep.cfsasbl.be/IMG/pdf/
       le_savoir_des_racistes.pdf

Kunst, M.
2018   Being True to the Catalogue. Pp. 29–32
       in *Words Matter*, eds. W. Modest and R.
       Lelijveld. Amsterdam: Research Centre for
       Material Culture.

Langer, C.
2017   Perspectives of Egyptologies and on Egyp-
       tologies in a Globalised World. Pp. xii–xx
       in *Global Egyptology: Negotiations in the
       Production of Knowledges on Ancient Egypt
       in Global Contexts*, ed. C. Langer. London:
       Golden House.

Larsen, M.
1989   Orientalism and Near Eastern Archaeology.
       Pp. 240–45 in *Domination and Resistance*,
       ed. D. Miller, M. Rowlands, and C. Tilley.
       London: Unwin Hyman.

Latour, B.
1986   Visualisation and Cognition: Drawing
       Things Together. *Knowledge and Society
       Studies in the Sociology of Culture Past and
       Present* 6: 1–40.

Lowenthal, D.
2006   Archives, Heritage, and History. Pp. 193–206
       in *Archives, Documentation, and Institutions
       of Social Memory*, ed. F. X. Blouin and W. G.
       Rosenberg. Ann Arbor, MI: University of
       Michigan.

Malarkey, T.
2006   *Resurrection*. New York: Riverhead.

Malfliet, K.; Van Aerschot, M.; and Bekers, T.
2016   *Wie zal haar vinden?: Het genderactieplan
       aan KU Leuven*. Leuven: Katholieke Uni-
       versiteit Leuven.

Marstine, J.
2011   *The Routledge Companion to Museum Ethics*.
       London: Routledge.

Mbembe, A.
2002   The Power of the Archive and its Limits.
       Pp. 19–26 in *Refiguring the Archive*, ed. C.
       Hamilton, V. Harris, J. Taylor, M. Pickover,
       G. Reid, and R. Saleh. Dordrecht: Kluwer
       Academic.
2015   Decolonizing Knowledge and the Question
       of the Archive. Paper presented at the *Wits
       Institute for Social and Economic Research*, Jo-
       hannesburg. https://africaisacountry.atavist.
       com/decolonizing-knowledge-and-the-
       question-of-the-archive

McKee, H. A., and Porter, J. E.
2012   The Ethics of Archival Research. *College Com-
       position and Communication* 64.1: 59–81.

Mickel, A.
2019   Essential Excavation Experts: Alienation
       and Agency in the History of Archaeologi-
       cal Labor. *Archaeologies* 15: 181–205.

Modest, W.
2018   Words Matter. Pp. 13–16 in *Words Matter*,
       eds. W. Modest and R. Lelijveld. Amster-
       dam: Research Centre for Material Culture.

Modest, W., and Lelijveld, R. (eds.)
2018   *Words Matter*. Amsterdam: Research Cen-
       tre for Material Culture.

Moro-Abadía, O.
2006   The History of Archaeology as a 'Colo-
       nial Discourse.' *Bulletin of the History of
       Archaeology* 16.2: 4–17.

Morra, L. M.
2020   *Moving Archives*. Waterloo, ON: Wilfrid
       Laurier University.

Moser, S.
2007   On Disciplinary Culture: Archaeology as
       Fieldwork and its Gendered Associations.
       *Journal of Archaeological Method and Theo-
       ry* 14.3: 235–63.

Nice Matin
1949   Plus fort que le trésor de Tout-Ank-Am-
       mon: Douze volumes du IIIe siècle exhu-
       més d'une grotte égyptienne remettent en
       question l'histoire des débuts du Christia-
       nisme. *Nice Matin*, June 2, 1949.

Omar, H.
2015   The State of the Archive: Manipulating
       Memory in Modern Egypt and the Writing
       of Egyptological Histories. Pp. 174–84 in
       *Histories of Egyptology: Interdisciplinary
       Measures*, ed. W. E. Carruthers. New York:
       Routledge.

Perry, S., and Challis, D.
2013   Flinders Petrie and the Curation of Heads.
       Interdisciplinary Science Reviews 38.3: 275–
       89.

Phillips, T., and Gilchrist, R.
2012   Inclusive, Accessible, Archaeology: En-
       abling Persons with Disabilities. Pp. 673–93
       in: *The Oxford Handbook of Public Archaeo-
       logy*, ed. J. Carmen and R. Skeates. Oxford:
       Oxford University.

Piacentini, P.
2013   The Antiquities Path: From the Sale Room
       of the Egyptian Museum in Cairo, through
       Dealers, to Private and Public Collections.
       A Work in Progress, Pp. 105–30 in *Form-
       ing Material Egypt*, ed. P. Piacentini, C.
       Orsenigo and S. Quirke. Milan: Libreria
       Antiquaria Pontremoli.

Pollock, S.
2010   Decolonizing Archaeology: Political Eco-
        nomy and Archaeological Practice in the
        Middle East. Pp. 196–216 in *Controlling the
        Past, Owning the Future: The Political Uses
        of Archaeology in the Middle East*, ed. R.
        Boytner, L. S. Dodd and B. J. Parker. Tucson,
        AZ: University of Arizona.

Porter, B. W.
2010   Near Eastern Archaeology: Imperial Pasts,
        Postcolonial Presents, and the Possibili-
        ties of a Decolonized Future. In *Handbook
        of Postcolonial Archaeology*, ed. J. Lydon
        and U. Z. Rizvi. Abingdon: Routledge.
        https://doi.org/10.4324/9781315427690

Pratt, M. L.
1991   Arts of the Contact Zone. *Profession* 1991:
        33–49.
1992   *Imperial Eyes: Studies in Travel Writing and
        Transculturation*. London: Routledge.

Puech, H. C.; Quispel, G.; and Van Unnik, W. C.
1955   *The Jung Codex*, trans. F. L. Cross. London:
        Mowbray.

Quirke, S.
2010   *Hidden Hands: Egyptian Workforces in Pet-
        rie Excavation Archives, 1880–1924*. London:
        Duckworth.

Rassart-Debergh, M.
2004   Dons et legs Doresse et Pfister en Belgique
        et au Vatican: Quelques documents relatifs
        à Antinoé. Pp. 73–105 in *Riding Costume
        in Egypt*, ed. C. Fluck and G. Vogelsang-
        Eastwood. Leiden: Brill.

Rassart-Debergh, M., and Fuchs, G.
2016   Les dons de Jean Doresse. *Bulletin de la Société
        d'histoire naturelle et d'ethnographie de Col-
        mar* 73: 71–83. https://www.museumcolmar.
        org/sites/museum/files/2019-09/4_1611_
        SHNEC_Bulletin%2073_M%20RASSART-
        DEBERGH_71-83.pdf

Reid, D. M.
1985   Indigenous Egyptology: The Decoloniza-
        tion of a Profession? *Journal of the Ameri-
        can Oriental Society* 105.2: 233–46.

2002   *Whose Pharaohs?: Archaeology, Museums,
        and Egyptian National Identity from Na-
        poleon to World War I*. Berkeley, CA: Uni-
        versity of California.

Riggs, C.
2016   The Body in the Box: Archiving the Egyp-
        tian Mummy. *Archival Science* 17: 125–50.
2019   *Photographing Tutankhamun: Archaeology,
        Ancient Egypt, and the Archive*. London:
        Routledge.

Robinson, J. M.
2014   *The Nag Hammadi Story*. Leiden: Brill.

Schoonderwoerd, S.
2018   Foreword. Pp. 7–10 in *Words Matter*, ed.
        W. Modest and R. Lelijveld. Amsterdam:
        Research Centre for Material Culture.

Schwartz, J. M.
2006   "Records of Simple Truth and Precision":
        Photography, Archives, and the Illusion of
        Control. Pp. 61–83 in *Archives, Documenta-
        tion, and Institutions of Social Memory*, ed. F.
        X. Blouin and W. G. Rosenberg. Ann Arbor,
        MI: University of Michigan.

Schwartz, J. M., and Cook, T.
2002   Archives, Records, and Power: The Mak-
        ing of Modern Memory. *Archival Science*
        2: 1–19.

Smith, C.; Garvey, J.; Burke, H.; and Sanz, I. D.
2015   Success Strategies for a Career in Archaeo-
        logy. *Archaeologies* 11: 300–36.

Spieker, S.
2008   *The Big Archive: Art from Bureaucracy*.
        Cambridge, MA: MIT.

Stevenson, A.
2019   *Scattered Finds: Archaeology, Egyptology
        and Museums*. London: UCL.

Stoler, A. L.
2002   Colonial Archives and the Arts of Gover-
        nance. *Archival Science* 2: 87–109.
2009   *Along the Archival Grain: Epistemic Anxiet-
        ies and Colonial Common Sense*. Princeton,
        NJ: Princeton University.

Thakur, G. B.
2020 *Postcolonial Lack: Identity, Culture, Surplus.* New York: SUNY.

Thompson, J.
2002 *Taking Responsibility for the Past: Reparation and Historical Justice.* Cambridge: Polity.

Van de Ven, A.
2022 Artefacts and Their Texts: Contextualising Ancient Near Eastern Collections from Excavation to Display. *Papers from the Institute of Archaeology* 33.1. https://doi.org/10.14324/111.444.2041-9015.1373

Chapter 10

Decolonization, Western Civilization, and the Incredible Whiteness of Being in Black Athena

Louise A. Hitchcock

ABSTRACT

The reception of Martin Bernal's *Black Athena* in 1987 by classicists focused on Bernal's errors of fact rather than on the content of his message. The thrust of this message was that Classics is a Eurocentric project that systematically excluded the Levantine and Egyptian contribution to European civilization. In 1996, I was hired to develop a *Black Athena* course to counter the Afrocentric view that black people were systematically excluded from their contribution to the fetishization of "Western Civilization" in Classics, Near Eastern Studies, Art History, and History, among other fields of study. I chose to avoid devaluating Afrocentric views or valorizing traditional views of Greece as the ethnically pure fount of European civilization. Instead, the course structure underscored that a thorough interrogation of the evidence could promote inclusive and multicultural histories by focusing on how civilization began in the east. Fast forward to the present: classicists have embarked on numerous projects to decolonize the fields of ancient studies through outreach, "colorizing" the Classics, and by recruiting people of color to reshape these fields. In considering the ethical issues involved in this project to decolonize Classics and related areas of research, I argue that the institutional positionality of a discipline that inscribes itself as central can never de-colonize itself but should de-center its privileged position in favor of a broader approach including neighboring regions.

INTRODUCTION

This chapter takes into account the reception, practical, and ethical challenges of teaching the ideas promoted by Martin Bernal's 1987 book, *Black Athena* and its sequels (popularly referred to as the *Bernaliad).* I will begin with a discussion of how I came to teach *Black Athena*. I will proceed to discuss the reception of the issues raised by *Black Athena* by classicists in the present and recent past, followed by a review of these issues at the time of its publication. I will conclude with a discussion of how the pedagogical landscape regarding the teaching of cultural interactions and identities has changed in recent times, the ethical issues raised, and the role that *Black Athena* played in these changes.

The ethical issues I discuss involve stepping outside a white heteronormative hermeneutic, in order to re-conceive the ancient Mediterranean and its cultures as an area of study that is broader and more complex than has been presented in the past. In doing so, teachers and academics are challenged to address the multicultural background of our society as actively engaged in this past, rather than as passive (and grateful) inheritors of a classical tradition. Teaching a multicultural past challenges both the legitimacy and the ability of white academics to speak for the colonized and for the "Other." From the perspective of conservative traditionalism we are also challenged to address the accusation that we are abandoning truth, evidence, or objectivity in favor of promoting "squishy," feel-good history catering to self-esteem rather than inquiry (e.g., Lefkowitz 1996). These tensions are addressed below. For those unfamiliar with the *Black Athena* project, the thrust of Bernal's (1987) message was that Classics is a Eurocentric project (the Aryan model) that systematically excluded the Levantine and Egyptian contributions to "European" civilization (the Ancient model).

B(L)ACK TO THE FUTURE: TEACHING BLACK ATHENA

Teaching *Black Athena* for six years, from 1996–2002, and designing it as a new subject from scratch presented many challenges and obstacles, institutional and pedagogical. My own interest in *Black Athena* began with the publication of volume 1. This period coincided with difficulties I was having as a student with my own teachers and fellow students in pursuing my study of Aegean archaeology from the perspective of being a Near Eastern historian and not a classicist. The majority of Aegeanists I interacted with and continue to interact with came out of a Classics background, rather than making a lateral move from one geographic region to another. The small, state university where I taught *Black Athena*

did not offer ancient history, languages, or any subjects dealing with the ancient Mediterranean. Instead, Africana studies was offered to the student body, which was largely made up of people of color (hereafter POC). Foremost among the challenges I faced was finding a way to work out a format to teach the intellectual debates presented in *Black Athena* that also included enough information about the past to students with no background in ancient history, languages, or archaeology to have a grasp as to why the debates were significant. Another challenge was to decide how to approach the issues raised in *Black Athena*: to dismiss them, embrace them, or develop a different approach.

In developing and teaching the subject, I was mandated by the head of the Sociology program who hired me to counter (if not dismiss) the Afrocentric view taught in the Africana studies department. In short, the Afrocentric view purported that the contribution of black people and black civilizations was systematically excluded in our fetishization of "Western Civilization," a modern category.[1] The students and their teachers believed that European literature, history, and philosophy was stolen from a black Egyptian civilization and that Eurocentric histories excluded things like the idea that Cleopatra was a beautiful black African queen. The demand for Africana studies programs in the US at this time was negatively impacted by the lack of enough scholars with PhDs to teach them, and the number of dedicated PhD programs remains small (Zeleza 2011: 24). This was one extreme end of the spectrum. At the other extreme end of this spectrum was the validation and promotion of the traditional view of Greece as the ethnically-pure fount of European civilization.

---

1   See the various lengthy blog articles of Rebecca Futo Kennedy on Classics at the Intersections (https://rfk classics.blogspot.com/) also frequently republished in Eidolon. To my mind, Futo Kennedy comes the closest to not only making an impassioned case for a new Classics but outlines what such a discipline might look like and teach. Her posts focus on many timely topics, not the least of which include blackness, Blood and Soil, the Dorian Invasion, as well as many teaching materials. See also Shanks and Tilley 1987a: 190.

My interest in the *Black Athena* project was influenced by the following: my Masters coursework in the ancient history, literature, religion, and languages of ancient Mesopotamia; my own ethnic background of being half-Lebanese—which is not clear from my name, making me, I suppose, a sort of stealth Arab; and finally, by the general ignorance of and disdain for the contributions of the Near East and Bronze Age cultures of Greece among many of the classicists that I interacted with. This last point refers to my experiences during three years of undertaking research (1990–1993) for my PhD on Aegean Art at the American School of Classical Studies in Athens. The ethnocentric disdain for examining the Near Eastern and African interactions with the rest of the Mediterranean was an approach that permeated the discipline until recently. Unlike many Aegeanists that are first trained in Classics, I made a lateral move from one set of Bronze Age cultures to another.

In teaching *Black Athena* in a polarized academic milieu of Afro- vs. Euro-centrism, I sought to find and inhabit the center, the space of the "vs." Thus, I chose to avoid devaluing Afrocentric views and by extension the students who held these views, many of which were plain wrong. I also chose to avoid embracing the classicist views that are extremely biased and teach a different and more creative kind of history and historiography. I endeavoured to demonstrate that a thorough interrogation of the evidence could promote an inclusive and multicultural history illustrating how "European" civilization began in the east. In designing my *Black Athena* subject and in popular and academic work published since, I was also influenced by the writings of Shanks and Tilley (1987a; 1987b), which raise still many unanswered challenges.

Shanks and Tilley challenged academics to question why the histories we write are ignored or dismissed by the public, preferring their histories to ours. They portray a picture of archaeology as an academic discipline of elite specialists, highly educated, and mostly white males that are alienated from the public. They note a gap between popular archaeology and academic archaeology.

Expert accounts are written to be passively consumed (or not) by the public (Shanks and Tilley 1987b: 25). For example, it might be suggested that black students who reject western history in favor of Afrocentric conspiracy theories do so because they do not recognize themselves in traditional histories, except as a commodity, that is, as slaves. Similarly, today, the right-wing "manosphere" as written about by Zukerberg (2018), not only does not recognize itself in "woke" history and literature, they perceive such accounts as undermining what made the "democratic west" great. They seek refuge and affirmation in alt-right podcasts and in right-wing think tanks. There is dissatisfaction all around. Rather than simply dismissing or setting aside popular accounts of the past, Shanks and Tilley urged archaeologists to question themselves regarding why the public embraces "Other" or fictional archaeologies.[2] Writing thick histories or archaeological accounts that are accessible is possible. It is not easy, yet it is always interesting and rewarding. Teaching *Black Athena* required going beyond *Black Athena*, requiring a great deal of additional reading and synthesizing to clarify the presentation of history and historiography in *Black Athena*. I did gently debunk what I perceived to be some of the Afrocentrist ideologies. For example, I questioned students as to why they clung to Cleopatra VII as someone worth focusing on or heroizing.[3] I portrayed her as a bit of a failure, who lost Egypt to the Romans. Instead, I used the work of Frank Snowden (1970; 1983) and Shelly Haley (1993) as well as books on Nubian archaeology to develop lectures on blacks in antiquity and on the Nubian kingdom of the Kushites that conquered Egypt. In doing this, I provided some background on the ancient Near East as well. Writing inclusive histories required a lot of extra work on my part, but if one puts in

2   "Other" archaeologies were alternative books and television shows in their era and have today exploded as Twitterized and YouTube accounts of histories that reject ours; see also Holtorf 2004.

3   I downplayed Cleopatra in order to move the subject along; however, I also brought up Shelly Haley's (1993) more nuanced discussion of her approach to the subject, which dealt with the fact that there was an unknown individual in Cleopatra's ancestry.

that work and looks beyond the silo, it becomes fun and easy. The more difficult part of teaching the subject was teaching *Black Athena* vol. 1 itself, as detailed below.

Another suggestion by Shanks and Tilley is to embrace the "Otherness" of the past. In a sense that involves abandoning our tidy modern ethnic categories, which were never as tidy as we might imagine. For example, if we consider the identity of the 15th/16th-century pirate Hayreddin Barbarossa, we realize that his father was Albanian Muslim, his mother was Orthodox Christian, he was born on Lesbos, and he served the Ottoman Empire (Capponi 2007: 30). Embracing the liminality of islands and Mediterranean coastal regions can help us better to understand it as a network of culturally entangled groups.

For anyone who has built a subject around the text of a very thick book that is a synthetic work, you re-read the book with a new goal—how you will make the book understandable to students rather than something you passively consume for your own purposes. Reading *Black Athena* for myself, I felt empowered in terms of the validation I felt in studying Near Eastern influences on the Aegean, and I worked hard to do this without falling back into a diffusionist model. In re-reading *Black Athena* in order to teach students about the reception of ancient Egypt and the Levant in European history, and how that evolved and changed, I realized that despite my admiration for Bernal, *Black Athena* is aimed at readers with a great deal of background knowledge, but as a textbook, it can be perceived as convoluted. It is lacking in background information, context, and generally fails to make sense to anyone without prior knowledge of what he's discussing. As a historian, Bernal is also frustratingly uncritical in the sense that he accepts the ancient Greek reception of Egypt as history and ancient Greek accounts of the Egyptian influence on Greek prehistory, privileging historical data over archaeology.[4] Critiquing *Black Athena* also requires philological, historical, historiographic,

and archaeological knowledge—combined knowledge sets that are uncommon. The only way for me to explain Bernal's ancient model and the centrality of the reception of ancient Egypt in early European history was to undertake a great deal of additional research. This meant in-depth research on Freemasonry, Rosicrucianism, alchemy, Kabbalism, Hermeticism, Orientalism, and colonialism, among other things. The significance of some of these movements lay in the European belief that Egypt represented an older, earlier mysticism that could heal religious schisms in Europe. In seeking this knowledge, elites sought magical and esoteric knowledge, believing it would usher in a new millennium. The works of Frances Yates (1986; 1991; also Copenhaver 1992), were especially valuable in explaining the significance of the ancient model espoused by Bernal and the privileging of the reception of Egypt in early Europe. Studying Orientalism (Said 1978) and lecturing on it was also necessary to explain the contemporary reception and study of Egypt by modern European scholars.[5] Explaining the rise of the Aryan model, replacing Egypt and the East with Greece as the foundational civilization for European civilization, required an explanation of how and why this changed. My approach was to explain how the disciplines of Egyptology, Near Eastern studies and languages, and Aegean archaeology were fairly new, beginning in the 19th and 20th centuries. This stands in great contrast to classical languages, which have been continuously studied for more than 2000 years.[6] It was only with Champollion's reading of the Rosetta Stone, a trilingual inscription, in 1824, followed by the first Egyptian dictionary in the 1860s that European scholars began to suspect that the world was much older than the Bible indicated. And it was only with Schliemann's excavations at Troy in 1871 and Mycenae in 1876 that the reality of an

---

4   Because of Bernal's general lack of understanding of archaeology and archaeological methods, I chose to focus on the historiography rather than on his later volumes.

5   An understanding of Orientalism is also necessary to understand the embeddedness of whiteness and patriarchy in our scholarship, as discussed by Nakhai in this volume.

6   It should be noted that the emphasis on what constituted "classical" languages varied over time between Greek, Hebrew, and Latin, as biblical languages were also emphasized. I'm grateful to Josephine Quinn for pointing this out.

Aegean Bronze Age of heroes was revealed as fact rather than myth (e.g., Wood 1998). When the father of Art History, Johann Joachim Winckelmann, writing in the *Geschichte der Kunst des Alterthums* in the 18th century, compared Egyptian and Near Eastern art to trees that were stunted and failing to develop in contrast to the Greeks whose art emphasized freedom, youth, and serenity, the realism of the Amarna style of Akhenaten and of Minoan art were not at all known (e.g., Clifton 2019; MacGillivray, Driessen, and Sackett 2000). Thus, teaching *Black Athena* also became both an exercise and an opportunity in explaining how the European views of Egypt and the East were not only frequently biased, they were frequently wrong. Instead, such views were based on centuries of reception rather than on recently discovered facts that emanate more slowly into the broad academic discourse, and this has become a main source of error. Then, it was necessary to project into the future how to go about change.

My interactions with both students and other academics regarding the critique of contemporary emphasis on Western Civilization gave me pause in terms of asking myself, How do you accessibly present the non-western and pre-classical features of civilization in an abbreviated public forum such as a twenty-minute talk? This is based on an experience where I was critical of a panel on Western Civilization at a conference and was told that it is not possible to address the longer history of civilization in a short format. In subsequent debate on this topic, I began by acknowledging that civilization does not begin in the west—this is a fiction. I proceeded by observing that there were multiple cradles of civilizations developing the technologies, social structures, and institutions that created the basis and the infrastructure for everything that came afterward. Just as Classics has broadened its approach to its objects of study, in Ancient Near Eastern and Egyptian studies there is much to be learned through examining the institutions and infrastructures developed in these regions, and no doubt in civilizations further to the east.[7]

The study of ancient technology, pre-monetary economy, maritime movements, and proof of trade in perishable items was still underdeveloped even when Bernal was undertaking his *Black Athena* project. We can now easily break down facile views of Greek ingenuity simply by listing the technological and institutional achievements that were developed in the Bronze Age, which made the development of later civilizations possible. We can think of the ancient Mediterranean, Aegean, Near East, Egypt, and Indus region as Cradles of Civilization that bit by bit achieved the following: writing, monotheism, astronomy, calendars, law codes, contracts, the administrative state, mythology and epic, art, realism, fresco painting, textile technology, concrete, maritime trade, navigation, ceramics technology, mining and metallurgy, monumental architectural constructions, optical refinements, quarrying, diplomacy, domestication of plants and animals, perfume making, use of spices, cheese production, sexagesimal number system still used in time keeping, and much, much more. Later civilizations only developed because these institutions and technologies were already in place, serving as a foundational infrastructure for further change.[8]

---

7   I do not know as much as I would like about civilizations further east, but I chanced to learn that smallpox

inoculation was developed in China, then spread to Ottoman Turkey, where an English woman learned it from a Greek doctor. Eventually, the technique was brought to the American colonies by an African slave, and George Washington used it to save the continental army from certain death (e.g., Chernow 2010).

8   This list is not exhaustive, and I only started thinking in terms of technology when someone challenged me to include the Ancient Near East into the discussion of civilization in a 20-minute lecture. Given the reverence for science in Western scholarship, technological advancements seemed like unassailable criteria in briefly illustrating the contributions of the Near East. I recently "road-tested" this list in a one-hour debate on Western Civilization at the Friedman Conference in Australia, July 11, 2020 (Marar et al. 2020). Without a doubt the concept "civilization" is problematic; however, dropping it also raises the issue of withdrawing the concept from other cultures.

Joining the 21st Century, Classics Decolonizes Itself

Since I last taught *Black Athena* in 2002 and published *Theory for Classics* in 2008, a lot has changed in the field of Classics. The discipline of Classics has embarked on numerous and ambitious projects to broaden its accessibility and appeal among the public, different socio-economic groups, and BAME/BIPOC/POC,[9] through teaching, research, and public facing activities. An exciting series of initiatives undertaken by professional organizations, institutions, groups, and individuals is pursuing this process through initiatives in broadening accessibility and inclusivity.[10] These initiatives include a greater emphasis on public outreach through public intellectual activity, mentoring for socially disadvantaged classicists and Classics students, pushing back against right-wing and alt-right personalities and think-tanks that are appropriating particular aspects of classical scholarship, broadening the scope of Classics beyond the Greek and Roman worlds, recruitment of a greater variety of researchers through promoting ethnic and gender balance in conference panels—sometimes referred to as "manels." These activities are taking place against the active appropriation of various strands of Classics by activity among the right and the alt-right, as well as by conservatives employed by educational institutions, and think-tanks that are slandering and stereotyping academics, labeling them as post-modern/Marxist/feminist/socialists. Examples of some of these now numerous initiatives will be presented here, as a thorough presentation is beyond the scope of

this chapter. Indeed, following these initiatives in detail leads not just down a rabbit hole, but can easily expand into the entire warren! The ethical importance of these initiatives lies in exposing the past to a socially and ethnically broader audience, as well as bringing a more fact-based past to audiences at all levels.

Tradition, the Right and the Alt-Right

The heavy weight of scholarly inertia and interests suggests that traditional histories of the classical world and the particularistic aspects of philology will continue to make up a very large segment of Classics. It is likely that such approaches will continue even if the privileged positions of these areas of Classics are de-centered. In *Theory for Classics*,[11] I posed the question, "What is Classics?" In Australia, where I taught, it is restricted to the study of classical languages, primarily Greek and Latin texts. Yet, in recent times, Michael Ventris's now-famous radio announcement in 1952 that Mycenaean tablets written in the Linear B script were an early form of Greek, and the discovery earlier in the 20th century that Hittite was an Indo-European language, extended the study of classical languages and Indo-European dialect into the Bronze Age. Interest both in the context of classical inscriptions and in the Minoan predecessors of the Mycenaean Greeks extends the boundaries of Classics for some further into archaeology, prehistory, and art history, with art history itself owing much of its development as a discipline to classical archaeology. Comparative research that studies the world of the Greeks beyond Greece is gaining traction, and more scholars beginning as classicists are benefiting from engaging with organizations such as ASOR.[12] Classics maintains disciplinary linkages with philosophy, comparative literature, history, biblical and Near Eastern studies, art history, and anthropology. These

9   Black and Middle Eastern or Black Asian Minority Ethnic or Black and Minority Ethnic, Black, Indigenous and People of Color, People of Color. The author identifies as BAME. For convenience, the abbreviation POC will be used throughout this chapter.

10   Since the original writing of this paper for the Heterodox Classics Session at the Australasian Society for Classical Studies Meeting in Otago, we have witnessed the horrific murder of George Floyd, which has resulted in a massive institutional initiative to press the project of decolonization forward at an accelerated pace previously not thought possible, at least in word if not in deed.

11   The following discussion is excerpted from the introduction of Hitchcock 2008.

12   For example, the work of Hyun Jin Kim (2021), examines interaction between the Greeks and the peoples of the "Far East."

linkages are particularly evident in the United States.

These different trajectories are contributing to a certain level of anxiety in the self-described white cultures of the Anglophone world. It manifests itself in a seemingly endless proliferation of conservative think tanks, foundations, and "liberty" conferences. YouTubers, podcasters, influencers, publicity seekers, and public intellectuals have formed a "griftocracy" that often sells itself as promoting and protecting Western Civilization while frequently portraying academics as strawmen, as noted above. An example of such a "think-tank" is the Ramsay Centre,[13] which used its eponymous bequest to set up controversial BA programs in Western Civilization in partnership with several Australian universities. In addition, online lectures, symposia, and boardroom lunches for business elites are enjoying new popularity. In the US, but with global reach through YouTube, it is the Freedom Academy, founded by conservative classicist, *National Review* contributor, and public intellectual Victor Davis Hanson.[14] These organizations and initiatives portray the fiction of contemporary "Western" Civilization as something originating in Greece and Rome, fully developed like Athena from the head of Zeus, that is threatened by multiculturalism and critical studies, placing "Western" Civilization in danger of extinction. Until recently, Classics has also been valorized as a type of "fetish,"[15] something that all cultures and ethnicities should want to benefit from, aspire to, and even undertake

as a pathway to upward social mobility (read "whiteness").[16] All of these neglect the fact that "Western" Civilization is an imagined community, a phrase not coined until the mid-19th century, that didn't really enter the common discourse with an explicit connection to whiteness and connected to Classics until the 20th century.[17]

More insidious within the alt-right has been the appropriation of inaccurate histories and DNA studies to promote white supremacy, anti-feminist agendas, and/or anti-Muslim and POC bigotry by podcasters and YouTubers such as Stefan Molyneux, Lauren Southern, and Jordan Peterson.[18] The *Pharos: Doing Justice to the Classics* blog written by Curtis Dozier of Vassar College takes aim at exposing the errors found in online alt-right appropriations of classical scholarship to promote racism and Eurocentrism.[19] The purpose of this exposure is to both raise awareness of these activities in the scholarly community and to provide resources in the form of response essays that promote inclusion. The appropriation of misogynistic rhetoric found in classical authors, which has been appropriated and amplified by INCELS (Involuntarily Celibate), PUA (Pick-up Artists), and MGTOWs (Men Going Their Own Way), has been detailed by Zuckerberg (2018) with similar goals in mind. Zuckerberg is also the founder and editor of the online journal *Eidolon*,[20] which

---

13 See https://www.ramsaycentre.org/. The curriculum focuses on "Great Books," excluding contributions of the non-west. The Centre has extended its reach to the U.S., awarding scholarships for Australian students to obtain a Masters Degree in studying "Great Books" at St. John's College, Annapolis.

14 Hanson's place in the "culture wars" with regard to Classics, his opposition to what he characterized as anti-Western political views, and his laying blame for a declining interest in Classics on its practitioners is detailed in Adler 2016: 173–212.

15 Invested with an immanent value severed from reality and superseding the real; see the discussion of the simulacrum in "Jean Baudrillard" (Hitchcock 2008: 76). I was once asked if I became an archaeologist because I could not "cut the languages."

16 For a brief overview on the history of and motivation for Black studies of the Classics, see Haley 1993. Haley served as president of the Society for Classical Studies (formerly APA) from 2021.

17 For a detailed discussion of "Western" Civilization and its increasing linkages to the right, see Kennedy 2019.

18 Molyneux was removed from YouTube in April 2021, while Southern, who was recently featured in the documentary "White Noise" (Lombroso 2020), has drifted away from the movement.

19 *Pharos'* mission statement is to serve as a platform to educate scholars and the public about the appropriation of classical antiquity by online hate groups and provide resources on how to respond to these. See http://pages.vassar.edu/pharos/. Dozier has also been active in holding round tables on combatting white supremacy at the Society for Classical Studies meetings.

20 For the mission statement, see https://eidolon.pub/welcome-to-the-new-eidolon-3b8a4230da5b. Unfortunately, *Eidolon* ceased publication at the end of 2020, with articles remaining available.

sought to foster a poly-vocalic, progressive, and informal voice for pedagogy in Classics. *Eidolon* also includes reception, Near Eastern studies, and teaching materials.

Sarah E. Bond of the University of Iowa has been extremely active in public facing research through her column in *Forbes*, blogging, writing for *Hyperallergic*,[21] and even collaborating with entertainers such as Samantha Bee of *Full Frontal* in her video segment "White at the Museum" (Bond and Bee 2019). Meanwhile, other initiatives are making a sincere effort to prevent the extinction of Classics as a discipline by recruiting or hiring people of color to inject a non-Western positionality into research, as seen in the work of Dan-el Padilla Peralta (Princeton), and the recruitment of people of color, as well as providing support to economically disadvantaged students through the Sportula microgrants project (Padilla Peralta 2017). There are also many active micro-bloggers on Twitter, particularly under the hashtag of #ClassicsTwitter. The benefits of such venues are the role they play in reaching the public and in stimulating immediacy, collaboration, and connectedness in scholarly debate as well as collapsing geographical space between scholars in ways that are not possible with the more cumbersome peer review process.

COST OF ACTIVISM

Activism, espousing progressive views, or even simply presenting a broader and more factual history does not come without a cost. In fact, views need not even be progressive to attract "troll storms." For example, Sarah Bond has been demonized and harassed for writing about the use of vibrant and vivid colors in Greek sculpture and architecture, despite the fact that this is widely known and has been taught in first year ancient art subjects for decades. I recently received a comment for a YouTube podcast on Bronze Age Cyprus that took the form of a mani-

festo incorporating terminology that referenced Covid-truther beliefs, northern European racial ideology, and anti-Semitic tropes, along with QAnon and anti-New World Order conspiracy theories. At the 2019 Society for Classical Studies Meeting, Dan-el Padilla Peralta of Princeton was accused by a casual lecturer of getting his job because he is black. Anyone even remotely familiar with the additional obstacles faced by people of color in seeking academic advancement knows how ludicrous such accusations are. Anyone venturing into the world of public facing scholarship unfortunately needs to be emotionally and intellectually prepared for the possibility of such an onslaught.

ETHICS

Although the efforts of contemporary classicists to broaden the field are noble, interesting, and important, they also raise a number of ethical issues alluded to in the introduction. Can the colonizers—e.g., white academics—sincerely speak for the colonized, and what does it mean to be the "colonized?" As long as there are not enough academics who are POC to teach these discourses, can we excuse white academics for teaching the history of the "Other"? If POC conform to or are appropriated by colonizing discourses, thereby abandoning the voice of the sub-altern, is the situation somehow better or improved?[22] It is important to note that among early decolonizing efforts was the expulsion of the British from its American colonies, leading to a decolonized population who were also colonizers. During the time of the Crusades, the descendants of Crusaders inhabiting the Holy Land fought side-by-side with Muslims inhabiting the region to expel new waves of European Crusaders. Drawing on these wide-ranging events can help some rethink their own positionalities. Lived experience also plays a role in the academic approach to scholarship that engages with different cultures. Is decolonization achieved by POC who pursue an aspirational goal to ultimately become part of a Eurocentric

---

21 More wide-ranging than *Eidolon*, *Hyperallergic* provides a forum for serious, progressive, and playful commentary on art around the world; see https://eidolon.pub/welcome-to-the-new-eidolon-3b8a4230da5b.

22 For example, contrast the perspectives of Frank Snowden (1996) and Shelley Haley (1993).

hierarchy? Or is there a responsibility for them to change what Classics means with regard to its engagement with other civilizations, how far it extends geographically and temporally? And, how far does the responsibility extend to engage with how the Classics are studied and how many more civilizations should be included? Should the struggles of black classicists be regarded as unique and privileged over the struggles of other scholars who may face obstacles based on their ethnicity, religion, gender, or theoretical orientation, such as peoples of India, Palestine, Africa, Asia, Indigenous peoples of Australia and the Americas, and peoples of mixed ethnicities? Does breaking down the rules of exclusion for one oppressed group claiming special pleading only set up new rules of exclusion for others? My point is that there is a lot more to implementing a decolonization of Classics than simply working to include and promote more African American students in Classics and in careers in teaching Classics, though this is important without a doubt.[23]

There is also a subtext, and that is the survival of the Classics, particularly in the US. The demographics of the US have been changing for some time, with just 600 BA degrees awarded in Classics in 1994,[24] with white Americans destined to attain minority status in 20–30 years if not sooner, and college enrollments expected to potentially drop by 2026 as a result of the 2008 financial crisis, which resulted in a decline in birthrates. The white population in the US has dropped below 60% according to the most recent census. In contrast, despite a recent and sudden drop in international enrollments due to Covid 19, university enrollments in Australia are expected to increase by 25% in the future. Since WW II, the white population in Australia has dropped from 99% to 75%. Overseas-born residents represent approximately 30% of the population and 30%

of university students speak a second language at home. Indigenous Australians remain under-represented in universities and over-represented in prisons, indicators of structural racism. Only three indigenous Australians have completed PhDs in archaeology at the time of writing, with only one of these in classical archaeology. Ethnic minorities and women are still underrepresented in leadership positions worldwide. There has not been an opportunity here to address the ethical issues raised in this contribution with regard to Classics in Europe, in Africa, or in Asia. This lies beyond the scope of my expertise; however, I am aware that there are initiatives to bring about change taking place overseas.[25]

I would argue that while demographic changes may create an incentive to promote more multi-cultural discourses, there are other reasons for teaching them that do not depend on demo-graphic arguments. Students are eager to learn more about the daily life and contribution of ordinary people of all cultures, not just big men and big monuments. Archaeology is particularly well-suited to render aspects of culture not widely represented more broadly in texts, including women, children, foot-soldiers, workers, and enslaved individuals.

Not Out of Africa or Black Athena Shuts Up, The Early Reception of Black Athena

The early reception of *Black Athena* is lamented by contemporary scholarship as representing a missed opportunity within the larger discourse of classical studies. For example, McCoskey (2018) wrote that Classics' response to *Black Athena* is coming home to roost, in that classicists became bogged down in the minutiae of Bernal's arguments while resisting awareness of broader cultural interest in it. Furthermore, when classicists were acknowledging Near Eastern influences on ancient Greece, it was primarily as supplement. That is, what did the Near East contribute to Greece, rather than what was its

---

23 On the limitations of promoting a more diverse field, see Rankine 2019. On the broader and more complex issues related to decolonization, see Tuck and Yang 2012. For a more in-depth look at developing inclusive teaching strategies, see the chapter by Beeler, this volume.

24 Adler 2016: 185.

25 For example, the Council of University Classics Departments in the U.K.

centrality to understanding the present? The Phoenicians are frequently treated as important for giving the Greeks their alphabet rather than as a stand-alone culture, important in its own right (Bass, Richlin, and Bikai 1989). Phrases such as "the Bronze Age has been Greek enough even for sceptics since the decipherment of Linear B" (Morris 1989: 48) serve to illustrate this issue. Although the unique subject I designed and taught on *Black Athena* took place nearly ten years after the publication of the first volume, the reception of *Black Athena* in the 1980s and 1990s was already baked in. Classicists were seemingly tripping over themselves trying to demonstrate that they were not racists (although the languages and cultures they studied and privileged were Greek and Latin, not the more ancient cultures and cuneiform languages of the Near East). Simultaneously, many classicists gleefully continued to point out that *Black Athena* was riddled with so many errors that it couldn't be taken too seriously or even seriously at all. This is illustrated by the American Philological Association Presidential Panel held in 1989 and published soon after as a special volume of *Arethusa*, entitled *The Challenge of Black Athena: The Classicists Response* (Levine and Peradotto 1989) and followed up on again in 1996 with *Black Athena Revisited*, another set of essays that excluded Bernal and his advocates, and largely clung to the same issues and approaches (Lefkowitz and Rogers 1996). The *Arethusa* volume included a carefully curated (read: important) group of responses that spoke to the panel, among them George Bass who directed the Uluburun excavations and Patricia Bikai who works on the Phoenicians (Bass, Richlin, and Bikai 1989). What the publication of those responses could not show was Bass shaking with emotion as he called *Black Athena* the most important book of the last twenty years and mentioned the outright hostility of classicists to the Near Eastern origins of or connections to Greek civilization. Bikai noted that the privileging of Greek civilization over contributions of the Phoenicians and the Canaanites in university teaching reinforced the bias. I mention these over the more well-known

contributions in the volume, as the small amount of establishment support for Bernal's views during this period tends to be overlooked. When I mentioned to one classicist who happily inserted herself into the debate (and its accompanying notoriety) that Bernal was planning a sequel called *Black Athena Writes Back*, her response was to express a desire for a volume entitled "Black Athena shuts up." These contentions were going on against the backdrop of a secondary debate on how we study culture: cultural diffusionism vs. indigenous development. In the late 19th to late 20th centuries, archaeology was practiced against this debate.

An example of this is the career of Sir Arthur Evans, who discovered, and some say invented, the Minoan civilization.[26] Evans sought to explain every development of Minoan and Mycenaean civilization as deriving from an earlier, eastern civilization in order to trace it back to an original form or earlier culture, which it had diffused or spread from. In contrast, theories of cultural diffusion were utterly rejected by the New or Processual Archaeology of the early 1970s.[27] Thus, it became the fashion to attribute every cultural change to indigenous or local development with no outside or earlier influence, and this was exemplified in Aegean Archaeology by the early work of Renfrew (1972). Things have greatly changed since these two extremes dominated academic discourse, with an acknowledgement that seafaring, a quest for metals, and eventually for other exotic and imported objects brought the cultures of the Mediterranean into regular contact primarily through coastal and island interaction networks whereby ideas, people, and goods were exchanged (e.g., Wachsmann 2008; Emanuel 2017). It is no longer forbidden or even unusual to regard the Bronze Age as the first era of globalization or to examine that cultures were changing and interacting without necessarily abandoning their cultural boundaries but occasionally merging them (Hitchcock 2020). Instead, it is now common to discuss cultural and ethnic

---

26 Critiqued by papers in Hamilakis 2002.

27 Most notably found in the work of Binford (1972) and brought into Aegean Archaeology by Renfew (1972).

entanglement (Stockhammer 2012), stimulus diffusion (Killebrew 2009), and limited migration.

I'm OK, You're Not OK, and You'll Never Be Ok: Black Athena's Revenge

To conclude, we are all embedded in, as well as constrained and enabled by regimes of power, from the first-year student, to the Emeritus professor, to the boards and councils that shape our institutions. *Black Athena* has an easy message to embrace or reject, but it is a difficult book or series of books to reckon with. It is easy to dismiss, seemingly impossible to thoughtfully critique, and frustratingly difficult to teach. In addition, when pressed, many classicists will admit to not having the background in Near Eastern languages and/or Bronze Age archaeology that might be viewed as requisite to inscribe these areas as central.[28] Yet, embracing the Ancient Model of *Black Athena* allows space for creativity and inclusivity in writing. *Black Athena* gave me and other colleagues the permission to do the type of research we wanted to do. To put it bluntly: If you do not let me investigate interactions between Greece and the Near East, you are a racist. In that regard, *Black Athena* has achieved its goal. We do not need a political ideology or an agenda to tell the truth or be inclusive—we have material culture, facts, and many histories available to do this. Rather than destroying modern democracy or Western civilization, knowing the long and illustrious path of human civilization explains how democracy and many other features of the Iron Age and succeeding periods could develop. My feeling and my opinion, however, is that Classics cannot decolonize itself and remains haunted by its missed opportunities. While it is great, if you are a classicist, to extol the joys of Greek and Latin to the socially disadvantaged or to study the incorporation of Egyptian deities into Roman religion, Classics cannot help but inscribe itself as central through its elevation of classical languages and texts as central. Many classicists remain co-opted within a white patriarchal discourse, regardless of gender and ethnicity.[29] Once one acknowledges that Greece and Rome are not central, but that Near Eastern languages and Bronze Age archaeology are also central, then it is no longer Classics, it is something else: Mediterranean studies, human civilizations, Ancient World Studies, or something not yet clearly labeled and neatly categorized.

Acknowledgments

I would like to thank Sarah Costello and Sarah Lepinski for inviting me to submit my paper to this volume. I am also grateful to the anonymous reviewers and to Josephine Quinn for their comments, which have no doubt improved the text. This is the extension of a paper presented at the annual meeting of the Australasian Society for Classical Studies and funded by the University of Melbourne. I am grateful to Megan Daniels and James Kierstead for inviting me to contribute to their session on Heterodox Classics. Some of the ideas presented here were also tested in brief contributions to the *Neos Kosmos* newspaper and at the Friedman conference, both in Australia. I am especially grateful to David Churchman for hiring me to teach at California State University at Dominguez Hills and to the students I taught there—I am sure that I learned more from them than they did from me.

References

Adler, E.
2016   *Classics, The Culture Wars, and Beyond.* Ann Arbor, MI: University of Michigan.

Bass, G. F.; Richlin, A.; and Bikai, P. M.
1989   Responses. *The Challenge of Black Athena, Special issue, Arethusa* 22.1: 111–14.

---

28 There still remain many institutional hurdles to opening up the Classics. I was informed by a colleague that he had a difficult time getting permission for a PhD student to substitute ancient Hebrew for Latin (Palaima, pers. comm.).

29 Also discussed in the chapter by Van de Ven, this volume, with regard to dead heroes and a canon of scholars that have defined our field.

Bernal, M.
1987   *Black Athena: The Afroasiatic Roots of Classical Civilization*, Vol. 1, *The Fabrication of Ancient Greece 1785–1985*. New Brunswick, NJ: Rutgers University.

Binford, L.
1972   *An Archaeological Perspective*, New York: Seminar.

Bond, S., and Bee, S.
2019   White at the Museum. *Full Frontal on TBS with Samantha Bee*, April 3, 2019. https:// www.youtube.com/watch?v=TkwUCUwt3 Rs&feature=youtu.be (accessed 29 August 2021).

Chernow, R.
2010   *Washington: A Life*. New York: Penguin.

Capponi, N.
2007   *Victory of the West: The Great Christian-Muslim Clash at the Battle of Lepanto*. Cambridge: Da Capo.

Clifton, R.
2019   Art and Identity in the Age of Akhenaten. PhD dissertation, University of Melbourne.

Copenhaver, B.
1992   *Hermetica*, Cambridge: Cambridge University.

Emanuel, J. P.
2017   *Black Ships and Sea Raiders: The Late Bronze–Early Iron Age Context of Odysseus' Second Cretan Lie*, Lanham, MD: Lexington.

Haley, S. P.
1993   Black Feminist Thought and Classics: Remembering, Re-claiming, Re-empowering. Pp. 23–43 in *Feminist Theory and the Classics*, ed. N.S. Rabinowitz and A. Richlin. New York: Routledge.

Hamilakis, Y. (ed.)
2002   *Labyrinth Revisited: Rethinking Minoan Archaeology*. Oxford: Oxbow.

Hitchcock, L. A.
2008   *Theory for Classics*. London: Routledge.

2020   Rise of the Minoans and Mycenaeans: The Global Aegean. *Ancient History Magazine* 26: 17–21.

Holtorf, C.
2004   *From Stonehenge to Las Vegas: Archaeology as Popular Culture*. Walnut Creek, CA: AltaMira.

Kennedy, R. F.
2019   On the History of "Western Civilization," Part 1. *Medium*, April 3, 2019. https:// medium.com/@rfutokennedy/on-the-history-of-western-civilization-part-1-3c7d6f3ebb10 (accessed 29 August 2021).

Killebrew, A. E.
2009   *Biblical Peoples and Ethnicity: An Archaeological Study of Egyptians, Canaanites, Philistines, and Early Israel (ca. 1300–1100 B.C.E.* Atlanta: Society of Biblical Literature.

Kim, H. J.
2021   Ethnic Identity and the "Barbarian" in Classical Greece and Early China: It's Origins and Distinctive Features. Pp. 440–42 in *Rulers and Ruled in Ancient Greece, Rome, and China*, ed. H. Beck and G. Vankeerberghen. Cambridge: Cambridge University.

Lefkowitz, M. R.
1996   *Not Out of Africa: How Afrocentrism Became an Excuse to Teach Myth as History*. New York: Basic.

Lefkowitz, M. R., and Rogers, G. M. (eds.)
1996   *Black Athena Revisited*. Chapel Hill, NC: University of North Carolina.

Levine, M. M., and Peradotto, J. (eds)
1989   *The Challenge of Black Athena, Special issue, Arethusa* 22:1.

Lombroso, D.
2020   *White Noise: Inside the Racist Right. Documentary Film*. The Atlantic. Boston: Atlantic Monthly.

MacGillivray, J. A.; Driessen, J. M.; and Sackett, L. H.
2000   *The Palaikastro Kouros: A Minoan Chryselephantine Statuette and Its Aegean Bronze*

Age Context. London: British School at Athens.

Marar, S.; Hitchcock, L. A.; Sufi, S.;
and Walker, K.
2020   *Friedman 2020// Western Civilization Debate*. Australian Taxpayers' Alliance, December 22, 2020. https://youtu.be/osQdxUwUgtM (accessed 29 August 2021).

McCoskey, D. E.
2018   Black Athena, White Power: Are We Paying the Price for Classics' Response to Bernal? *Eidolon*, November 16, 2018. Palimpsest Media LLC. https://eidolon.pub/black-athena-white-power-6bd1899a46f2 (accessed 29 August 2021).

Morris, S. P.
1989   Daidalos and Kadmos: Classicism and "Orientalism." *The Challenge of Black Athena, Special issue, Arethusa* 22.1: 39–54.

Padilla Peralta, D. E.
2017   Classics Beyond the Pale. *Eidolon*, February 21, 2017. Palimpsest Media LLC. https://eidolon.pub/classics-beyond-the-pale-534bdbb3601b (accessed 29 August 2021).

Rankine, P. D.
2019   The Classics, Race, and Community-Engaged or Public Scholarship. *American Journal of Philology* 140.2: 345–69.

Renfrew, C.
1972   *The Emergence of Civilization: The Cyclades and the Aegean in the Third Millennium B.C.* London: Methuen.

Said, E. W.
1978   *Orientalism*. New York: Pantheon.

Shanks, M., and Tilley, C.
1987a   *Social Theory and Archaeology*. Cambridge: Polity.
1987b   *Reconstructing Archaeology*. Cambridge: Cambridge University.

Snowden, F. M.
1970   *Blacks in Antiquity: Ethiopians in the Greco Roman Experience*. Cambridge, MA: Belknap, Harvard University.
1983   *Before Color Prejudice: The Ancient View of Blacks*. Cambridge, MA: Harvard University.
1996   Bernal's "Blacks" and the Afrocentrists. Pp. 112-28 in *Black Athena Revisited*, ed. M. R. Lefkowitz and G. M. Rogers. Chapel Hill, NC: University of North Carolina.

Stockhammer, P. W.
2012   Performing the Practice Turn in Archaeology. *Transcultural Studies* 3.1: 7–42.

Tuck, E., and Yang, K. W.
2012   Decolonization is not a Metaphor. *Decolonization, Indigeneity, Education & Society* 1.1: 1–40.

Wachsmann, S.
2008   *Seagoing Ships and Seamanship in the Bronze Age Levant*. College Station, TX: Texas A & M University.

Wood, M.
1998   *In Search of the Trojan War*. Berkeley, CA: University of California.

Yates, F. A.
1986   *The Rosicrucian Enlightenment*. London: Routledge and Keegan Paul.
1991   *Giordano Bruno and the Hermetic Tradition*, Chicago: University of Chicago.

Zeleza, P. T.
2011   Building Intellectual Bridges: From African Studies and African American Studies to Africana Studies in the United States. *Africa Focus* 24.2: 9–31.

Zuckerberg, D.
2018   *Not All Dead White Men: Classics and Misogyny in the Digital Age*. Cambridge, MA: Harvard University.

Chapter 11

Digging on Borrowed Time

The Climate Crisis, Cultural Heritage, and the Future of Middle Eastern Archaeology

Benjamin W. Porter

ABSTRACT

Climate scientists project that rising global temperatures will substantially transform the Middle East during the remaining decades of this century. These changes will also impact the region's cultural heritage, particularly its documentation and management. This chapter reflects on how ethical issues already under discussion in Middle Eastern cultural heritage management are complicated by the challenges that climate change brings, or will bring, to the region. Archaeologists can respond to these changes in several ways, such as considering the impacts of their research practices on Middle Eastern communities and their cultural heritage, and prioritizing the documentation and preservation of cultural heritage sites in the most threatened zones.

INTRODUCTION

Climate scientists widely concur that concentrations of carbon dioxide in the Earth's atmosphere are greater than at any other time in the last 800,000 years.[1] The presence of such large amounts of greenhouse gases in the atmosphere has brought about several measurable changes. The Earth's atmosphere and oceans are warming, sea levels are rising, and snow and ice levels are declining (Intergovernmental Panel on Climate Change 2014). Since 1880, global temperatures have increased by one degree Celsius. If greenhouse gases continue to be issued into the atmosphere at the current rate, scientists forecast a global temperature increase of between two and four degrees Celsius before 2100, and even possibly by 2050. The consequences of these temperature changes will include more frequent and higher intensity heat waves and precipitation events, warmer and acidified oceans, and the inundation of coastlines due to a rise in sea levels.

---

1 This chapter was written in late 2020 and revised in 2021 during the COVID-19 pandemic.

The Middle East will certainly not be immune to these changes. Scientists have warned, in fact, that it will likely be one of the hardest hit regions in the world, posing significant challenges to the millions of people who will live there in the decades to come (Pal and Eltahir 2016; Waha et al. 2017).

The fact that the Middle East is sitting on the precipice—or perhaps already in the midst—of a dramatic climate crisis may not necessarily alarm scholars familiar with the region's deep history. Archaeologists and historians have long documented the role that changes in climate have—and have not—impacted the region's past societies, whether it was the Neolithic Era's Younger Dryas (Bar-Yosef 2011) or briefer episodes of change (e.g., Langgut et al 2014; Kaniewski, Guiot, and Van Campo 2015; Raphael 2013). Today, archaeologists have an unprecedented, but admittedly still partial, grasp of the Middle East's environmental record thanks to scientific tools and techniques available to collect environmental proxy data (e.g., palynology, speleothems). Research during the second half of the twentieth century often over-interpreted the impact that climate change had on the region's ancient societies, seeing settlement abandonment and human migration as symptoms of collapse. A balance has been struck in more recent scholarship that recognizes the human capacity to not only stand resilient in the face of climate change (e.g., Porter 2013; Wilkinson et al. 2007), but to also play a significant role in instigating such changes (Cardova 2007; Rosen 2007). Scholars now understand that Middle Eastern societies and natural phenomena often play equally powerful roles in co-creating the environment.

Given Middle Eastern societies' documented resilience in the face of climate change, it may therefore appear to be an act of crying wolf when sounding the alarm amid a growing body of evidence pointing to the emerging climate crisis toward which the entire planet—and the Middle East in particular—is headed. The coming climate crisis will certainly not spell the end of Middle Eastern society, but it will substantially transform where, when, and how people live in

the region. Climate scientists, policy makers, and social scientists are in the early stages of planning how governments and societies should respond to these changes.

Not to be forgotten is the impact that the climate crisis will have on the Middle East's cultural heritage and the various stakeholders who value and manage it. Most cultural heritage is a non-renewable resource that is not only a well-spring from which communities can materialize their identities but is also an important archive documenting the Middle East's contributions to human history. Yet for those objects, practices, and places that come to be semiotically defined within the category of "heritage," they are often entangled in contested political, economic, and cultural conflicts, both subtle and public. In this chapter, I summarize and reflect on the challenges that lie ahead for practices surrounding cultural heritage in the Middle East, including archaeology, historic preservation, museums, and collections repositories. An overview of the most recent climate change projections for the region is presented as well as the likely human responses to these new conditions. Following this is a discussion on climate change impacts on cultural heritage resources and practices. The chapter then explores how an acknowledgment of these impacts can lead archaeologists to make ethically-informed adaptations to their research and preservation practices that prioritize Middle Eastern communities and their cultural heritage.

THE MIDDLE EAST'S CLIMATE CRISIS

The current climate of the Middle East[2] ranges from mostly temperate in its northern half to extremely arid in its southern half. Precipitation falls mainly November through April, the most abundant amounts falling in the region's northern half. May through October see substantially less or no precipitation throughout the entire region. These environmental conditions, especially the timing and abundance of precipitation, play

---

2 North Africa is excluded from this review due to space constraints, although the region shares many challenges in common with the Middle East.

a key role in the region's economies, whether industry, tourism, or, perhaps most importantly, agriculture. The extent to which countries depend on agriculture for food and jobs varies across the region and is contingent on the availability of arable land, labor forces, and proximity to markets. Under currently constrained conditions, large amounts of foodstuffs are already imported to meet consumer demands, including wheat, barley, rice, and corn (Verner 2012). Naturally available resources and the industries organized around them play a significant role in each country's per capita annual gross domestic product (GDP), which varies substantially across the region. In 2018, Gulf countries such as Saudi Arabia and the United Arab Emirates were 18 and 53, respectively, in World Bank GDP rankings by country while Jordan and Yemen were listed at 91 and 104 out of 205 countries and territories (World Bank 2018). These disparities in wealth play a key role in countries' abilities to build or adapt infrastructure to climate risks (Waha et al. 2017). Exacerbating the current economic situation even more are the region's relatively high unemployment and underemployment levels coupled with the destabilizing events of the past decade, including international wars, civil wars, and the Arab Spring that have introduced volatility and uncertainty into local and national governance.

Models developed in the last decade that consider a two- and four-degree increase in global temperature levels before 2050 project substantial changes in global and regional climate patterns (Lelieveld et al. 2012; 2016).[3] These changes will impact the Middle East's environment in several ways, only some of which can be described here. Annual summer temperatures will increase and episodes of intense heat will become more common. Winter precipitation levels will also become more erratic; while the southern half of the region will see decreased levels, the northern half may experience extreme unpredictable storms that could cause flooding. High-altitude snowpack in the northern mountain zones that supply major river systems (e.g., the Euphrates, Tigris, Orontes) will have reduced input, leading to downstream supply being reduced. Subsurface aquifers that supply freshwater springs and oases will not be as fully recharged. At the same time, sea levels will rise, inundating coastlines and the freshwater river systems that drain into the Mediterranean Sea, the Red Sea, and the Persian/Arabian Gulf. Unpredictable extreme weather events, such as spikes in summer temperatures and sudden winter rainfalls, will further stress the region.

Studies considering global climate change impacts on human populations often point out that the Middle East will be among the hardest hit regions in the world, regardless of whether a two-, four-, or greater degree change is achieved (Jobbins and Giles 2015; Pal and Eltahir 2016; Waha et al. 2017). These drying conditions will stress the region's rural agricultural industries that are mainly based on crop and livestock production. A 2015 World Food Report anticipates that heat extremes and droughts will exacerbate food insecurities, stymieing farmers' capacities to grow food (Jobbins and Giles 2015: 4). As arid conditions increase, demand for water will increase, causing growers to compete for water that is government rationed or deplete naturally available ground water resources. Safe and efficient food delivery systems to consumers will be disrupted, requiring countries to depend more on food imports to meet consumers' basic needs. The agricultural sector's decline, the 2015 World Food Report projects, will reduce the most important employment sector in rural areas and will lower landowners' property values. The lagging economic conditions will encourage families to move to urban centers in search of new employment opportunities. This migration to urban and exurban spaces will increase the overall size and residential density of the region's cities, some of which currently face housing and infrastructure crises. To add to these health and wellness chal-

---

3 For the latest scientific results, see Climate Change 2021: The Physical Science Basis. Contribution of Working Group I to the Sixth Assessment Report of the Intergovernmental Panel on Climate Change at https://www.ipcc.ch/report/ar6/wg1/#FAQ. Consult the regional fact sheets for Europe and Asia for summaries of the Middle East and Mediterranean Basin.

lenges, chronic and contagious diseases, especially those that thrive in arid environments are predicted to increase, in part due to longer and warmer summers.

These economic and demographic projections are no doubt dire for the region, especially when considering that the Middle East's population is expected to dramatically increase by 2050 (United Nations, Department of Economic and Social Affairs, Population Division 2019), with some countries possibly experiencing a doubling in population. Planners emphasize that strong and transparent governance is key to successfully mitigating climate change. Local and national governing institutions, international aid organizations, and non-government organizations will have various degrees of strength to mitigate these changes. However, some, but not all, scholars have projected that climate change will catalyze political strife within and between countries in the region. A 2009 International Institute for Sustainable Development report focused on the Levant identified a half-dozen threats to regional security that include competition for scarce water resources, increased tensions over occupied lands and refugee communities, and the militarization of natural resources (IISD 2009). Conflict within countries is also projected, whether it is between regions, between urban and rural divisions, or between sectarian groups. Observers of the Syrian Civil War, now in its eleventh year at the time of this writing (and considered by most observers to be on the wane), debate the extent to which climate change instigated this dramatic war. Those seeing a correlation point to a substantial five-year drought, one of the worst on record, which began in 2007. The crisis pushed rural populations into cities where they faced overcrowding and underemployment, all of which fanned the flames of conflict (e.g., Kelley et al. 2015). But others caution that the correlation of such patterns does not necessarily mean climate change was the principal instigator of the civil war. Rather, the timing of the drought's beginning with the Syrian government's economic liberalization initiatives that saw the end of subsidies for rural communities exacerbated what was already going

to be a painful transition (Selby and Hulme 2015; el-Showk 2019). While this debate is a cautionary tale in using climate change to explain political and social upheaval in the coming decades, one can observe how the degraded conditions can be a force multiplier alongside other economic and cultural factors that create the context for violence and conflict.

Repeated World Bank reports express a frustration with countries' slow GDP growth and call for an increase in government transparency. Many governments and national economies are expected to remain in a fragile state during the next two decades unless job sectors are opened for the relatively well-educated population, the majority of which in most countries are now people under thirty years of age. A stable, if not growing, economy is key for mitigating climate change. Currently, only the region's wealthiest countries (e.g., Israel, Saudi Arabia, and some Gulf states) have the capacity to build and scale adaptive infrastructure that will sustain basic utilities for a challenged population, although many countries are developing implementation plans (IRENA 2020). Saudi Arabia, Israel, and some Gulf States are investing in renewable energy alternatives, particularly solar, wind, and hydroelectricity. These countries are also scaling desalination facilities that will provide clean water to make up for what can no longer be captured from precipitation.[4] Less wealthy countries are not investing in adaptive infrastructure and are instead maintaining their dependency on fossil fuels or tapping into groundwater aquifers that will see lower levels of recharging as arid conditions increase. In some instances, these countries are in the planning phases or are working with the international community to gain the expertise and funding to carry out these adaptive projects.

---

4   It should be noted, however, that current desalination technologies require carbon energies to operate, although efforts are being made to reduce emissions. They also generate a high degree of waste products that are not easily recycled.

Climate Change Impacts on Cultural Heritage

At first glance, it may appear insensitive to reflect on the future of cultural heritage in the Middle East given the severe impacts the climate crisis will have on the region's human and animal populations. However arbitrary the constructed category of cultural heritage may be (Jacobs and Porter 2009: 72–73), the objects, places, and, at times, practices that constitute it are nonetheless non-renewable resources that play an important role in the quality of life in the Middle East. Many cultural heritage sites serve as the basis for cultural, religious, and national identities, leading countries and their international partners to make significant investments in maintaining them. Despite its deep and sometimes unfortunate entanglements with politics, cultural heritage is, ultimately, maintained by institutions, communities, and individuals existing in webs of often-problematic relationships, large and small, a point that Meskell has illustrated in her rigorous treatment of UNESCO (Meskell 2018).

Cultural heritage has served and continues to serve as a key economic resource in the Middle East. The United Nations World Tourism Organization's report on the Middle East and North Africa (MENA) region recorded a ten-percent growth from the previous year's level in international tourist arrivals in the region (UNWTO 2019). This growth during the past few years signaled the region's recovery from internal conflicts and economic decline during the previous decade as well as the robust economies of developed nations with people with spending power to visit the region. Cultural heritage landmarks, including archaeological sites and museums, are among the most popular destinations for international and domestic visitors. Observers were predicting another seven- to ten-percent growth in the MENA region's tourism and travel sector before the outbreak of the COVID-19 pandemic brought international travel to a near standstill (World Tourism Organization 2019). While this recovery was good news for the overall industry, it would not have eased the tension between Middle East tourism's capacity to, on one hand, exacerbate inequities and create dependencies, while on the other hand stimulate entrepreneurship at all levels of society and create public and private sector jobs. The practices surrounding tourism also currently contribute to the region's climate crisis, especially the use of long-haul transportation technologies—airplanes, buses, and cars—that still largely depend on carbon fuels. The hospitality industry uses above average amounts of water to provide clean drinking water, showers, and swimming pools. Efforts to promote carbon-neutral "green" tourism in the region are only in their infancy and, at present, only the region's wealthier countries are investing in more energy-efficient infrastructure for airports and hotels.

There is currently a broad but largely tacit consensus that much of the Middle East's cultural heritage is already under threat regardless of the emerging climate crisis. Damage done to sites during armed conflict provides the most visible examples and receives heightened attention from the media and researchers (Emberling and Hanson 2008). The availability of free or inexpensive satellite imagery and remote sensing software have produced multiple studies demonstrating armed conflict's impact on archaeological sites during the Iraq War and the Syrian Civil War (Casana and Laugier 2017; Danti 2015). These well-documented instances of destruction during periods of conflict, however, distract from the everyday iterative threats that archaeological sites face. The region's dramatic and largely unplanned growth in population during the past two decades has created new demands for land and housing. Suburban growth that extends into the rural countryside has brought populations into greater contact with sites that were once relatively well protected due to their remote locations (Glausiusz 2020). Building construction can inadvertently lead to the destruction of cultural heritage in the private and public sector's haste to accommodate this growth. The increased value of private land is also introducing conflicts between governments and landowners over the extent to which antiquities on private lands should be managed by the government. Add to this the ongoing challenges around looting that destroys sites for the sake of extracting objects for sale in tourism and antiquity markets within the region or further afield (Kersel 2007). Animal grazing and the harvesting of building materials and agricultural soils from archaeological sites are additional activities on what is already a growing list of negative impacts. The first line of defense in mitigating these impacts is the national government agencies—ministries and departments of antiquities, cultural heritage, and tourism—who are often well-trained and passionate about what is a challenging mission. However, such agencies are chronically underfunded by their governments and will likely continue to be so in the future. Support and staffing for basic activities, such as site monitoring and guarding, and for infrastructure such as fences and signs are usually constrained at most sites, aside from the select number that draw large amounts of revenue from tourists.

Because climate change is a threat multiplier, the challenges facing cultural heritage in the Middle East will only be exacerbated in the decades to come as the climate crisis grows more acute. A 2016 study drew attention to the global challenges that climate change presents to destinations that have been granted UNESCO world heritage status (Markham et al. 2016). Changes in sea level, temperature, and precipitation will directly threaten the architectural integrity of some sites and pose unique challenges to their preservation and management. The Middle East, where nearly 100 UNESCO World Heritage sites are currently listed, is posed to be one of the hardest hit regions in the world. Many of the region's archaeological sites are located in rural agricultural areas that are predicted to decrease in population as agriculture becomes a less viable income source and families move to urban areas to pursue new livelihoods. Some areas of the Middle East, especially those now in arid and semi-arid zones, will become even more inaccessible as daytime temperatures climb and populations withdraw. With rural populations depleted, some impacts on sites, ironically, could be reduced, such as animal grazing and building

material harvesting. However, the protection afforded by those communities that do exercise even a casual level of stewardship over sites in their vicinity may be reduced. Increased aridity in areas with arable lands will see a decline in arable soil quality and abundance, leading farmers to mine nutrient rich aerosols from archaeological sites to fertilize fields. Museums and collection facilities that care for archaeological objects will also face challenges in the climate crisis. While new museums have recently opened or are scheduled to in the near future in the wealthiest of the region's countries, such as the Louvre Abu Dhabi, other national and regional museums remain chronically underfunded and often lack sufficient infrastructure and staffing. Even before the COVID-19 pandemic that disrupted international tourism (Gössling, Scott, and Hall 2020; Lew et al. 2020), forecasters were predicting a steady decline in all tourism sectors as warmer conditions set in, crippling the hospitality industry. For better or worse, Middle Eastern governments and non-profit organizations make decisions about the management of cultural heritage based on the revenue they earn from tourism. Declines in investment from the public and private sectors could see an overall reduction in cultural heritage management.

ARCHAEOLOGY AND THE MIDDLE EAST'S CLIMATE CRISIS

The fields that support the cultural heritage sector in the Middle East will need to confront the challenges of the global climate crisis in the coming decades. The most important question to consider is what steps should be taken now to prepare for these changes. While fields such as tourism and hospitality studies (e.g., Dubois and Ceron 2006; Kaján and Saarinen 2013) and historic preservation (e.g., Veerkamp 2015; Xiao et al. 2019) began this conversation in their respective communities of research and practice more than a decade ago, archaeology is only beginning this important discussion. Two recent collections of studies authored by archaeologists demonstrate a growing awareness of the situation, especially as it pertains to coastal and inland river flooding's impact on cultural heritage sites (Dawson et al. 2017; Meharry, Haboucha, and Comer 2017). Collectively, the authors stress the need to work with various publics, from government policy makers to community stewards and stakeholders, to mitigate the emerging crisis. Nearly all of these studies are based in the so-called developed world—North America, Europe, Japan, and Australia—and, notably, none are concerned with the Middle East.

How then should one start to think about the practice of Middle Eastern archaeology within the context of the region's climate crisis? Rather than begin with the discipline's instinct to "preserve" and "protect" the archaeological record, we must instead start by recognizing the now-settled uncomfortable truth that Middle Eastern archaeology's nineteenth-century foundation and early twentieth-century development was entangled in European imperialism and, later, colonialism (Porter 2010). Since World War Two, archaeology has continuously benefited from European, North American, and now East Asian interests in the Middle East's carbon resources. Critics continue to describe Middle Eastern archaeology as a neo-colonialist enterprise that extracts evidence for Western research priorities under the guise of ethical "salvaging" of global cultural heritage (Meskell 2020). This critique is not entirely fair, of course—some of archaeology's most important contributions to the governments that host their research is the discovery and documentation of monuments on which national cultural heritage and tourism destinations are based. However, even if these contributions are viewed positively, they also serve as reminders that Middle Eastern archaeology is not and has never been a neutral bystander in the region's local and national politics (Meskell 1998).

Invoking archaeology's historical legacy while reflecting on the climate crisis is important because it situates archaeological practice, regardless of the position of its practitioners, within a systemic regime that has already proved harmful to Middle Eastern societies. Setting aside the well-documented examples of archaeologists who contributed their research to the region's ethno-national narratives (e.g., Israel's Yigael Yadin, among others), archaeological practice can create tacit inequities despite the well-intentioned motives of researchers. For instance, local communities that live adjacent to cultural heritage sites often receive limited benefits beyond seasonal labor and small business patronage despite their participation in the research and site interpretation process (Mickel 2021). In some instances, in fact, archaeological research and site development projects have displaced entire communities in the name of preservation and security, such as the relocation of families living in or alongside the archaeological sites of Umm Qais (Brand 2001) and Petra (Comer 2012) in northern and southern Jordan, respectively.

Growing awareness of the negative impacts that Middle Eastern communities can experience have led archaeologists to develop more ethically-engaged sensibilities and practices in their research programs. To do so, they have drawn on community archaeology models that consider local groups as stakeholders in the documentation and interpretation of cultural heritage. Indeed, these collaborative programs have grown common in archaeological practice around the world, especially in North American and Australian projects that bring indigenous communities together with archaeologists to achieve shared goals (e.g., Silliman 2008; Smith and Wobst 2005). Over the past two decades in the Middle East, archaeologists have adopted community archaeology as a framework that can potentially reverse the discipline's imperialist and colonialist legacy. Despite early enthusiasm for the approach, collaborative and community archaeology programs have not been widely adopted. Only a handful of projects have risen in visibility, such as the largely privately funded Umm al-Jimal Project in northern Jordan and the USAID-funded Sustainable Cultural Heritage Through Engagement of Local Communities Project, or SCHEP. So far, both projects have been successful in collaborating with local stakeholders in site development, interpretation, and educational programs. While the reasons that prevented the widespread adoption of these practices among other projects—lack of sustained funding, internal and international conflicts, failed partnerships—require examination elsewhere, they nevertheless speak to the challenges that archaeologists face in building and sustaining community partnerships in the early decades of the twenty-first century. If these initiatives cannot be forged during these early years of the climate crisis, how can they possibly be developed under the more dire conditions to come?

This brief autopsy of community archaeology in the Middle East is key because it is likely the local rural and suburban communities that live alongside archaeological sites that stand to be the most affected by changing climate conditions. As described earlier, rural communities who are responsible for supplying a significant portion of the region's food supply will be stressed by warming conditions, erratic winter weather patterns, and increased erosion of valuable soils. Archaeological projects, regardless of the extent to which they collaborate with host communities in their research, remain dependent on communities and their businesses for basic services. As these services grow scarce, will archaeological projects place an undue burden on these communities struggling for survival? A conversation regarding the ethics of working in resource-taxed areas near communities experiencing trauma and upheaval is necessary.

Middle Eastern archaeology already contributes to the climate crisis and, at times, the destruction of cultural heritage sites. Before active research even begins, participants often expend significant amounts of carbon fuels flying and driving long distances to reach their field sites. While in residence, research teams can generate large amounts of waste, much of which cannot be recycled due to the underdevelopment of recycling programs in the Middle East ("Waste Management in the Arab Region: Recycling on Trial" 2019). Field research also has potentially negative impacts directly on archaeological sites. Many ancient Middle Eastern societies modified, and in some instances, desiccated the environments around their settlements through agriculture, quarrying, and other land-intensive activities. Ancient anthrosols created through

everyday activities now offer habitats for animal and plant species that are attracted to the soils' nutrient levels. Upon excavating these deposits, archaeologists often disturb these plant and animal communities. Archaeologists also have an unfortunate habit of leaving their research sites in disarray. Excavation activities create spoil heaps and rock piles that make follow-on site management projects challenging. Trenches collapse if they are not backfilled after excavation, leading to the erosion of intact cultural deposits. One immediate step archaeologists can take is to design and carry out sensible site management practices in the course of field research rather than waiting until active excavation is completed to "clean up" a site for visitor interpretation projects. Such steps are relatively inexpensive and reversible, such as backfilling excavation trenches, building terraces and walls from unused soils and stone, and, when appropriate, planting drought resistant native plants to reduce erosion.

Even with proper site management strategies in place, many archaeological sites will become inaccessible to researchers in the coming decades. Increased daytime temperatures and unpredictable severe weather events will make sustained archaeological research impossible in some regions, especially in arid zones. Likewise, as sea levels rise, sites preserved along coastlines and next to interior rivers will become submerged. Sites on the edges of major population centers will likely see destruction as cities expand to accommodate new communities. Populations living in these regions will have no choice but to move to larger urban centers with better employment and services, or leave the Middle East altogether. National government agencies should consider whether or not documenting sites in these at-risk regions is a priority. If so, domestic and foreign archaeological teams can carry out salvage operations, much as they have done ahead of major dam construction projects (Dissard 2011). Of course, the impacts of this research on local communities must be taken into consideration as well.

As the region's cultural heritage is destroyed or rendered inaccessible, previously excavated collections and their associated information will soon be among the only remaining testimony to the past societies of the Middle East. Scholars will come to depend on this evidence to conduct their research. Properly managed archaeological collection facilities where evidence can be curated and made available for research and teaching will be essential. Currently, facilities that care for Middle Eastern collections already exist around the world in museums, research universities, and government agencies. However, no matter where they are located, collections facilities are chronically underfunded and understaffed, and often lack the physical infrastructure and technologies to properly care for collections. Likewise, the information associated with these collections requires careful curation. Today, field notes, maps, architectural plans, object descriptions, and other documents containing information about archaeological sites and associated collections are distributed in even more diffuse locations than physical collections (Kansa and Kansa 2014). Even when this information is well cared for in physical archives, its discoverability is limited and often disassociated from the physical collections they describe. Successful and sustainable online searchable databases such as Open Context and The Digital Archaeological Record (tDAR) have been established in recent decades to address archaeology's information crisis.[5] Both physical and digital data information repositories are fast becoming essential research infrastructure for archaeology around the world. Like archaeological collections facilities, digital data require sustainability plans to ensure these resources are available in the coming decades. Granting agencies already require applicants to describe data management and archiving plans for their projects, but more investment in physical and digital repositories are required to sustain them into the future.

Disciplinary Adaptations

These acknowledgments call for a careful re-thinking of Middle Eastern archaeology, ahead

of the anticipated changes that climate change will bring. The question that arises, then, is what should these adaptations be in light of Middle Eastern archaeology's duty-of-care to both the people and the cultural heritage in the countries that host their research? For ideas to inform a response, consider two ambitious and largely opposing political and economic paradigms that currently dominate planning conversations around the climate crisis. Although neither paradigm offers satisfying off-the-shelf solutions, they are nevertheless worth considering, as both provide glimpses into how global economies might change over the next century. These paradigms are also helpful for archaeologists to think with as they consider which disciplinary adaptations are needed in the coming decades. The first paradigm, known throughout the developed world by the moniker "green growth," argues that the climate crisis can be managed through public- and private-sector investments that will retire carbon-based energy technologies and replace them with renewable energy technologies based on wind, solar, hydropower, and more.[6] Building and maintaining these new technologies will create a large number of jobs that will employ people who would otherwise be working in carbon-based sectors (e.g., mining, oil refineries, pipeline construction). De-carbonized economies, green growth advocates argue, will transform the everyday lives of people, from how they travel to their workplace to how they prepare their food, concomitantly reducing greenhouse gasses in the atmosphere (to the extent possible), restoring biodiversity, and sustaining standards-of-living during the process.

It is in this last point—the claim that societies will continue to enjoy the same levels of wealth and opportunity that they did in a carbonized economy—where proponents of the degrowth paradigm disagree with green growth proposals. Noting green growth programs' emphasis on

---

5   Visit Open Context at https://opencontext.org/ and The Digital Archaeological Record (tDAR) at https://core.tdar.org/.

6   Green growth legislation is now often known as "Green Deal," or, sometimes, "Green New Deal," programs (Green New Deal Group 2008). Other national governments, think-tanks, and non-governmental organizations have developed and continue to develop their own documents.

economic growth as a principal solution to de-carbonizing society, degrowth advocates argue that the plan still does not eliminate the neoliberal capitalist basis of the economy whose growth, they believe, created the now multi-century devastation of the planet's natural resources. Nor do green growth programs offer reasonable pathways for countries with still-developing economies to make these transitions to de-carbonized economies, especially those who depend on the extraction and export of non-renewable resources to developed countries who will, purportedly, be transitioning to home-grown renewable energy sources. Green growth programs, in other words, will continue to hold back the economies of developing countries, increase global poverty levels, and promote the structural inequalities that have been attributed to global capitalism's rise over the past two centuries.[7]

Degrowth advocates focus instead on the consequences that economic growth has had on the climate, especially since the middle of the twentieth century. The extraction and consumption of non-renewable energy sources has largely supported this growth, beginning with coal in the nineteenth century and continuing with oil and natural gas in the twentieth century. Degrowth models predict that this economic growth experienced by much of the developed world will eventually subside while those in developing countries will see their standards of living rise to match the new reduced levels of the developed world.[8] As wealth and resources are more equitably distributed across the planet, a significant transformation in the organi-zation of labor will occur, with people dedicating their time and energy to meet the needs of their immediate communities. So too will the organization of leisure activities such as tourism change to focus on affordable and sustainable practices.[9]

These are admittedly thumbnail sketches of what are complex political, economic, and philosophical programs; there is no space here to provide anything more than cursory overviews.[10] Worth noting for the present discussion is how cultural heritage research and management are implicated in both programs. Cultural resource management firms already support private and public development projects, including those in non-renewable energy sectors. Green growth legislation promises to fund or stimulate the construction of large renewable energy infrastructure projects that will require the participation of cultural resource management firms. Archaeologists will continue to find employment in government and private sectors in countries with cultural heritage preservation laws. Critics, however, have argued that archaeological firms have too eagerly supported the neoliberal capitalist projects that have brought on the climate crisis, the construction of oil pipelines in North American being but one example. Time and again, critics argue, archaeologists were paid low wages for exhausting, sometimes dangerous work. Worried that green growth infrastructure projects will continue to exploit professional archaeologists, the conversation has turned recently to what degrowth paradigms can offer professionals in terms of collective resistance toward what they argue will otherwise be business as usual.[11]

7 Green growth plans often include foreign aid to developing countries to encourage these adaptations toward clean energy economies. Some understand this foreign aid as reparations for the environmental harms that industrialized countries have had on the less economically developed Global South, which is disproportionally experiencing climate change effects.

8 Before, during, and following the COVID-19 epidemic, sustained conservations about the degrowth of multiple industries have occurred. Most relevant here are discussions about the future of tourism, especially as the global industry saw a significant downturn during 2020. See the 2019 issue (vol. 27, no. 12) of the *Journal of Sustainable Tourism* for a collection of articles addressing the topic.

9 Degrowth scholarship is growing in prominence despite its foundational ideas dating to the late twentieth century. See D'Alisa et al. 2014; Kallis 2018; Kallis et al. 2020; and Latouche 2009 for overviews.

10 Likewise, this characterization of green growth and degrowth paradigms as diametrically opposed to each other is also misleading. There are areas of overlap, of course. Readers encouraged to explore the programs should look to this publication's bibliography.

11 See Flexner 2020 as well as Zorzin 2021 (and various responses in the same journal issue) for thoughtful discussions on the role of the professional archaeologist in green growth and degrowth movements.

Clues as to how archaeologists might participate in renewable energy development projects in the Middle East, if indeed they are invited to participate, can be garnered from their participation in the dam projects that took place in the second half of the twentieth century. Although opinions today are divided on whether or not the benefits that large dam projects are worth the negative impacts on the surrounding environment, dams were mostly well-regarded throughout the twentieth century as civil engineering technologies that provided hydroelectric power, large-scale freshwater storage, and flood control, all of which are today considered desirable in a decarbonized future in the coming climate crisis. Egypt, Iraq, Jordan, Syria, Turkey, and other neighboring countries have constructed dams of various sizes on major rivers such as the Nile, Euphrates, and Tigris Rivers, as well as smaller drainages (e.g., the Wadi al-Mujib in Jordan). Middle Eastern countries carried out these projects, sometimes with international aid, to increase their energy independence, exercising their sovereign right to develop resources within their territorial borders. Because the large lakes that accumulate behind dams inadvertently submerge cultural heritage (as well as displace communities and destroy species' habitats), domestic and foreign archaeologists have been employed to conduct multi-year surveys and emergency excavations. Their work also recovered enormous amounts of evidence, of course, that contributed to the discipline's knowledge of the region's past. Only in some instances were efforts made to preserve cultural heritage sites, notably the dramatic move of Egypt's Abu Simbel temple complex in the mid-1960s. More often, cultural heritage sites were and continue to be destroyed.[12] Whether or not archaeologists will be called upon to conduct cultural resource management projects in support of upcoming green growth projects is difficult to predict. Instead of documenting sites in danger of flooding, archaeologists could be conducting salvage work ahead of the construction of photovoltaic power stations (i.e., solar farms), desalinization facilities, or even nuclear power plants.

Similarly, pathways of degrowth in Middle Eastern archaeological research can be envisioned by recalling the episodic periods of unplanned disruptions during the past century. Following the 1979 Islamic Revolution in Iran, nearly all foreign research activities in the country were suspended, with only archaeologists from countries with diplomatic relationships being allowed to return eventually. In the United States, an entire generation of archaeologists who had worked in the country for decades saw their research activities abruptly end. The ensuing Iraq-Iran War between 1980 and 1988 and the subsequent wars between Iraq and the United States and their allies in 1991 and again in 2003 (with an occupation lasting until 2011) also saw the disruption of research activities. The Lebanese Civil War between 1975 and 1990 and the more recent Syrian Civil War that began in 2011 likewise saw the near-complete cessation of research activities. Archaeologists have become deft at navigating these conflicts, moving their research from one area to another (and back again), such as the noticeable shift of Mesopotamian specialists from Iraq and Iran to Syria and Turkey during the 1980s and 1990s, and then, quite abruptly, back to Iraq a few years after the 2003 conflict subsided. As the climate crisis unfolds, archaeologists may continue to follow this hopscotching pattern across the region as conditions in specific regions shift between hospitable and inhospitable. This lurching between projects often has negative effects on research, with excavation and development projects placed on hiatus or going unfinished and accumulated evidence stored near research sites going unstudied and often lost. Unplanned degrowth also has direct negative impacts on cultural heritage sites, and, most importantly, the civil servants that manage them and the communities that live near them. The looting, site destruction, and even murder of site stewards during the Syrian Civil War, for instance, offers a grim prediction of what could happen in the future.

These observations about the recent past, of course, offer imperfect lessons that nevertheless

---

12 See Dissard 2011 and Luke 2018 for two extensive studies on the economic and cultural impacts that resource extraction has had on either end of Turkey.

remind one of archaeology's entanglements with Middle Eastern societies and their governments and economies, as critics who characterize the discipline's practices as extractive remind us (Meskell 2020). As much as one may argue that foreign-led research activities should cease in light of these political entanglements and, now, the climate crisis, it is unlikely that the discipline will suddenly come to a complete halt. Rather, those who actually conduct archaeological research in the region should think carefully about how the discipline can make thoughtful ethically-informed adaptations. One need not entirely subscribe to either green growth or degrowth programs to gather ideas for the discipline's future. The network of institutions that are involved in the investigation and management of the region's cultural heritage—Middle Eastern government agencies and universities, overseas research centers, funding agencies, museums, and non-government institutions—must play a leading role in shaping policies. European and North American professional societies, in particular, can set carbon-neutral level goals. In-person conferences can be scheduled less frequently while intellectual exchanges can be scheduled through digital remote platforms. Organizations with publication programs can adopt green and, ideally, gold open access models that make knowledge about the Middle East more freely available to scholars and public stakeholders. Publishers can offer print-on-demand subscriptions to decrease paper consumption and carbon fuels required for shipping. Professional societies can develop new curricula for the next generation of professionals that include training in heritage site, collections, and information management, all of which will be increasingly valuable in the coming decades.

CONCLUSION

This brief essay has sought to define the current circumstances and establish a context for future discussions about which adaptations are necessary and how to carry them out. In doing so, it has painted an admittedly bleak picture of cultural heritage's future in the Middle East. Rest

assured that it is more likely than not that professional disciplines dedicated to investigating the region's past will likely always exist in one form or another. Nevertheless, in 2022, archaeologists find themselves at an inflection point, although they may only come to recognize it in hindsight. The decision to adapt key practices must be made soon, or the discipline will proceed down an unplanned and uncontrolled path that will likely see the field crippled beyond recognition. Can archaeologists instead envision sensible plans that will sustain the production of new knowledge about the past and, at the same time, guide it toward a more ethical and sustainable horizon? This is a difficult question to ask, admittedly, as so many of the institutions that support cultural heritage research count on growth models for their financial sustainability and are therefore guided by profit and scholarly impact when making decisions about the future. Funding agencies and private foundations that reward scholars carrying out ambitious research programs do not yet request applicants to describe how their research activities are designed to reduce climate impacts, such as calculating carbon expenditures. Middle Eastern archaeology is resultantly embedded in the modern capitalist enterprise that values growth and the accumulation of capital, even if that capital comes in the form of new knowledge about the ancient world. Whether or not archaeologists can envision thoughtful and responsible adaptations to mitigate the sharp abatement of research activities in the coming decades remains to be seen.

If, by some impossibly good fortune, the climate projections for the Middle East are inaccurate, that global temperature rise will not ultimately exceed even two degrees Celsius, will archaeologists have wasted their time adapting to what was, in fact, a false alarm? Certainly not. In fact, by making these changes, archaeologists will have become better stewards of cultural heritage resources and the communities that live around and draw inspiration from them. They will also have become better stewards of archaeological evidence and their associated information. If there is a silver lining to be salvaged from the threats that the climate crisis promises, it is the possibility of a more accountable and ethically engaged discipline. Clarion calls for these changes in practice have existed since the 1990s, well before climate scientists forecasted the future of the Middle East. Ironically and, perhaps, sadly, it may be the discipline's self-interested attempts to preserve itself that motivates Middle Eastern archaeologists to commit themselves finally to these ethical practices. The likelihood that global climate projections are somehow in error is, ultimately, the stuff of magical thinking to preoccupy one's mind while digging on borrowed time.

REFERENCES

Bar-Yosef, O.
2011   Climatic Fluctuations and Early Farming in West and East Asia. *Current Anthropology* 52: 175–93. https://doi.org/10.1086/659784

Brand, L. A.
2001   Displacement for Development? The Impact of Changing State-Society Relations. *World Development* 29: 961–76. https://doi.org/10.1016/S0305-750X(01)00024-9

Casana, J., and Lauier, E. J.
2017   Satellite Imagery-Based Monitoring of Archaeological Site Damage in the Syrian Civil War. *PLoS ONE* 12.11: e0188589. https://doi.org/10.1371/journal.pone.0188589

Comer, D. C. (ed.)
2012   *Tourism and Archaeological Heritage Management at Petra: Driver to Development or Destruction.* New York: Springer.

Cordova, C.
2007   *Millennial Landscape Change in Jordan: Geoarchaeology and Cultural Ecology.* Tucson, AZ: University of Arizona.

D'Alisa, G.; Giorgos Kallis, G.; and Demaria, F.
2014   *Degrowth: A Vocabulary for a New Era.* London: Taylor and Francis.

Danti, M.
2015   Ground-Based Observations of Cultural Heritage Incidents in Syria and Iraq. *Near Eastern Archaeology* 78.3: 132–41. https://doi.org/10.5615/neareastarch.78.3.0132

Dawson, T.; Nimura, C.; López-Romero, E.; and Daire, M.-Y. (eds.)
2017   *Public Archaeology and Climate Change.* Oxford: Oxbow.

Dissard, L.
2011   Submerged Stories from the Sidelines of Archaeological Science: The History and Politics of the Keban Dam Rescue Project (1967–1975) in Eastern Turkey. PhD dissertation, University of California, Berkeley. https://escholarship.org/uc/item/28s978db

Dubois, G., and Ceron, J.-P.
2006   Tourism and Climate Change: Proposals for a Research Agenda. *Journal of Sustainable Tourism* 14: 399–415. https://doi.org/10.2167/jost539.0

Emberling, G., and Hanson, K.
2008   *Catastrophe! The Looting and Destruction of Iraq's Past.* Chicago: Oriental Institute Museum. https://isac.uchicago.edu/sites/default/files/uploads/shared/docs/oimp28.pdf

Flexner, J.
2020   Degrowth and a Sustainable Future for Archaeology. *Archaeological Dialogues:* 27.2: 159–71. https://doi.org/10.1017/S1380203820000203

Glausiusz. J.
2020   Paving over the Past. *Nature* 582: 474–77.

Gössling, S.; Scott, D.; and Hall, C. M.
2020   Pandemics, Tourism and Global Change: A Rapid Assessment of COVID-19. *Journal of Sustainable Tourism* 29.1: 1–20. https://doi.org/10.1080/09669582.2020.1758708

International Institute for Sustainable Development (IISD)
2009   IISD Annual Report 2009–2010. Winnipeg, Canada. https://www.iisd.org/publications/annual-report/iisd-annual-report-2009-2010

International Renewable Energy Agency (IRENA)

2020   *Power Sector Planning in Arab Countries: Incorporating Variable Renewables.* Abu Dhabi: International Renewable Energy Agency.

Jacobs, J., and Porter, B. W

2009   Excavating *Turaath*: Documenting Local and National Heritage Discourses in Jordan. Pp. 71-88 in *Archaeologies and Ethnographies: Iterations of "Heritage" and the Archaeological Past,* ed. L. Mortenson and J. Hollowell. Gainesville, FL: University of Florida.

Jobbins, G., and Giles, H.

2015   *Food in an Uncertain Future: The Impacts of Climate Change on Food Security and Nutrition in the Middle East and North Africa.* London: Overseas Development Institute; Rome: World Food Programme.

Kaján, E., and Saarinen, J.

2013   Tourism, Climate Change and Adaptation: A Review. *Current Issues in Tourism* 16: 167–95. https://doi.org/10.1080/13683500.2013.774323

Kallis, G.

2018   *Degrowth.* Newcastle upon Tyne: Agenda.

Kallis, G.; Paulson, S.; D'Alisa, G.; and Demaria, F.

2020   *The Case for Degrowth.* Cambridge: Polity.

Kaniewski, D.; Guiot, J.; and Van Campo, E.

2015   Drought and Societal Collapse 3200 Years Ago in the Eastern Mediterranean: A Review. *WIREs Climate Change* 6: 369–82. https://doi.org/10.1002/wcc.345

Kansa, S. W., and Kansa, E.

2014   Data Publishing and Archaeology's Information Ecosystem. *Near Eastern Archaeology* 77: 223–27. https://doi.org/10.5615/neareastarch.77.3.0223

Kelley, C. P.; Shahrzad, M.; Cane, M. A.; Seager R.; and Yochanan, K.

2015   Climate Change in the Fertile Crescent and Implications of the Recent Syrian Drought. *Proceedings of the National Academy of Sciences of the United States of America* 112: 3241–46. https://doi.org/10.1073/pnas.1421533112

Kersel, M.

2007   Transcending Borders: Objects on the Move. *Archaeologies* 3.2: 81–98. https://doi.org/10.1007/s11759-007-9013-0

Langgut, D.; Frank, H. N.; Mordechai, S.; Allon, W.; Elisa, J. K.; Elisabetta, B.; and Finkelstein I.

2014   Dead Sea Pollen Record and History of Human Activity in the Judean Highlands (Israel) from the Intermediate Bronze into the Iron Ages (~2500–500 BCE). *Palynology* 38: 280–302. https://doi.org/10.1080/01916122.2014.906001

Latouche, S.

2009   *Farewell to Growth.* Cambridge: Polity.

Lelieveld, J.; Hadjinicolaou, P.; Kostopoulou, E.; Chenoweth, J.; El Maayar, M.; Giannakopoulos, C.; Hannides, C.; Lange, M. A.; Tanarhte, M.; Tyrlis, E.; and Xoplaki, E.

2012   Climate Change and Impacts in the Eastern Mediterranean and the Middle East. *Climatic Change* 114: 667–87. https://doi.org/10.1007/s10584-012-0418-4

Lelieveld, J.; Proestos, Y.; Hadjinicolaou, P.; Tanarhte, M.; Tyrlis, E.; and Zittis, G.

2016   Strongly Increasing Heat Extremes in the Middle East and North Africa (MENA) in the 21st Century. *Climatic Change* 137: 245–60. https://doi.org/10.1007/s10584-016-1665-6

Luke, C.

2018   *A Pearl in Peril: Heritage and Diplomacy in Turkey.* Oxford: Oxford University.

Markham, A.; Osipova, E.; Lafrenz Samuels, K.; and Caldas, A.

2016   *World Heritage and Tourism in a Changing Climate.* Nairobi: United Nations Environment Programme; Paris: United Nations Educational, Scientific and Cultural Organization.

Meharry, J. E.; Haboucha, R.; and Comer, M.
(eds.)
2017   On the Edge of the Anthropocene? Modern Climate Change and the Practice of Archaeology. *Archaeological Review from Cambridge* 32.2.

Meskell, L. (ed.)
1998   *Archaeology Under Fire: Nationalism, Politics and Heritage in the Eastern Mediterranean and Middle East.* New York: Routledge.

Meskell, L.
2018   *A Future in Ruins: UNESCO, World Heritage, and the Dream of Peace.* Oxford: Oxford University.
2020   Imperialism, Internationalism, and Archaeology in the Un/Making of the Middle East. *American Anthropologist* 122: 554–67. https://doi.org/10.1111/aman.13413

Mickel, A.
2021   *Why those who Shovel are Silent: A History of Local Archaeological Knowledge and Labor.* Louisville, CO: University of Colorado.

n.a.
2019   Waste Management in the Arab Region: Recycling on Trial. *Global Recycling.* https://global-recycling.info/archives/2620 (accessed November 10, 2019).

Pal, J. S.; and Eltahir, E. A. B.
2016   Future Temperature in Southwest Asia Projected to Exceed a Threshold for Human Adaptability. *Nature Climate Change* 6: 197–200. https://doi.org/10.1038/nclimate2833

Porter, B .W.
2010   Near Eastern Archaeology: Imperial Pasts, Postcolonial Presents, and the Possibilities of a Decolonized Future. Pp. 49–57 in *The World Archaeological Congress Handbook on Postcolonialism and Archaeology,* ed. J. Lydon and U. Rizvi. Walnut Creek, CA: Left Coast.
2013   *Complex Communities: The Archaeology of Early Iron Age West-Central Jordan.* Tucson, AZ: University of Arizona.

Raphael, S. K.
2013   *Climate and Political Climate: Environmental Disasters in the Medieval Levant.* Leiden: Brill.

Rosen, A. M.
2007   *Civilizing Climate: Social Responses to Climate Change in the Ancient Near East.* Lanham, MD: Altamira.

Shelby, J., and Hulme, M.
2015   Is Climate Change really to Blame for Syria's Civil War? *The Guardian,* November 29.

El-Showk, S.
2019   The Challenges of Linking Climate Change, Conflict and Migration. *Nature Middle East,* February 20, 2019. https://doi.org/10.1038/nmiddleeast.2019.19

Silliman, S. W. (ed.)
2008   *Collaborating at the Trowel's Edge: Teaching and Learning in Indigenous Archaeology.* Tucson, AZ: University of Arizona.

Smith, C., and Wobst, H. M. (eds.)
2005   *Indigenous Archaeologies: Decolonizing Theory and Practice.* London: Routledge.

The Green New Deal Group
2008   *A Green New Deal.* London: New Economics Foundation.

The Intergovernmental Panel on Climate Change
2014   *Climate Change 2014: Synthesis Report. Contribution of Working Groups I, II and III to the Fifth Assessment Report of the Intergovernmental Panel on Climate Change.* Geneva: The Intergovernmental Panel on Climate Change.

United Nations, Department of Economic and Social Affairs, Population Division
2019   *World Population Prospects 2019.*

United Nations, World Tourism Organization (UNWTO)
2019   International Tourism Highlights 2019. https://www.e-unwto.org/doi/book/10.18111/9789284421152

Veerkamp, A.

2015   Preservation in a Changing Climate: Time to Pick Up the Tab. *Forum Journal* 29.4: 9–18. https://doi.org/10.1353/fmj.2015.a587537

Verner, D.

2012   *Adaptation to a Changing Climate in the Arab Countries: A Case for Adaptation Governance and Leadership in Building Climate Resilience.* Washington, DC: World Bank.

Waha, K.; Krummenauer, L.; Adams, S.; Aich, V.; Baarsch, F.; Coumou, D.; Fader, M.; Hoff, H.; Jobbins, G.; Marcus, R.; Mengel, M.; Otto, I. M.; Perrette, M.; Rocha, M.; Robinson, A.; and Schleussner, C.-F.

2017   Climate Change Impacts in the Middle East and Northern Africa (MENA) Region and their Implications for Vulnerable Population Groups. *Regional Environmental Change* 17: 1623–38. https://doi.org/10.1007/s10113-017-1144-2

Wilkinson, T. J.; Christiansen, J. H.; Ur, J.; Widell, M.; and Altaweel, M.

2007   Urbanization within a Dynamic Environment: Modeling Bronze Age Communities in Upper Mesopotamia. *American Anthropologist* 109: 52–68. https://doi.org/10.1525/aa.2007.109.1.52

World Bank

2018   GDP Ranking. https://datacatalog.worldbank.org/dataset/gdp-ranking (accessed November 10, 2019).

Xiao, X.; Seekamp, E.; van der Burg, M. P.; Eaton, M.; Fatorić, S.; and McCreary, A.

2019   Optimizing Historic Preservation under Climate Change: Decision Support for Cultural Resource Adaptation Planning in National Parks. *Land Use Policy* 83: 379–89. https://doi.org/10.1016/j.landusepol.2019.02.011

Zorzin, N.

2021   Is Archaeology Conceivable within the Degrowth Movement? *Archaeological Dialogues* 28.1: 1–16. https://doi.org/10.1017/S1380203821000015

Contributors

Maggie Beeler is a Teaching Assistant Professor of Mediterranean Art and Archaeology in the Department of Classics at the University of Pittsburgh. Maggie's research and teaching focus on issues of social identity and critical theory in the ancient Mediterranean.

maggie.beeler@pitt.edu

Sarah Kielt Costello is Professor of Art History at University of Houston – Clear Lake. Her research areas include early Mesopotamian art and archaeology, as well as museum and heritage studies.

costello@uhcl.edu

Grace Erny is an Assistant Professor in the Department of Ancient Greek and Roman Studies at the University of California, Berkeley. Her research focuses on settlement patterns and social differentiation in Archaic and Classical Crete.

gkerny@berkeley.edu

Laura Heath-Stout (she/her) uses qualitative and quantitative social science methods to study equity issues and knowledge production in archaeology. She is currently a postdoctoral fellow at the Stanford Archaeology Center and a member of the Disabled Archaeologists Network's Leadership Team.

www.lauraheathstout.com
lheathst@stanford.edu

Nadhira Hill is an Assistant Professor of Classics and Archaeology at Randolph-Macon College. Her archaeological fieldwork has primarily taken place in Greece and her research explores the intersections of ceramic production, cultural interaction, and commensal practices in the Greek world.

nyhill@umich.edu
NadhiraHill@rmc.edu

Louise A. Hitchcock is an Independent Researcher. She has written or collaborated on over 120 articles on Mediterranean Archaeology as well as on five books including *Aegean Art and Architecture* and *Plagues in Antiquity*. She served as area supervisor on the Tell es-Safi/Gath Excavation Project for ten years.

minoanarchitecture@gmail.com

Sarah Lepinski is Curator, Department of Greek and Roman Art, The Metropolitan Museum of Art, New York City, and former Senior Program Officer in the Division of Preservation and Access and the Office of Challenge Grants, at the National Endowment for the Humanities, Washington, DC. Her work focuses on Roman art and archaeology, as well as collections stewardship and cultural heritage stewardship.

sarah.lepinski@metmuseum.org

Dimitri Nakassis is Professor in the Department of Classics at the University of Colorado Boulder. He is co-director of the Western Argolid Regional

Project, an archaeological survey in Greece, and of the Pylos Tablets Digital Project.
dimitri.nakassis@colorado.edu

Beth Alpert Nakhai is a Professor Emerita in the Arizona Center for Judaic Studies at the University of Arizona. She received her MTS from Harvard Divinity School, and her MA and PhD from the University of Arizona. Her publications focus on the lives of women in antiquity, Canaanite and Israelite religion and culture, Israelite ethnogenesis and village life, and women working in the field of Near Eastern archaeology. She chaired ASOR's Initiative on the Status of Women and is an officer of the W. F. Albright School of Archaeological Research in Jerusalem.
bnakhai@arizona.edu
http://www.judaic.arizona.edu

Benjamin W. Porter is an Associate Professor of Middle Eastern Archaeology at the University of California, Berkeley, and Curator of Middle Eastern Archaeology at the Phoebe A. Hearst Museum of Anthropology.
bwporter@berkeley.edu

Mason J. Shrader is a PhD student at the Joukowsky Institute for Archaeology and the Ancient World at Brown University. He also has an MA in Classics and an MA in Anthropology from Texas Tech University. He studies the bio-archaeology of disability and impairment in the ancient Mediterranean, focusing specifically on Late Antiquity and early Christianity.
mason_shrader@brown.edu

Debby Sneed is an Assistant Professor of Classics at California State University, Long Beach. She has a PhD in Archaeology from UCLA, an MA in Classics from the University of Colorado at Boulder, and a BA in English and History from the University of Wyoming. She studies physical disability in ancient Greece.
debby.sneed@csulb.edu

Tuğba Tanyeri-Erdemir is the coordinator of ADL's Task Force on Middle East Minorities and the co-chair of International Religious Freedom Roundtable's Middle East Working Group. She has a PhD in Archaeology from Boston University, an MA and a BA in Art History and Archaeology from Bilkent University. Previously, she worked as a lecturer, researcher, and a museum director at the Middle East University, Ankara, Turkey. Her research focuses on minority rights in the Middle East, cultural heritage management of sacred sites, converted and contested religious buildings, and re-utilization and museumification of religious heritage.
ttanyeri-erdemir@adl.org

Christopher Thornton is Director of Research Programs at the National Endowment for the Humanities and former acting Director of Grants program and Senior Director of Cultural Heritage, National Geographic Society, both in Washington, DC.
cthornton@neh.gov

Annelies Van de Ven is an FNRS-funded postdoctoral researcher in archaeology at the Université catholique de Louvain in collaboration with Musée L. She previously completed her PhD at The University of Melbourne where she also worked as a teaching and curatorial assistant.
vandevena1@gmail.com